Magnetics 2022

Orlando, Florida, USA
8-9 February 2022

ISBN: 978-1-7138-5214-8

Printed from e-media with permission by:

Curran Associates, Inc.
57 Morehouse Lane
Red Hook, NY 12571

Some format issues inherent in the e-media version may also appear in this print version.

TWST Events
622 3rd Ave, 34th FL
New York, NY 10017
USA

twstevents.com

Additional copies of this publication are available from:

Curran Associates, Inc.
57 Morehouse Lane
Red Hook, NY 12571 USA
Phone: 845-758-0400
Fax: 845-758-2633
Email: curran@proceedings.com
Web: www.proceedings.com

TABLE OF CONTENTS

The Global Permanent Magnet Industry 2020-2030

A comprehensive study authored by
Walter T. Benecki, Steve Constantinides, John Ormerod, Stan Trout

Presented by Stan Trout
Spontaneous Materials

Magnetics 2022
February 8-9, 2022
Orlando, FL

www.MagnetReport.com

Outline

- Why take on this project?
- Who are we?
- What is in this report?
- The next decade: 2020 to 2030
- How is the report useful to me?
- Conclusions

Why take on this project?

- Our last study was published in 2010
  - There has been a seismic shift in the industry, material situation and applications
- Myriad of canned market/industry studies available with suspect content
  - Most studies are performed by industry outsiders and conducted by phone interview and e-mail
  - Most make little or no use of industry experts – those with extensive experience and networks for research and fact-checking
- This new study offers value to magnet producers, customers, government agencies, investors, university and research institutions, etc.

  - - and we'll show why

The Global Permanent Magnet Industry 2020 - 2030

Who are we?

Walter T. Benecki

Walt holds B.S. and M.S. Degrees from Pennsylvania State University and an M.B.A. from the University of Pittsburgh. In 1989, Walt was named President of Arnold Magnetic Technologies. Walt was president of MMPA from 1994-1997 and served as a member of the Board of Great Western Minerals Group (2006-2009), and the Advisory Board of Bunting Magnetics Company (2002-2016). Since 2001, Walt has managed a consulting practice serving the global permanent magnet industry. In 2017, Walt published the 3rd Edition of "The Global Permanent Magnet Industry".
Magnet industry experience: 32 years

Steve Constantinides

Steve is a materials scientist with experience at Corning Inc., involved with glass ceramics, passive electronic components and manufacturing management systems. Steve joined tungsten carbide manufacturer GTE Valenite with responsibility for over 40 vacuum and atmospheric furnaces. In 1988 , Steve joined Crucible Magnetics as Manager of Technology and Quality Assurance. After joining Arnold Magnetic Technologies in 1992, Steve performed process and product development, manufacturing and applications engineering. From 2005 through 2016 he was Arnold's Director of Technology.
Magnet industry experience: 32 years.

Dr. John Ormerod

John graduated from the University of Manchester, UK with a B.Sc., M.Sc. and Ph.D. in Metallurgy. He has over twenty years of research, product development, and manufacturing experience in magnetics. John worked for Phillips and Arnold Engineering (now Arnold Magnetic Technologies). In 2002, John was named President of Res Manufacturing, a manufacturer of stamped metal components. John has provided expert ITC testimony regarding issues of patent invalidity on rare earth magnets. In 2015 John founded his consultancy serving the magnet and metals industries.
Magnet industry experience: 42 years.

Dr. Stanley R. Trout

Stan's experience includes corporate responsibilities with Molycorp, Magnequench, Hitachi Magnetics, Crucible Magnetics and Recoma. Stan started his Spontaneous Materials consulting practice in 2001, assisting clients with solutions to technical problems involving permanent magnets and rare earths. Stan is a registered professional engineer in Colorado and Pennsylvania, holds a B.S. in Physics from Lafayette College and a Ph.D. in Metallurgy and Materials Science from the University of Pennsylvania. Dr. Trout is a member of the IEEE and UK Magnetics Societies.
Magnet industry experience: 46 years

The Global Permanent Magnet Industry 2020 - 2030

What is in this report?

- First and foremost: Industry Statistics and forecasts, for example...

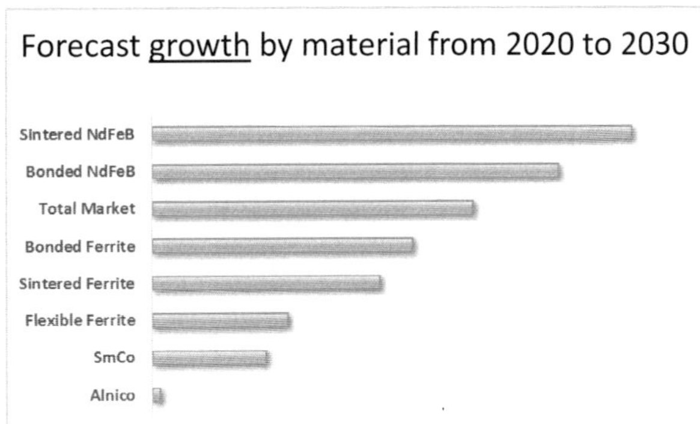

Industry Current Status

- Production statistics
  - By magnet material and country/region
- Applications for permanent magnets
  - Preferred materials and descriptions
- New technologies and their effects on the industry
  - Material substitutions have expanded product choices with regard to properties and price such as cerium use in Neo and in ferrite magnets
- Recycling within production facilities and at EOL (end of life)

Example data extracted from the report...

China Market Share, % by weight

	Actual				Forecast	
Material	**2005**	**2010**	**2015**	**2020**	**2025**	**2030**
Ferrite	49.6	49.2	54.2	56.7	57.3	56.5
NdFeB	37.2	71.9	73.1	83.8	85.7	86.7
SmCo	68.9	68.6	64.8	64.6	62.9	61.0
Alnico	60.3	59.8	59.8	60.9	61.3	61.8

The Next Decade

- Permanent Magnet Raw Materials
- Magnet Material Selection
- Raw Material and Magnet Pricing
- Production Quantities and Locations
- Usage Forecasts by Application

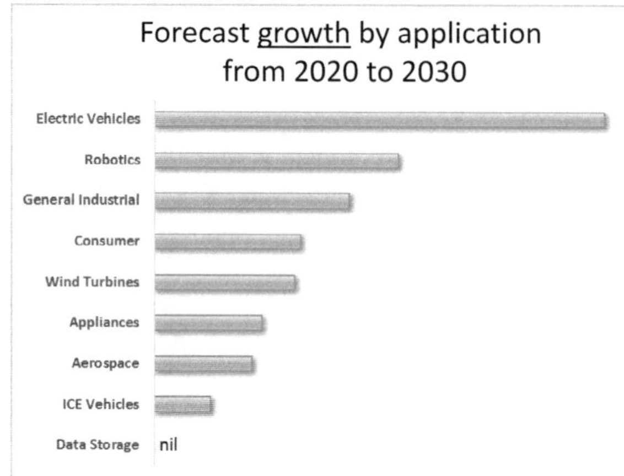

The Global Permanent Magnet Industry 2020 - 2030

Production Quantities and Locations

Countries/Regions covered

- China
- Japan
- Europe
- USA
- India
- Southeast Asia
- South America
- Other

Materials covered

- Alnico
- Ferrite and La,Co-Ferrite
- SmCo
- NdFeB and NdCeFeB
- SmFeN
- Bonded Magnets

The Global Permanent Magnet Industry 2020 - 2030

Usage Forecasts by Application

Combining the basic GWEC data with other industry information permits estimates of magnet consumption in wind power generating systems as per the following chart, Figure 8.5.

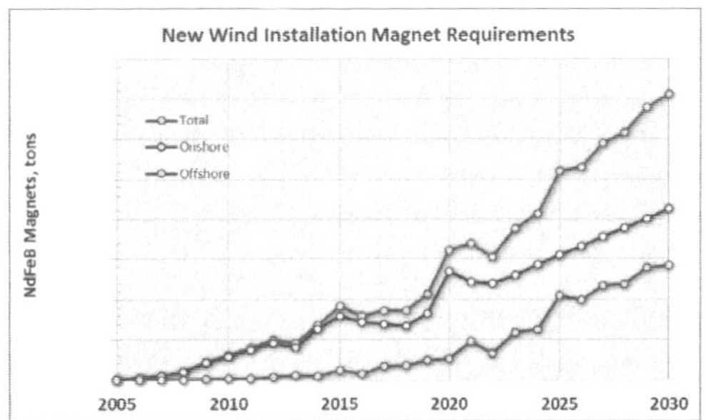

Figure 8.5. NdFeB Magnet Requirements in Support of Annual New Installations of Wind Power Electricity Generation

Between the years 2030 and 2040, a tapering in demand is expected for new installations of wind power. Concurrent with that will be end-of-life (EOL) for an increasing number of existing wind generators which have a design life of 20 years. At that time, a few options are available as follows. In many cases the tower, if properly maintained to prevent corrosion or structural

The Global
Permanent Magnet Industry
2020 - 2030

Usage Forecasts by Application

be required to satisfy the demands for the conversion of the drive systems?" Each vehicle type requires a different amount of magnet. A small passenger car such as the Prius hybrid uses 0.65 to 0.85 kilograms of magnet. At the other extreme, a semi tractor-trailer can require 5 kg or more of NdFeB magnets.

Magnet requirements have been calculated as shown in Figure 8.11. A steep ramp can be seen in demand from under 10,000 tons in 2020 to almost 80,000 tons in 2030 – an 8-fold increase – with the largest increase coming in the second half of the decade.

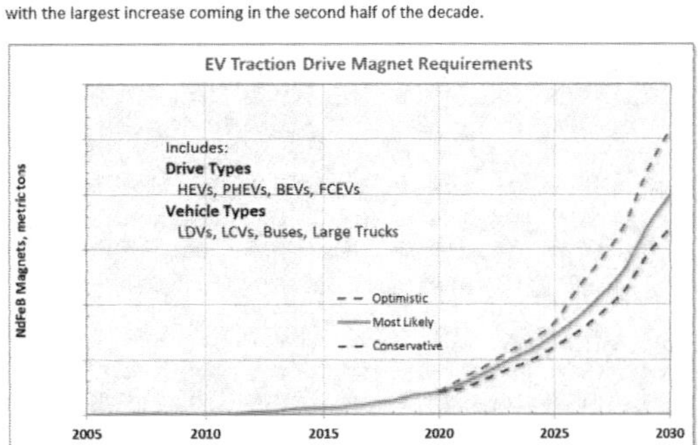

Figure 8.11. NdFeB Magnet Requirements to Meet Conversion from ICE to EVs

The Global
Permanent Magnet Industry
2020 - 2030

Raw Materials

- Supply of heavy rare earths will continue to be of importance
  - Dy and Tb
- Demand for the light rare earths is forecast to surge
  - Nd and Pr
- We could use more market development for rare earths which remain in excess
  - Ce and La
- Many rare earth mines have been identified, but...
- Mines take many years and a lot of money to bring on stream
  - New mines are a risky and slow-moving solution
- Let's not forget
  - Separation
  - Reduction to metal
  - Alloying

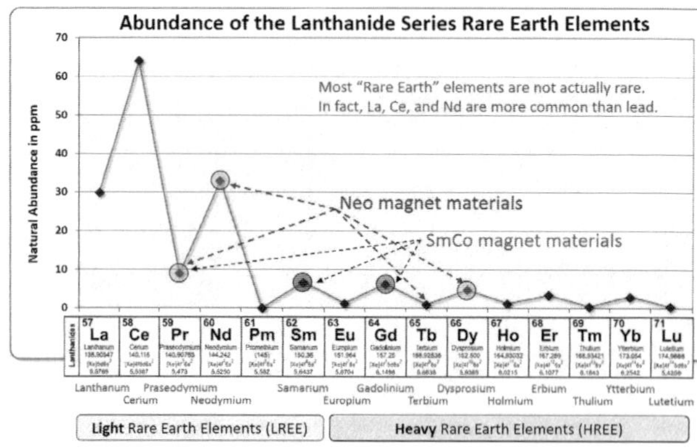

The Global
Permanent Magnet Industry
2020 - 2030

Material Selection

- Design optimization
  - Least material
  - Lowest overall cost
- Key points
  - Temperature range
  - Magnet material and grade choice
  - Minimizing magnet content in the design
- Smart material selection is a faster solution to material constraints than expansion of raw material supply

GE Haliade 6 MW generator construction showing magnets

The Global
Permanent Magnet Industry
2020 - 2030

Pricing and Forecasting

- What causes raw material price fluctuations?
  - Dislocation in supply vs. demand
- Do the study usage forecasts depend on product pricing?
  - Absolutely!
  - Possible scenarios: optimistic, pessimistic and most likely
  - Rapid price fluctuations are more of a problem than absolute prices
- How can fluctuations be reduced or eliminated?
  - Coordination between producers, consumers and investors

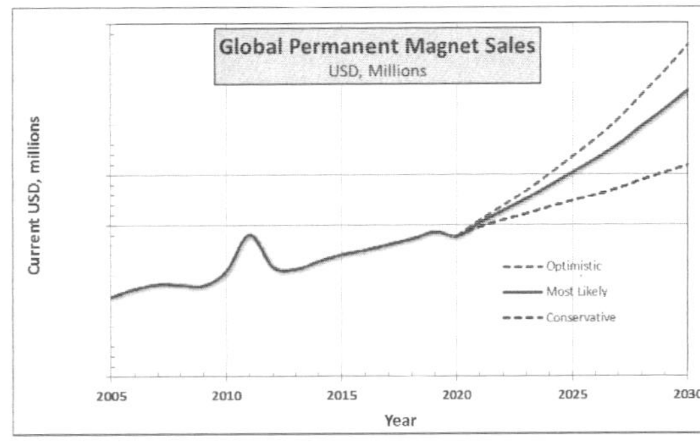

The Global Permanent Magnet Industry 2020 - 2030

Additional Information

- Government Policies and IP Issues
- Research Activities
- Industry Associations
- Magnet Industry Service Providers
  - Magnetizing and Measuring, Magnetic Design Software, Professional Societies, Industry Associations, Publications and Consultants
- Motor Efficiency Standards
  - 70% of permanent magnets are used in motors

The Global Permanent Magnet Industry 2020 - 2030

Magnet Manufacturing Processes

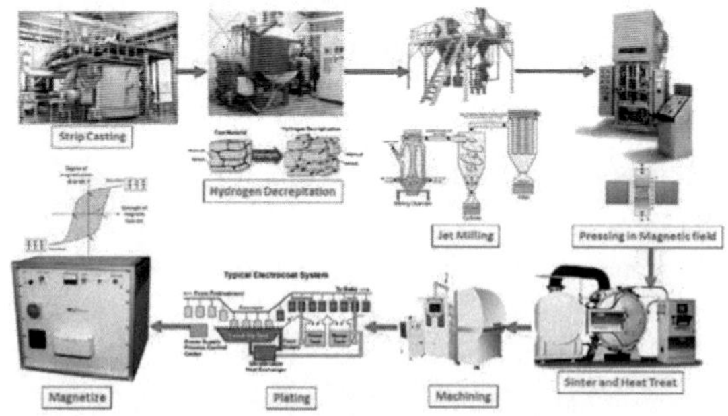

Figure 4.4. The Powder Metallurgical Processing of NdFeB Magnets

The precursor RE metals or master alloys are formed from separated RE oxides or mixed oxides which are reduced to the metallic state by the process of electrolytic reduction. An electric current is passed through a molten mixture of the oxide and a fluxing agent in an electrolytic cell to make the conversion to metal. Each rare earth oxide is processed separately. Keeping the oxygen, nitrogen, and carbon levels low is an important consideration for producing any RE metals because removing any impurity later in the process is impractical.

The Global
Permanent Magnet Industry
2020 - 2030

Reference Material, for example...

Property		Ferrite		Alnico	SmCo		NdFeB	
Symbol (Units)	Name	HF 16/19 p	Ceramic 8B	Alnico 5-7	REC-20	Recoma 30	MQ1-B	N42SH
B_r (T)	Remanence Residual Flux Density	0.265	0.42	1.35	0.9	1.12	0.69	1.34
$\alpha(B_r)$ (%/°C)	Temperature Coefficient of B_r	-0.19	-0.2	-0.02	-0.045	-0.035	-0.105	-0.12
$(BH)_{max}$ (kJ/m^3)	Energy Product	14	32.8	60	160	230	80	350
H_{cJ} (kA/m)	Intrinsic Coercivity	220	236	60	2400	1600	700	1600
$\alpha(H_{cJ})$ (%/°C)	Temperature Coefficient of H_{cJ}	0.3	0.4	0.03	-0.3	-0.3	-0.4	-0.6
H_s (kA/m)	Field Required to Saturate	800	800	240	1600	2400	2800	2800
T_c (°C)	Curie Temperature	450	450	890	727	825	360	310
ρ (g/cm^3)	Density	3.7	5	7	8.4	8.3	6	7.5
ρ (relative)	Electrical Resistivity	high	high	low	low	low	moderate	low
$/kg (relative)	Raw Material Cost	low	low	moderate	high	high	moderate to high	moderate to high
Processing Technology		Injection Molded	Sintered	Cast	Sintered, 1-5 alloy	Sintered, 2-17 alloy	Compression Bonded	Sintered

The Global
Permanent Magnet Industry
2020 - 2030

Key Industry Players, for example...

Beijing Jingci Magnetism Technology Co.
No.31 Shuntong Road
Shunyi District, Beijing 101300 **China**
Website: **www.bjmt.com.cn**
Phone: +86 10-89491701
Fax: +86 10-89492040
Email: **sales@bjmt.com.cn**

BJMT was founded in 1987. Today, they are a company with four factories and 400 employees, with an annual production capacity of 1000 metric tons of sintered NdFeB magnets. BJMT became a Sumitomo (now Hitachi) licensee for the production of sintered NdFeB magnets in 2000.

Beijing Zhongke San Huan High-Tech Co., Ltd.
27/F, Bldg. A, No. 66 East Road
Zhong Guan Cun, Hai Dian District, Beijing **China**
Website: **www.san-huan.com.cn**
Phone: +86 10 62553366
Fax: +86 10 62533386
Email: **e-business@zksanmag.com**

San Huan's principal activities are the research, development, manufacture and sale of sintered NdFeB rare earth permanent magnets and electrically operated bicycles. The group has numerous factories producing sintered NdFeB magnets and one major R&D facility. The company was the first Chinese licensee authorized by Sumitomo (now Hitachi) for the production of NdFeB magnets.

BGRIMM Magnetic Materials and Technology Co., Ltd.
No.2 Building, 10D Science Quarter
Fengtai District, Beijing **China**
Website: **www.magmat.com**
Phone: +86 010-63703380
Fax:
Email: **sales@magmat.com**

BGRIMM is a major supplier of Sr and Ba ferrite powders used for the manufacture of sintered ferrite and bonded ferrite magnets. The company also offers ferrite compound, sintered and flexible ferrite magnets and isotropic magnet rolls. BGRIMM is listed on the Shanghai Stock Exchange.

The Global
Permanent Magnet Industry
2020 - 2030

Magnetics Training Manual, for example...

The Three Vectors

Note this section is written in SI units. Section V discusses the CGS units for magnetism.

Most magnetic behavior is described in terms of three interrelated quantities.

B, Magnetic induction or flux density. A vector quantity, describing the concentration of magnetic flux at a point in space, expressed in terms of flux lines per unit of cross-sectional area. This quantity is reported in tesla (T) in SI (Système International d'Unités) units.[1]

H, Magnetic field. A vector, describing the magnetic field created by a field source, current moving through a wire or a permanent magnet, for example. The correct units are Ampere-turn/meter (A/m). Sometimes, it is more convenient to report the product $\mu_0 H$ rather than H, in this case the proper units are tesla.

M, Magnetization. A quantity describing the magnetic state of the material, representing the vector sum of individual atomic magnetic moments per unit volume. Magnetic moments arise from unpaired spinning electrons, typically in the 3d or 4f electron shell of each atom. The units for M are A/m, just like H. Like H, it is sometimes more convenient to report $\mu_0 M$ and the correct units are again, tesla. In addition, $\mu_0 M$ is called polarization, J, defined as $\mu_0 M = J$.

These three vectors are not independent but are related. Induction is always a combination of magnetization and magnetic field, and in SI Units it is written as

$$B = \mu_0(H + M) = \mu_0 H + J \qquad (1a)$$

The Global
Permanent Magnet Industry
2020 - 2030

Conclusions

- The coming decade should be a good one for the permanent magnet industry
- Use of permanent magnets is forecast to grow especially in key applications such as EVs and offshore wind power
- Both NdFeB and ferrite are growing
- Alnico and SmCo are expected to show little-to-modest growth
- The relationship between supply and demand will remain an ongoing challenge

The Global
Permanent Magnet Industry
2020 - 2030

Thank You for Your Kind Attention

Special Magnetics 2022 Offer
strout@ieee.org
www.magnetreport.com

A High-Efficiency Motor-Drive Architecture with Direct AC-AC Conversion

Dr. Somasundaram Essakiappan

Manager – R&D Engineering, QM Power

Who are we?

QM Power develops and commercializes electric motors and motor controllers

Q-Mag Motors

Q-Sync Controllers

2

Q-Mag Applications

- Electric Vehicle Motors

  - Torque: >400 Nm

- Electric Aircraft Motors

  - Power density: >50 kW/L, >10 kW/kg

3

Q-Mag Motors: Magnet-free Rotor + Patented Stator Geometries

Q-Mag Motors

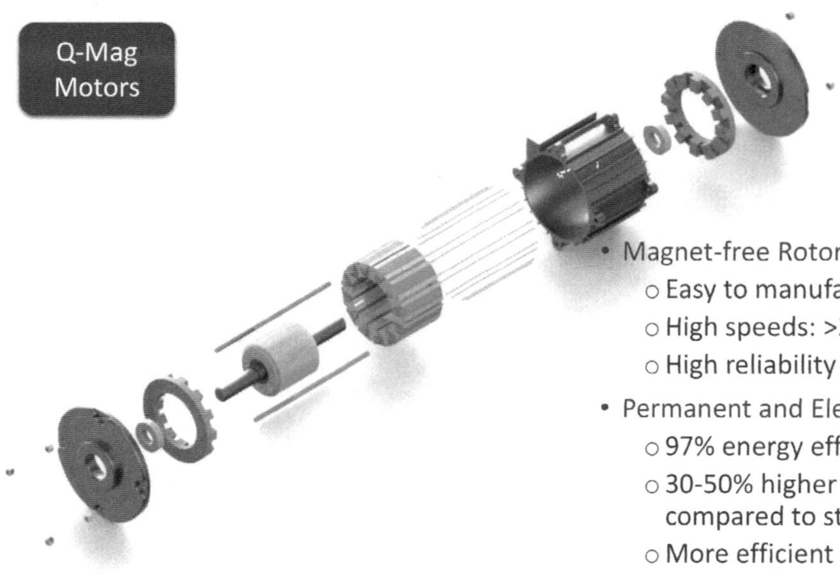

- Magnet-free Rotor
  - Easy to manufacture
  - High speeds: >25,000 RPM
  - High reliability
- Permanent and Electromagnets on Stator
  - 97% energy efficiency
  - 30-50% higher power densities compared to standard motors
  - More efficient cooling

4

Q-Sync Applications

- Commercial Refrigeration
  - Improved efficiency
  - Electricity savings

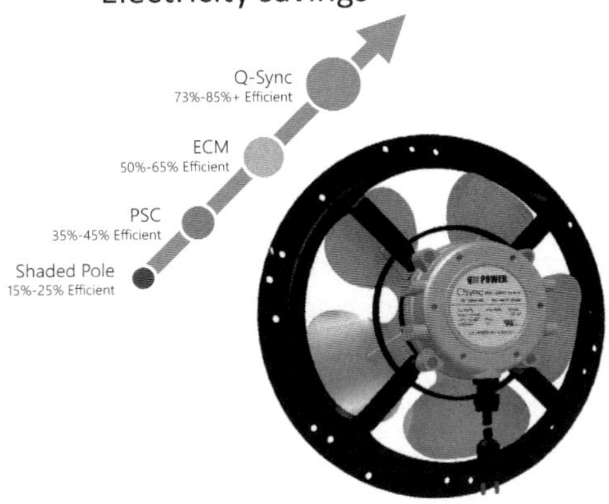

- Heating Ventilation Air Conditioning
  - Improved efficiency and SEER rating
  - Multi-speed capability
  - Reduces operating costs

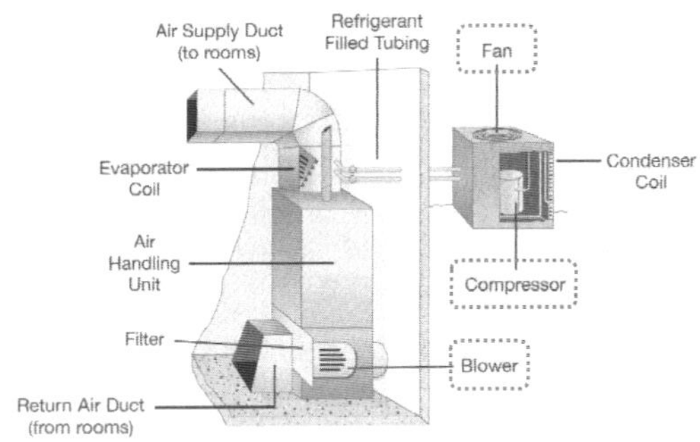

SEER: Seasonal Energy Efficiency Rating (BTU/W-h)

5

Motor Controller Topologies:

- Drive topologies for motors such as ECM's use a PWM inverter drive fed by a rectifier & dc link (two stage power conversion)
- Input power factor can be improved by using boost power factor correction or replacing the rectifier with an active front end

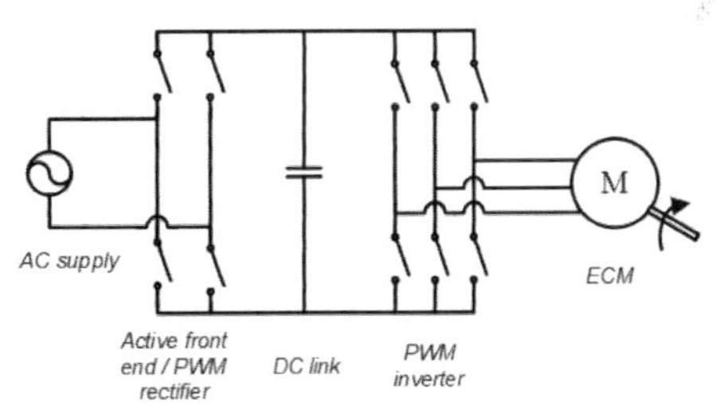

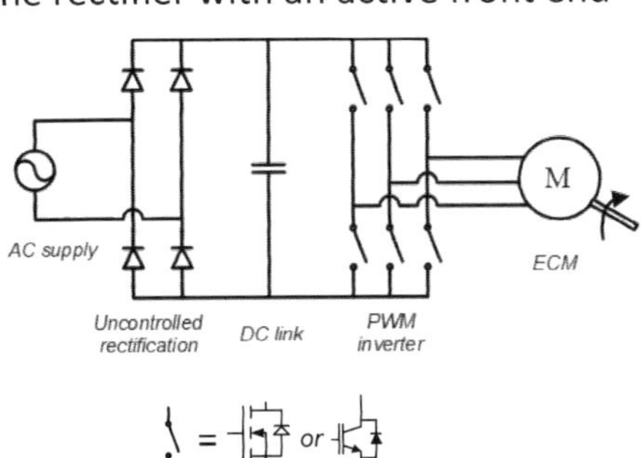

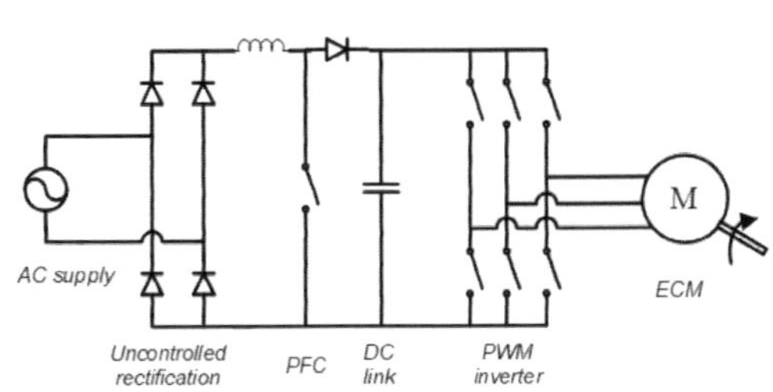

6

Q-Sync AC-AC Converter Topology

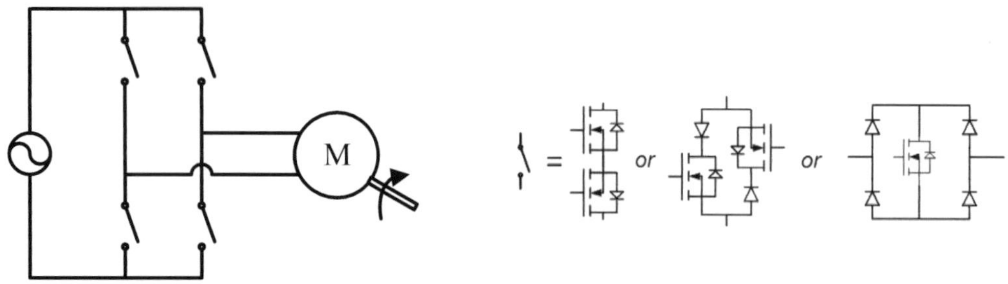

- Direct AC-to-AC Power Conversion
- Single-stage power conversion eliminates dc-link capacitor, improves reliability
- Pulse width modulation and output voltage polarity reversal are performed using the bidirectional devices to follow V/f ratio, below synchronous speeds – providing multi-speed capability
- Sync speed operation: one top device and one bottom device switched on, and sinusoidal input / output current has no distortion and very high displacement power factor

7

Q-Sync: AC to AC Motor Controller

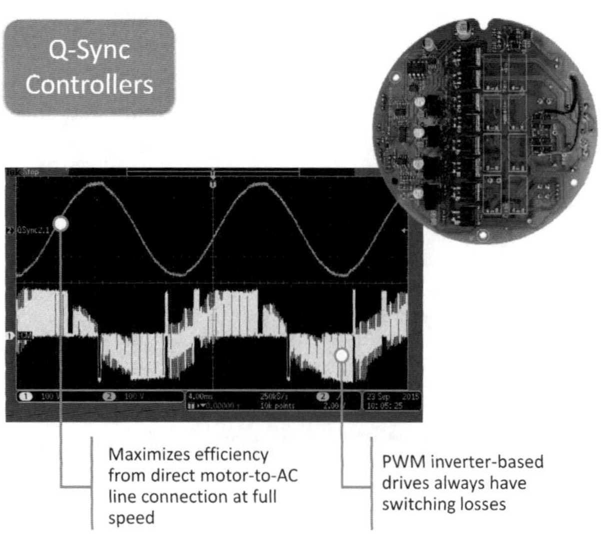

- Absence of switching losses at synchronous speeds provides very high efficiency performance
- Ability to modulate output voltage and frequency enables multi-speed operation
- Very high-power factor operation is realized at rated speed, since the input current is sinusoidal, compared to two-stage drives which require power factor correction

8

Q-Sync – Principle of Operation

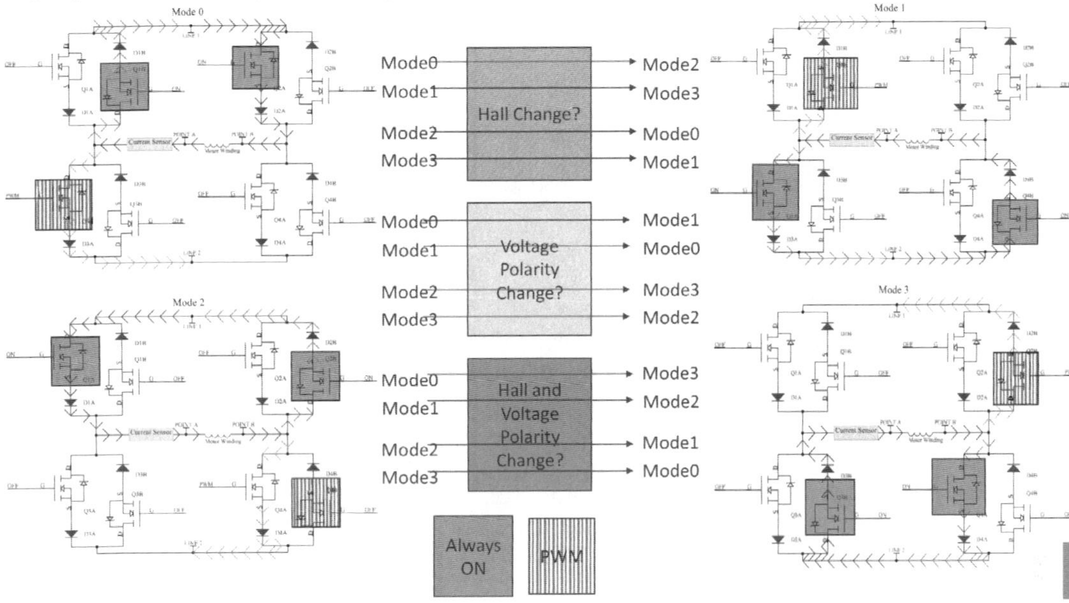

9

Q-Sync Controller-Driven Single-Phase PM (6-pole) Motor

- Rated power = 0.5 hp = 373 W at 1200 rpm
- Operation at **600 rpm (30 Hz)**

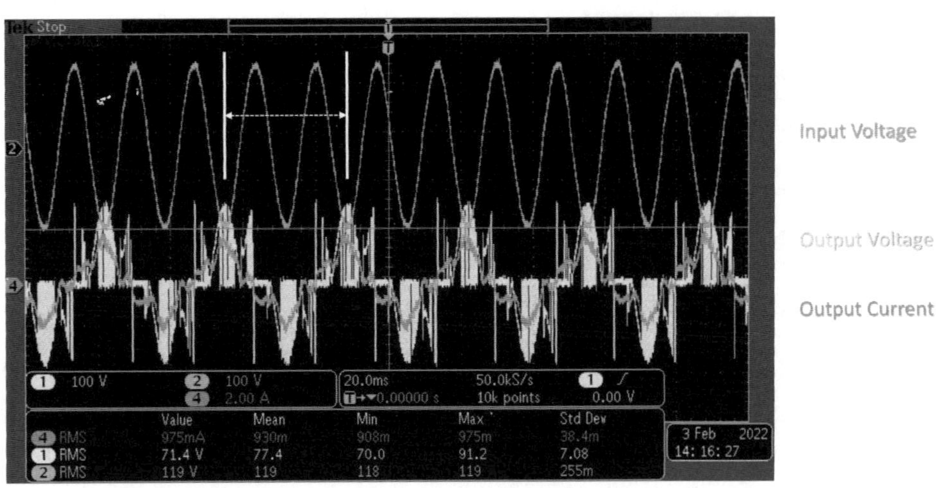

10

Q-Sync Controller-Driven Single-Phase PM (6-pole) Motor

- Rated power = 0.5 hp = 373 W at 1200 rpm
- Operation at **750 rpm (37 Hz)**

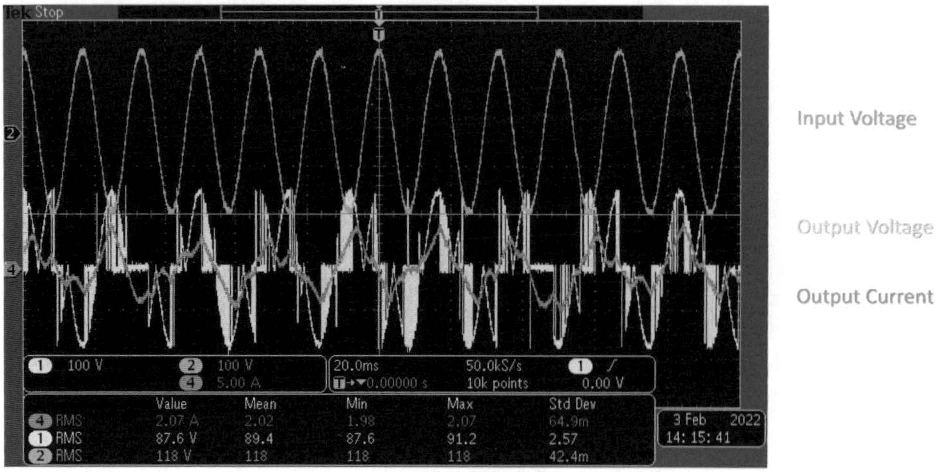

11

Q-Sync Controller-Driven Single-Phase PM (6-pole) Motor

- Rated power = 0.5 hp = 373 W at 1200 rpm
- Operation at **900 rpm (45 Hz)**

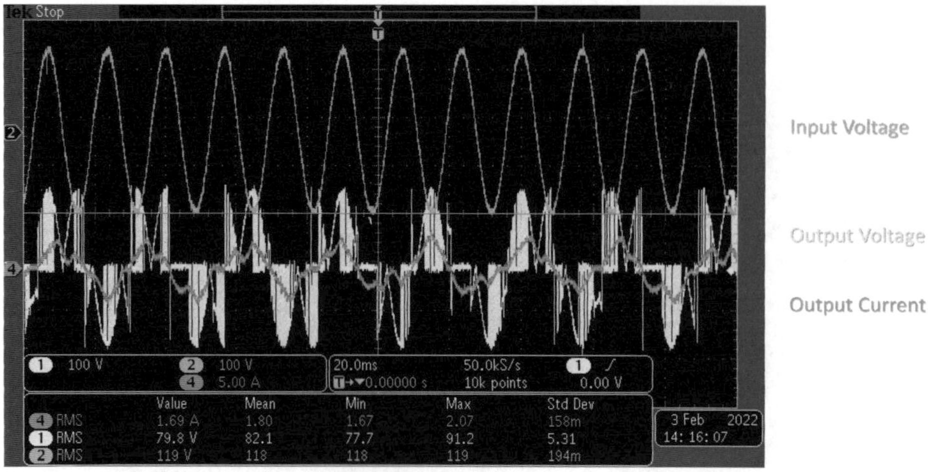

12

Q-Sync Controller-Driven Single-Phase PM (6-pole) Motor

- Rated power = 0.5 hp = 373 W at 1200 rpm
- Operation at **1200 rpm (60 Hz)**

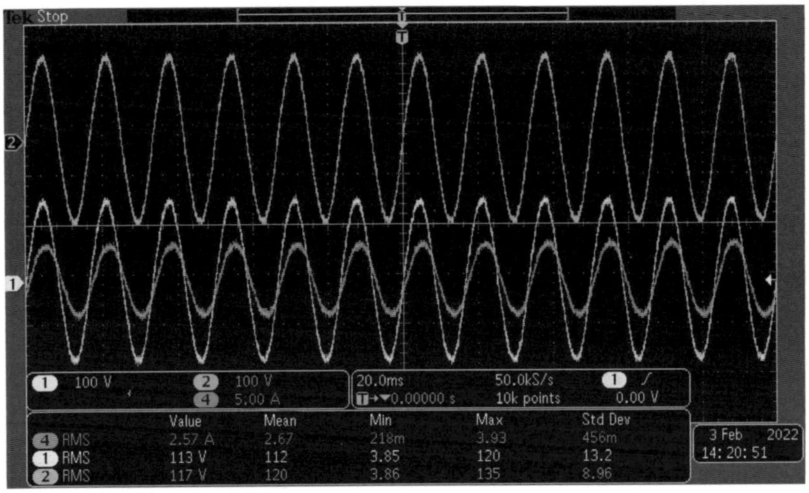

13

Q-Sync Impact

- New residential central air-conditioning and air-source heat pump systems in the US will be required to meet new minimum energy efficiency standards
- Using single-stage power conversion, high efficiency and power factor performance of Q-Sync, substantial maximization of performance ratings may be achieved

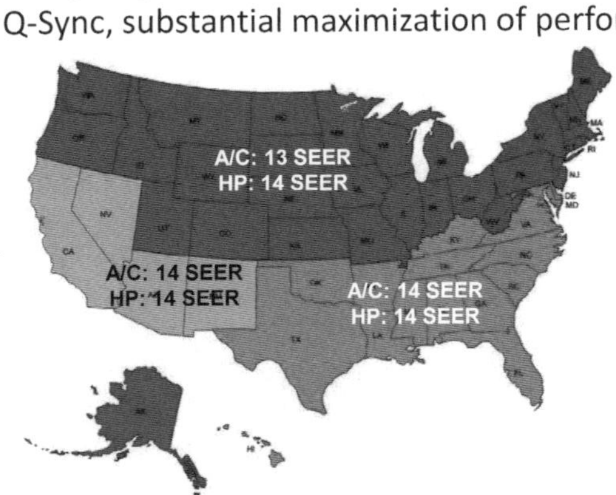

CURRENT REQUIREMENT

2023 REQUIREMENT

SEER: Seasonal Energy Efficiency Rating (BTU/W-h)

14

Q-Sync Impact

- Compared to state-of-the-art motors such as ECM's SEER gains of up to 1.2 have been achieved
- Large-scale deployment of Q-Sync single-phase controllers have the potential to reduce power consumption by applications such as HVAC units substantially

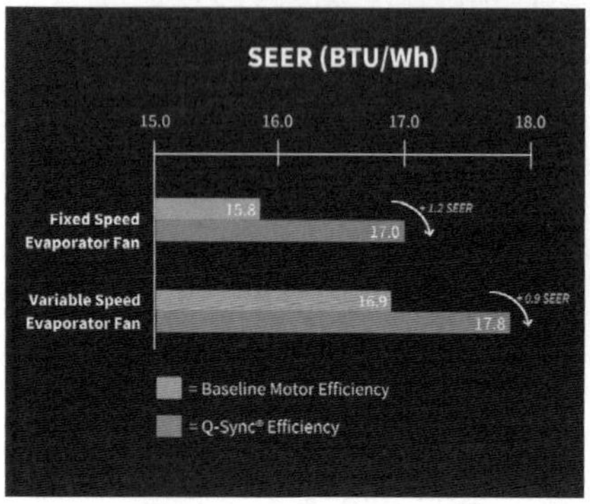

SEER: Seasonal Energy Efficiency Rating

Q-Sync full assembly: Motor + integrated drive module, with single phase ac input shown

15

Q-Sync Three-Phase

- A reduced switch 3-phase to 3-phase sparse matrix topology has been proposed to perform motor control / starting operations
- A 3x3 full matrix topology utilizes 9 bidirectional semiconductor devices (18 unidirectional devices)
- By using advanced control algorithms, a sparse topology which uses 6 bidirectional devices (12 unidirectional devices) has been proposed
- The converter performs PWM switching during ramp up and syncs-up to the grid for line frequency operation at rated speed, providing an adaptable starter solution for motors such as induction machines

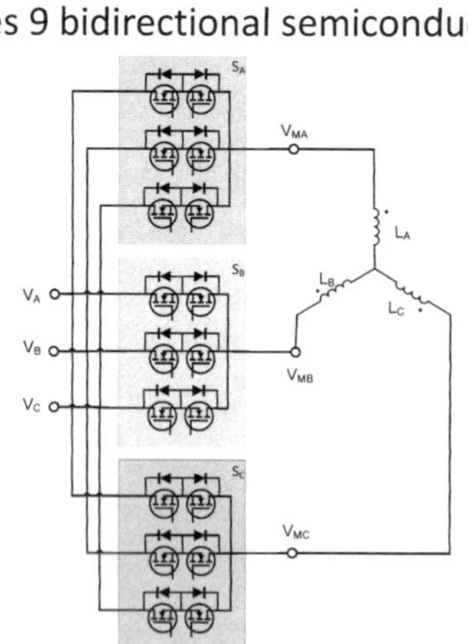

3-phase to 3-phase full matrix topology

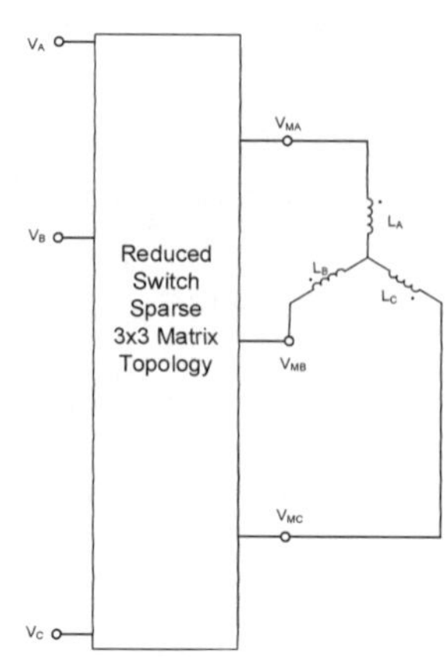

Reduced switch sparse matrix architecture

16

Q-Sync Three-Phase: Algorithm Evaluation

- Motor start-up ramp to half of rated speed (30 Hz)

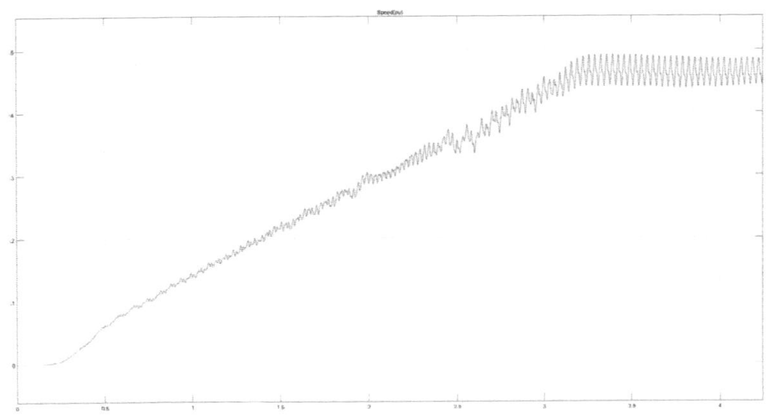

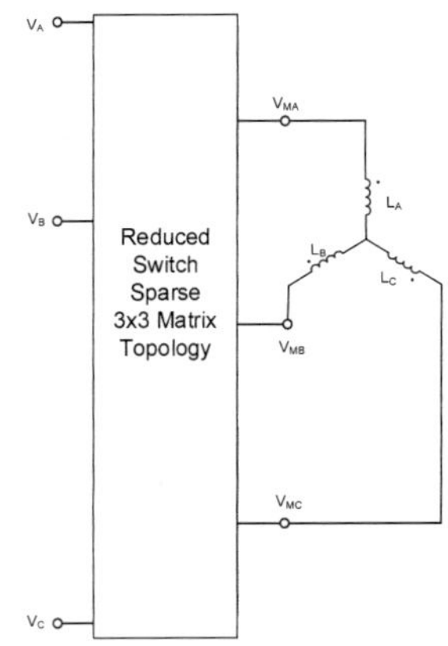

Reduced switch sparse matrix architecture

17

Q-Sync Three-Phase: Algorithm Evaluation

- Motor terminal applied voltages, speed ramping up to half of rated speed (30 Hz)

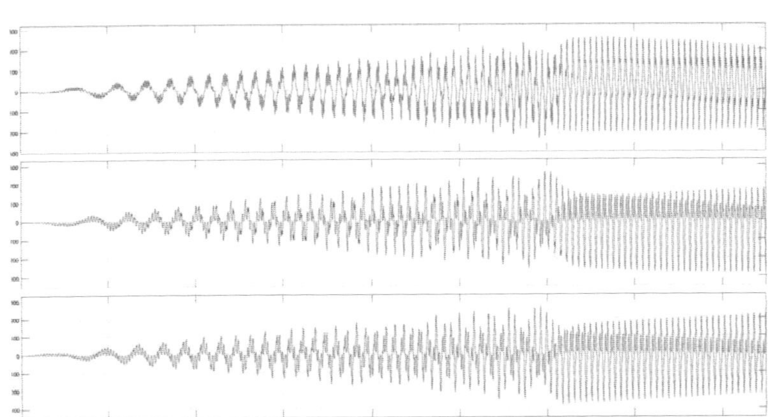

Switching frequency components filtered out for illustration

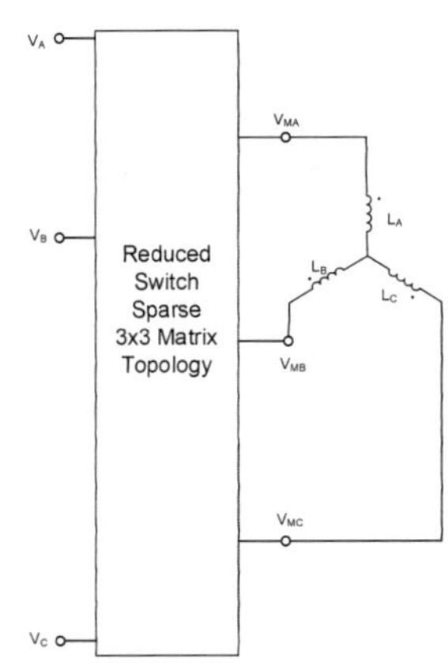

Reduced switch sparse matrix architecture

18

Q-Sync Three-Phase: Algorithm Evaluation

- Input and motor voltages and currents, speed ramping up to half of rated speed (30 Hz)

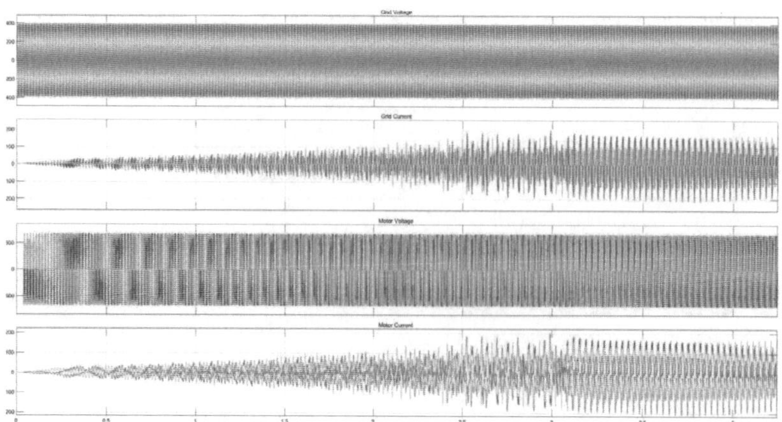

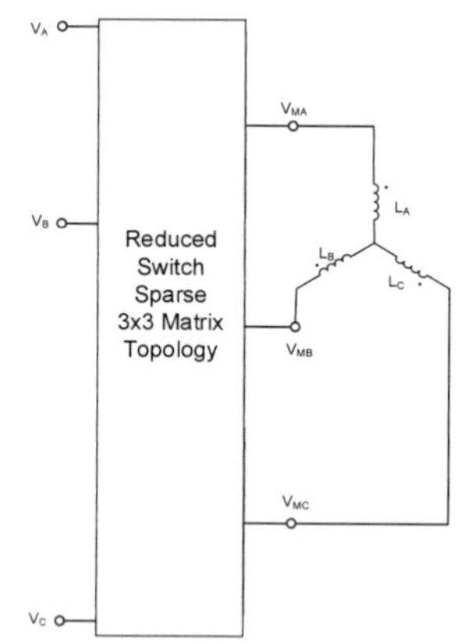

Reduced switch sparse matrix architecture

19

Conclusion

- The Q-Sync motor control technology with single-stage AC-AC power conversion has been presented
- Q-Sync architecture eliminates two-stage power conversion and dc link found in traditional drive systems, allowing for better efficiencies and reliability
- Q-Sync control logic eliminates PWM switching at synchronous speed operation, eliminating switching losses, providing higher efficiencies and power factor performance than state-of-the-art
- Q-Sync controllers and motors shown to yield performance metrics meeting / exceeding compliance targets in applications such as HVAC
- Continued development underway on scaling up Q-Sync technology to three-phase industrial motor starters and drives

20

QM
POWER
INC.
Thank you!

DELO
NEW ADHESIVES IN E-MOTORS: BOND STRENGTHS OF MORE THAN 20 MPA AT +180 °C

DELO

FAMILY-OWNED

€ 160 M. REVENUES

800 EMPLOYEES

DELO

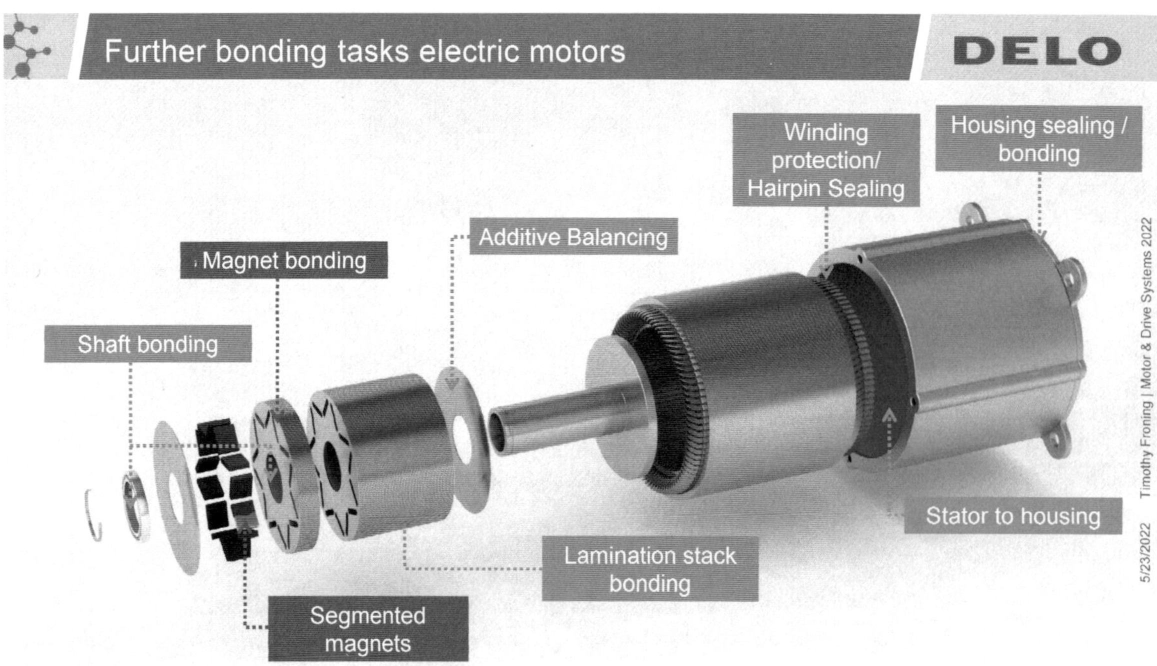
Further bonding tasks electric motors
DELO
Winding protection/ Hairpin Sealing
Housing sealing / bonding
Additive Balancing
Magnet bonding
Shaft bonding
Stator to housing
Lamination stack bonding
Segmented magnets
5/23/2022 Timothy Froning | Motor & Drive Systems 2022

Structural joining – overview

DELO

Many modification options (e.g. spacer, color, flow behavior, thermal conductivity)

Temperature range of use up to +220 °C

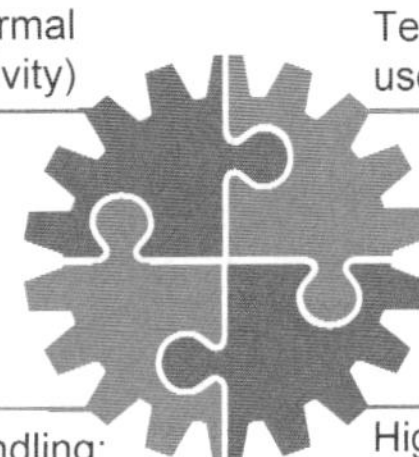

Easy handling; storage temperature 0 to 10 °C, long processing time, large containers possible

High reliability against different media (e.g. automotive typical media, oil)

- One-component epoxy adhesives
- Broad portfolio available for testing!

What are the benefits of the new HT adhesives?

DELO

- Highest temperature strength: >20 MPa @ +180 °C!
- Stable temperature resistance even after 10.000 h storage!
- Gap adjustment with spacers ~50 µm
- Fast curing: 10 min @ +150 °C
- Combination with light fixation possible
- Development of thermal conductivity

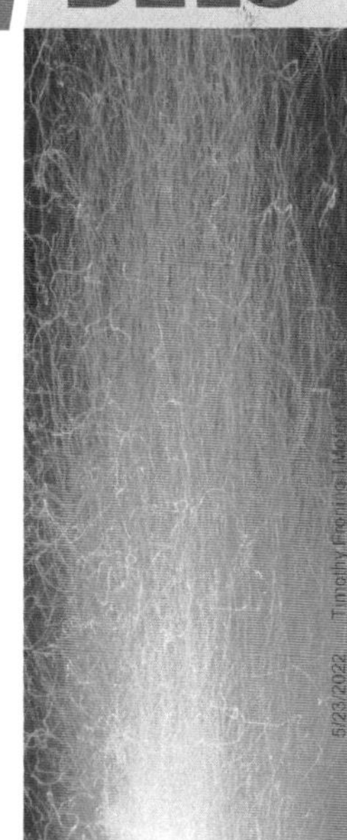

DELO MONOPOX HT2999

DELO

Properties	Standard 1C Epoxy	DELO MONOPOX HT2999
Colour	beige	grey
Fillers	minerals	minerals, glass spacer
Temperature range of use [°C]	-40 to +180	-55 to +220
Viscosity [mPas]	pasty	pasty
Glass transition temp. [°C] DMTA	134	180
Dielectric strength [kV/mm]	23	22
Curing parameter	40 min at +150 °C	10 min at +150 °C

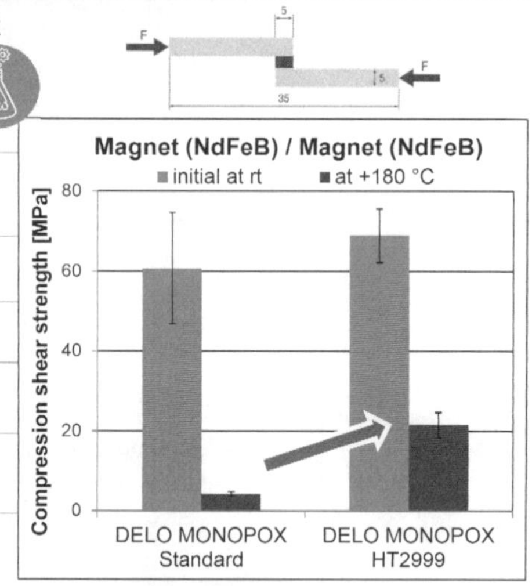

Advantages of DELO MONOPOX HT2999:

⇨ Best temperature strength, high glass transition temperature, fast heat curing, no CMR-listing

Timothy Froning | Motor & Drive Systems 2022 5/23/2022

Long-term stability of 10.000h!

DELO

Requirement: long-term stability – life time of final product for 8.000 h / 15 years

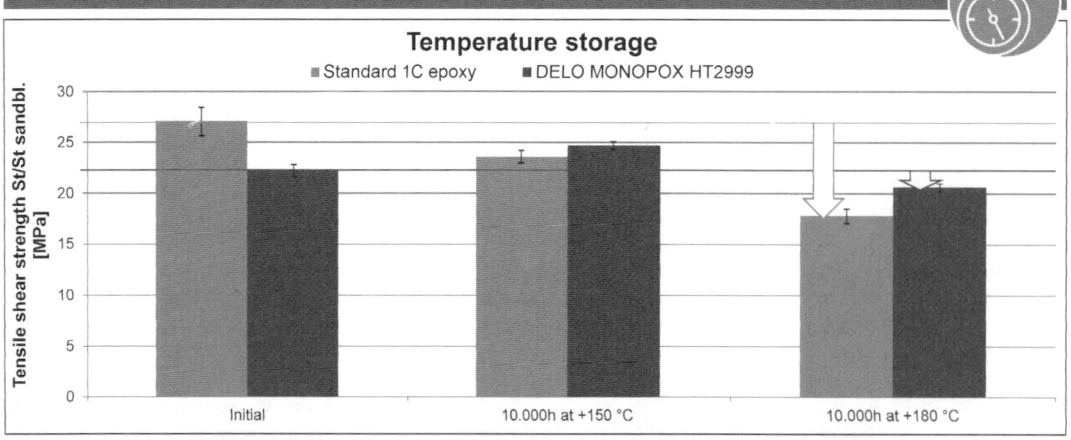

⇨ Stable results with new HT-MONOPOX, difference to standard products at +180 °C

Timothy Froning | Motor & Drive Systems 2022 5/23/2022

Optimization of curing parameters

DELO

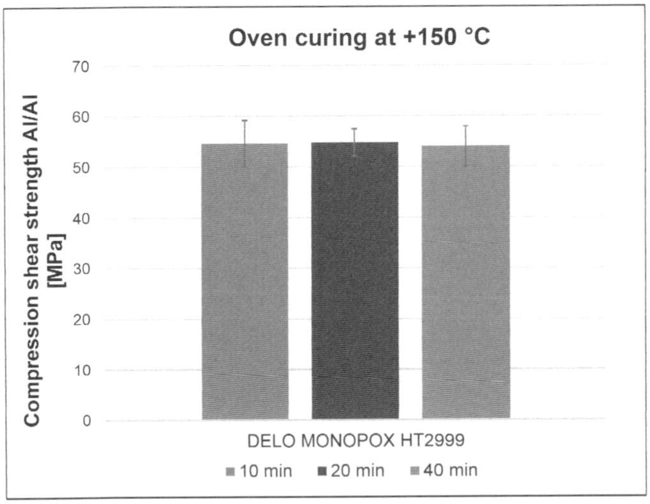

- *Oven curing of rotor stacks with DELO MONOPOX*

⇨ Equal strength level starting with 10 min @ +150 °C!
⇨ Faster curing than comparable HT-products in the market

Optimization of curing parameters – induction heating

DELO

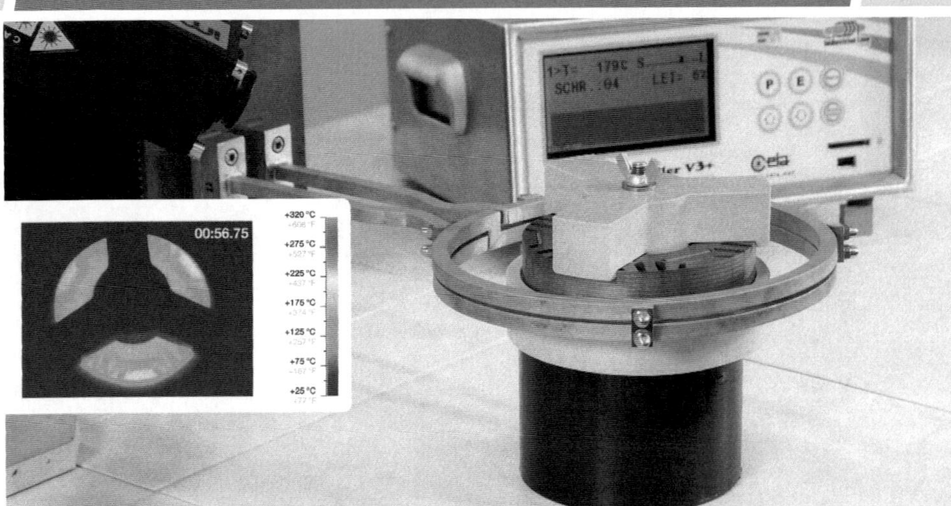

⇨ Equal strength level starting with 1 min at +180 °C!
⇨ Very fast production processes possible with heat curing materials!

5/23/2022 Timothy Froning | Motor & Drive Systems 2022

Application integrated permanent magnet bonding

DELO

Benefits with bonding technology

- No damage of magnets and coating due to joining method (magnetic flux not disturbed)
- High fixation strength of magnets
- Reliable fixation over life time
- Vibration protection/noise minimization
- Additional fixation of e-sheets
- Fast processes (e.g. induction heating, light fixation)

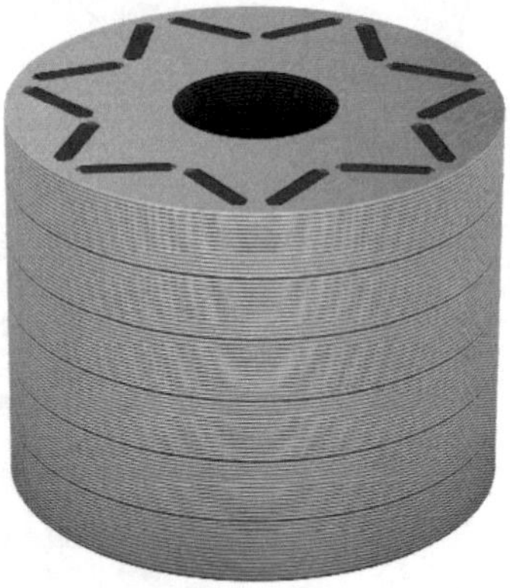

- *Complete rotor with several lamination stacks and bonded integrated permanent magnets*

5/23/2022 Timothy Froning | Motor & Drive Systems 2022

⇨ Focus on epoxy adhesives in traction motors for electric cars
⇨ Improved power density leads to higher requirements for temperature resistance

Magnet bonding with DELO MONOPOX HT2999

DELO

Temperature performance on rotor stacks

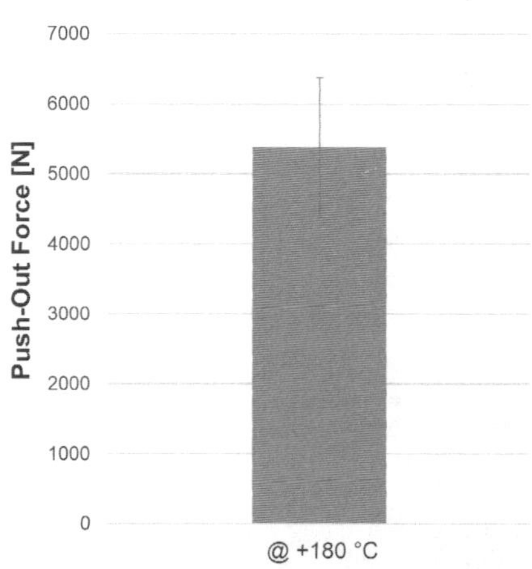

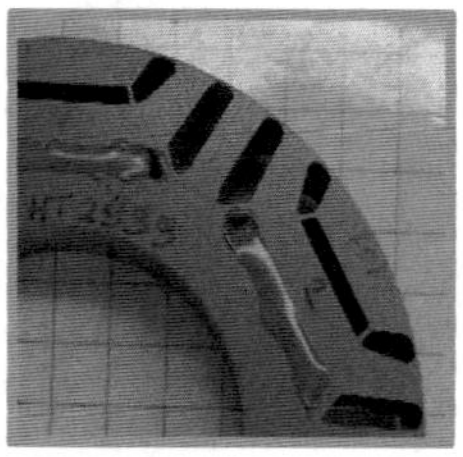

Dummy rotor placed on the lower clamp of the tensile unit within the temperature chamber

5/23/2022 Timothy Froning | Motor & Drive Systems 2022

⇨ Huge values for the fixation of magnets, even at highest temperatures!

Process: bonding with light fixation in side slots

DELO

DELO DUALBOND

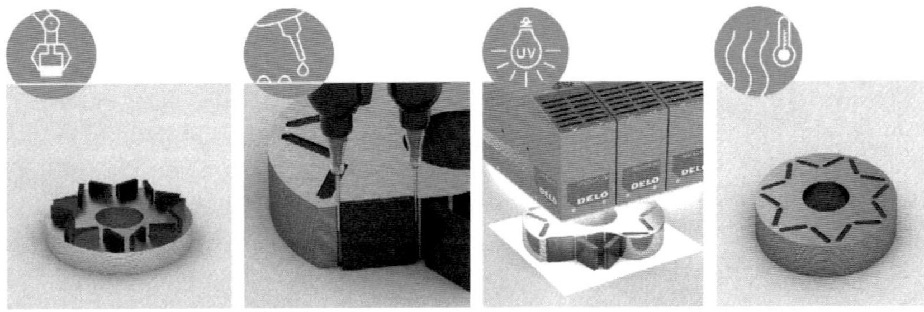

Magnet insertion *Dispensing* *Pre-fixation with light* *Curing*

Watch the video: https://www.youtube.com/watch?v=iPPj0QQiliU
Electric Motor Magnet Bonding –
Increasing UPH With Fixation-Aid-Free Process Design

- Also combination with high temperature performance adhesives
- In addition: focus on debonding technologies for end-of-life recycling

5/23/2022 Timothy Froning | Motor & Drive Systems 2022

Application segmented magnets

DELO

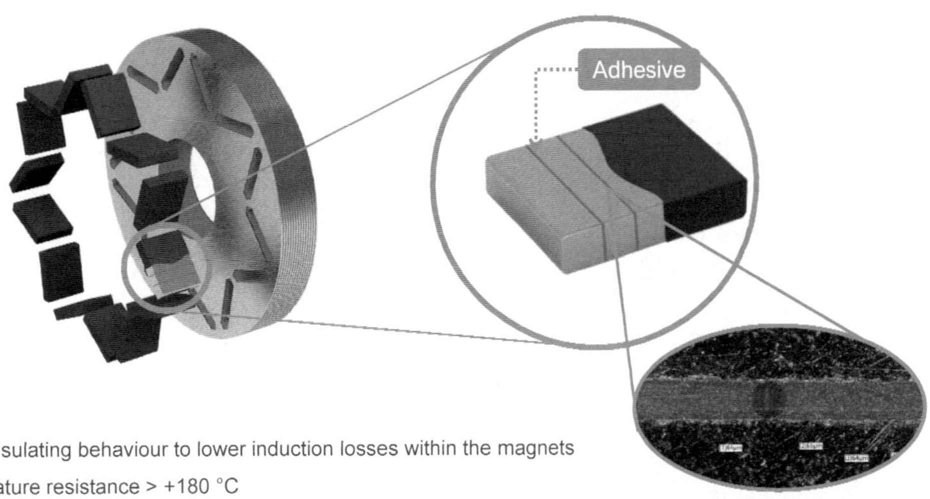

- Electrically insulating behaviour to lower induction losses within the magnets
- High temperature resistance > +180 °C
- Defined bondline thickness (50µm) with combined insulation

5/23/2022 Timothy Froning | Motor & Drive Systems 2022

Summary of product group DELO MONOPOX

DELO

- Typical containers: cartridges, buckets, hobbocks
- Easy handling, long processing time
- Well-adjusted portfolio for various applications
- Many process variations, fast heat curing
- Highest temperature resistance!
  → DELO MONOPOX HT2999

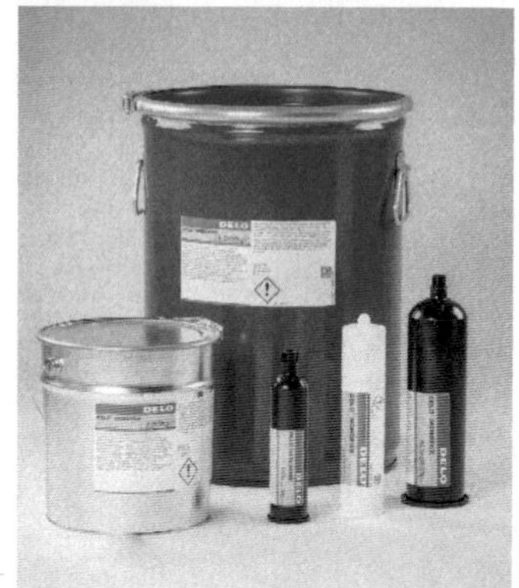

5/23/2022 Timothy Froning | Motor & Drive Systems 2022

The world's strongest adhesive – DELO MONOPOX

DELO

3 g of adhesive	17.5 t weight	World Record for DELO

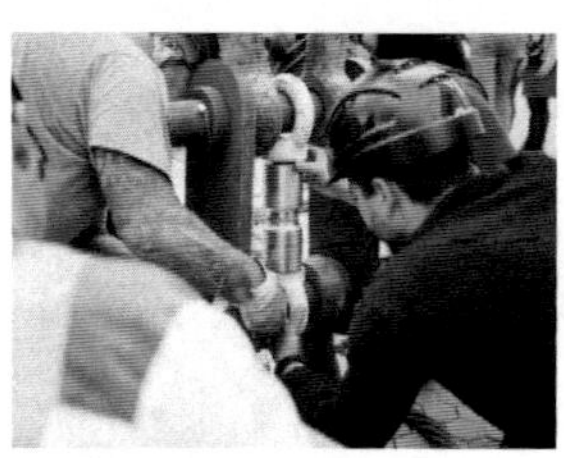

The bonded aluminum cylinder is put into position.

The truck hung at a height of 1 m for 1 hour.

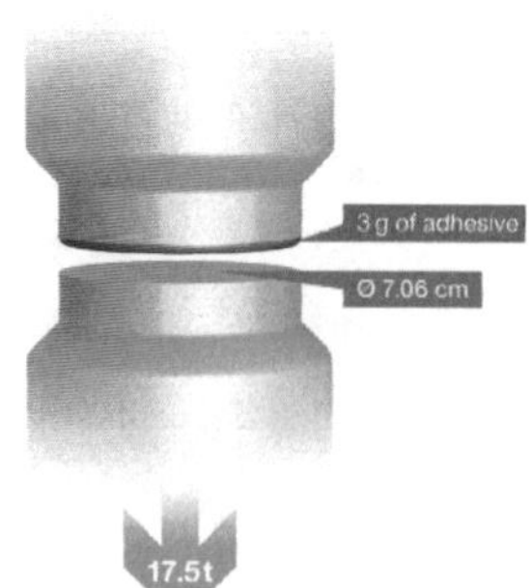

⇨ The strongest adhesive is a modification of a high-temperature-resistant, heat-curing DELO MONOPOX HT

*modification not available for commercial sale

5/23/2022 Roman Schlicher

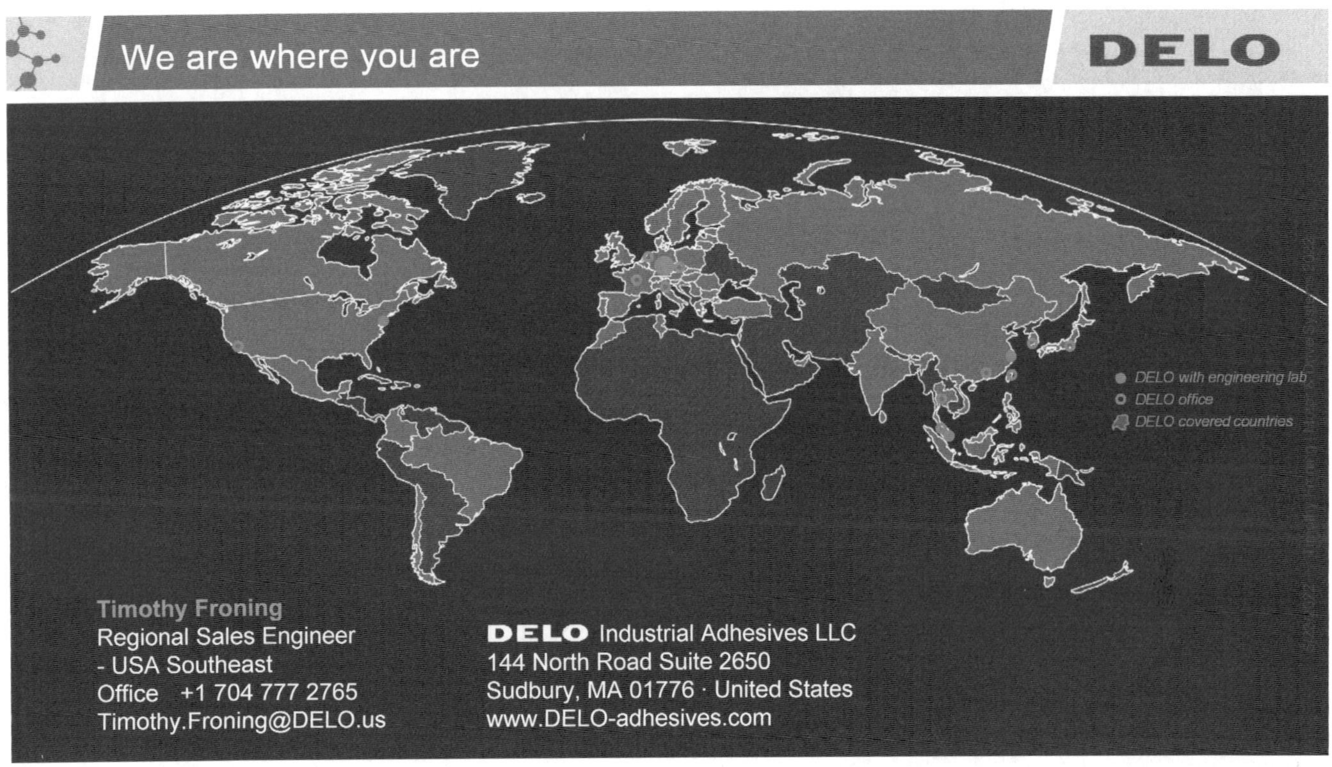
We are where you are
DELO
DELO with engineering lab
DELO office
DELO covered countries
Timothy Froning
Regional Sales Engineer
- USA Southeast
Office +1 704 777 2765
Timothy.Froning@DELO.us
DELO Industrial Adhesives LLC
144 North Road Suite 2650
Sudbury, MA 01776 · United States
www.DELO-adhesives.com

HBK
HOTTINGER BRÜEL & KJÆR

Measuring Power Losses in Electric Motors and Inverters

Learn more at
https://www.hbm.com/eDrive

HBM Brüel & Kjær

PUBLIC

eDrive testing

Agenda

1. Introduction
2. Inverter losses
3. Motor Losses
4. Measurement Uncertainty

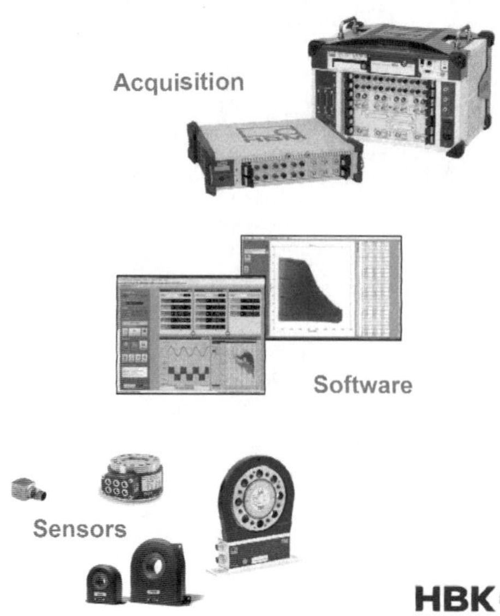

2 PUBLIC

HBK
HOTTINGER BRÜEL & KJÆR

UNRESTRICTED

Losses

- Each component has losses in energy between states
- Losses create heat
- Losses decrease range
- Losses result in increased weight/volume
- Characterize losses so we can:
  - Understand them
  - Mitigate them
  - Manage them

Heat

Vehicle Range

Weight & Volume

Inverter Losses

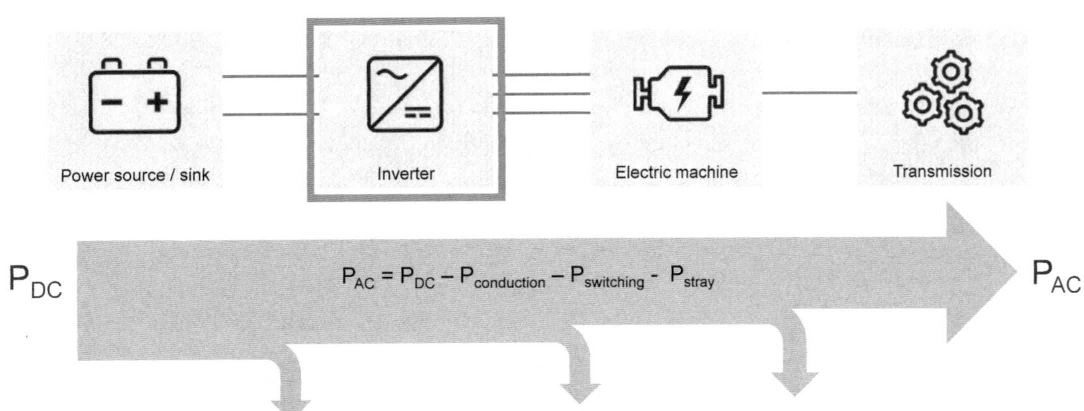

- Conduction Losses
  - Resistance of the switch
  - Resistance of the connections
- Switching Losses
  - Turn on losses
  - Turn off
- Stray Losses
  - off state
  - support circuits

Inverter Switch operation

- Conduction
  - Switch has an "on resistance"
  - Power loss = $I^2 R_{switchOn} = I_{ds} * V_{ds}$
  - Resistance is a function of temperature
- Turn on / Turn off Loss
  - $P = f*(E_{on} + E_{off}) = I_{ds} * V_{ds}$
  - Losses increase with frequency
  - Losses increase with on/off time
- Key to Measurement
  - Time aligned electric & mechanical
  - Calculations
  - Accuracy

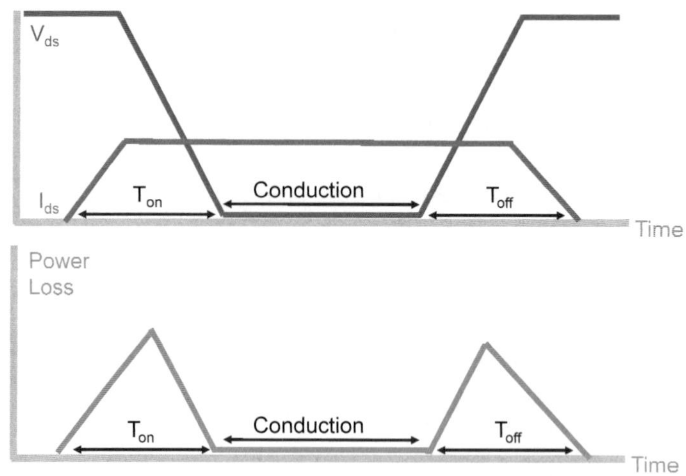

5 | PUBLIC

HBK HOTTINGER BRÜEL & KJÆR

UNRESTRICTED

Inverter Loss Measurement

- Accurately measure DC in & AC out
- Estimate On resistance with TC and equation
  - Calculate losses
  - Time aligned temperatures
- Measure P_{on} & P_{off} with differential measurement across switch
  - Scope card @ 250MS/s

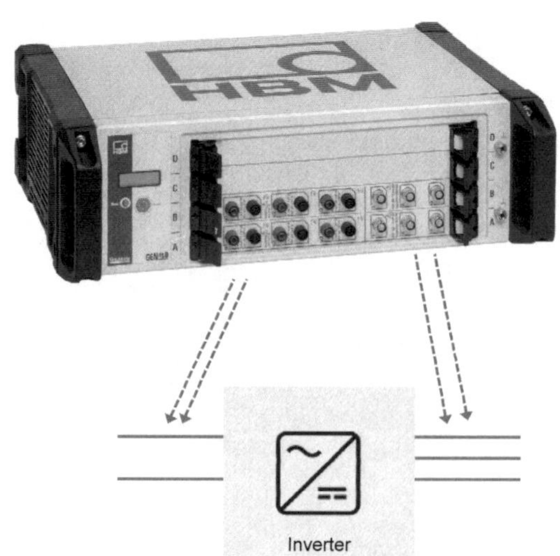

6 | PUBLIC

HBK HOTTINGER BRÜEL & KJÆR

UNRESTRICTED

Inverter Switch On and Off Example

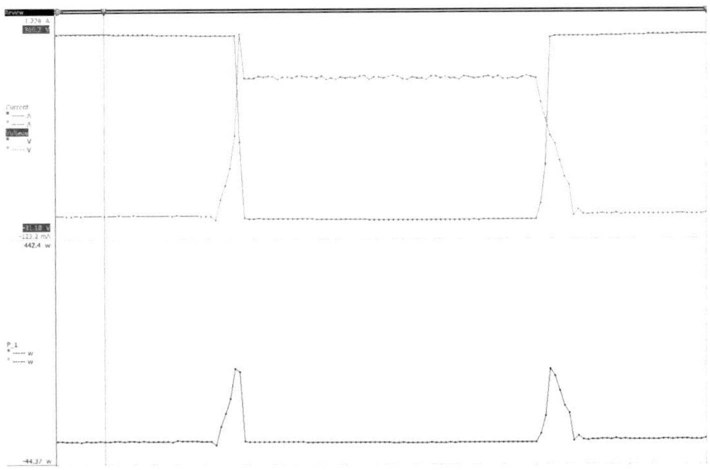

Motor Losses

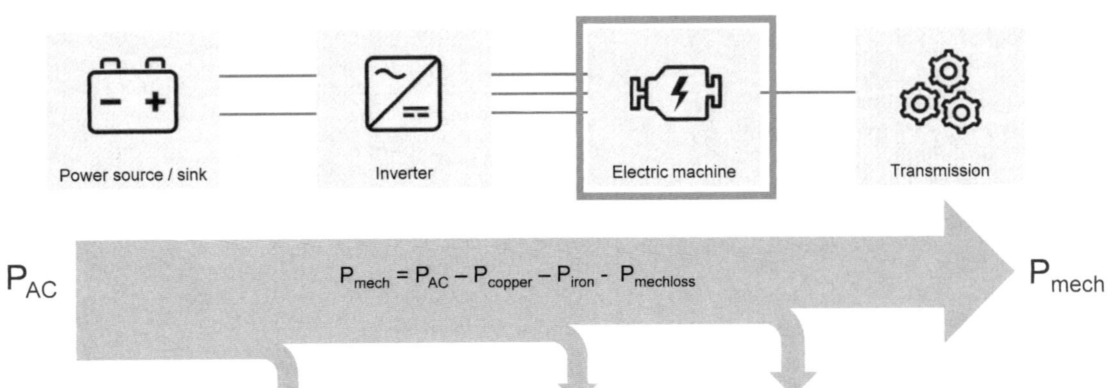

- Copper Losses
  - Resistive
  - Skin effect
- Iron Losses
  - Eddy currents
  - Hysteresis
- Mechanical Losses
  - Friction
  - Windage

Copper Losses - Resistive

- Losses due to resistance of the motor windings
- $P_{copper} = I_{ph}^2 * R_{windings}$
- Temperature dependent
  - $R_{winding} = R_0*(1+\alpha*(T-T_0))$
  - Temp → Ω
  - Can be reduced by cooling
- Measured with phase current and temperatures
- Key to Measurement
  - Time aligned electric & mechanical
  - Custom sensors and calculations
  - Accuracy

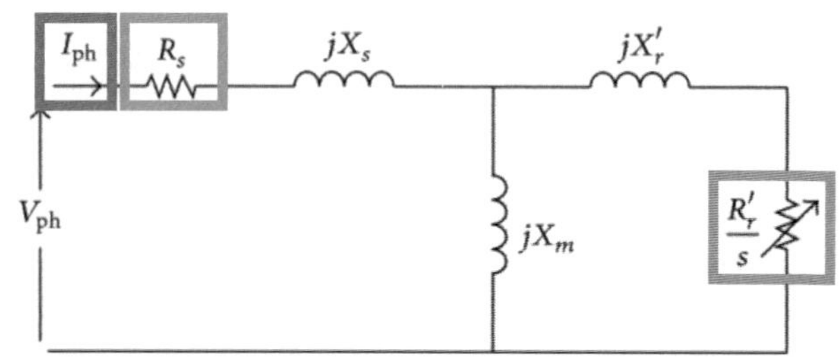

Motor Circuit equation highlighting the resistive element

HBK HOTTINGER BRÜEL & KJÆR

UNRESTRICTED

Iron Losses - Hysteresis

- Magnetizing iron requires energy
- Losses happen every sine wave
  - Property of the iron & permeability
- $P_b = \eta*f*V*B_{max}^n$
  - η – Steinmetz hysteresis coefficient (material property)
  - n - Steinmetz exponent (material property)
  - V – Volume
  - f – Frequency
  - B – Max flux density
- Key to Measurement
  - Data to understand variables → Sensitivity
  - Accuracy
  - Custom Calculations
  - Time aligned electric & mechanical

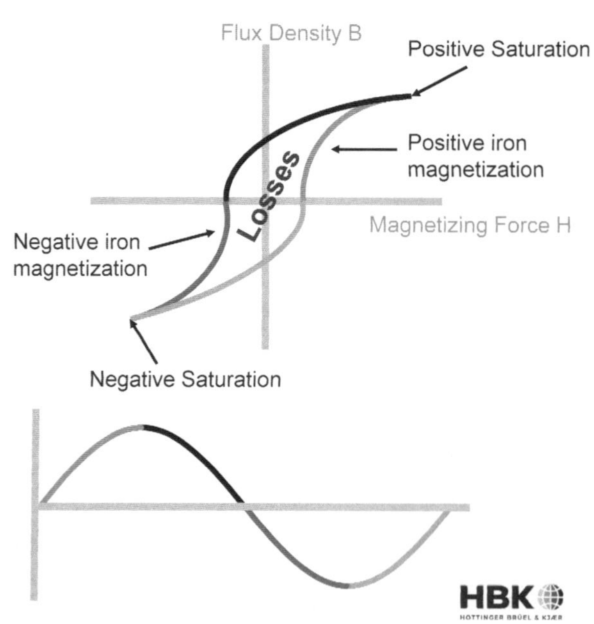

HBK HOTTINGER BRÜEL & KJÆR

UNRESTRICTED

Iron Losses - Eddy Currents

- Faraday's law states *"any change in the environment of a coil of wire will cause a voltage to be induced in the coil, regardless of how the magnetic change is produced"*
  - The magnetism of the flux will self induce EMF
  - Current will flow in the core → losses
  - Thinner laminations have a higher resistance

- $P_e = K_e * B_{max}^2 * f^2 * t^2 * V$
  - K_e – eddy current constant
  - B - Max flux density
  - f – frequency
  - t – Thickness
  - V – Volume

- Key to Measurement
  - Data to understand variables → Sensitivity
  - Accuracy
  - Custom Calculations

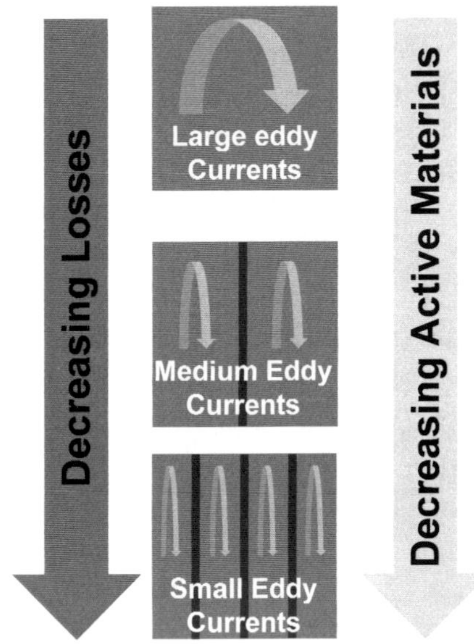

UNRESTRICTED

HBK HOTTINGER BRÜEL & KJÆR

Mechanical losses

- Internal windage
- Bearing Friction
- Misalignment
- Keys to measurement
  - Accuracy
  - Custom sensors

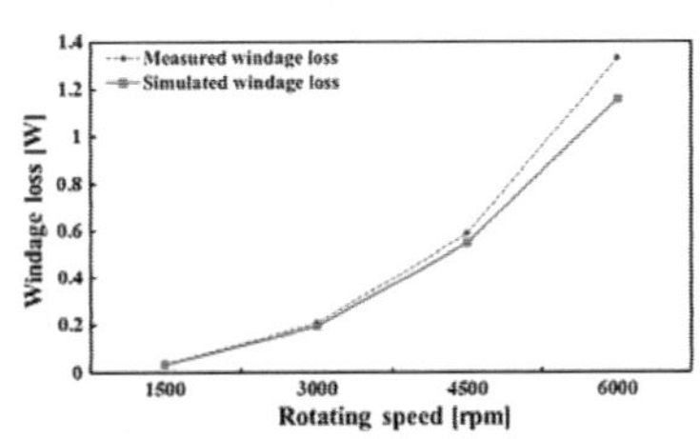

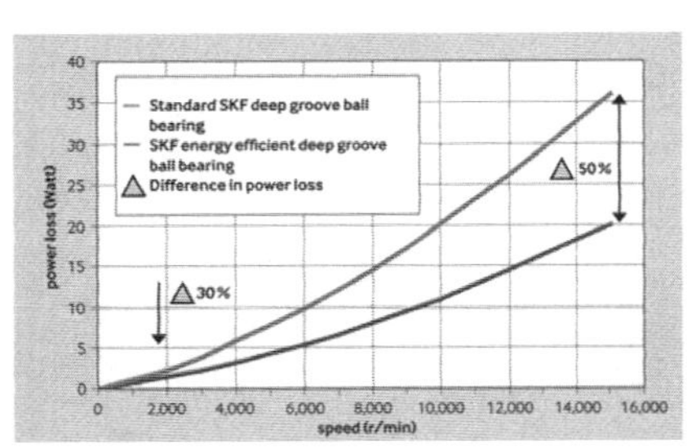

HBK HOTTINGER BRÜEL & KJÆR

UNRESTRICTED

Motor Loss Measurement

- Accurately measure AC in & Mechanical out
- Measure copper/iron losses thermocouples and equations
- Measure mechanical losses with equation or a curve based on measurement

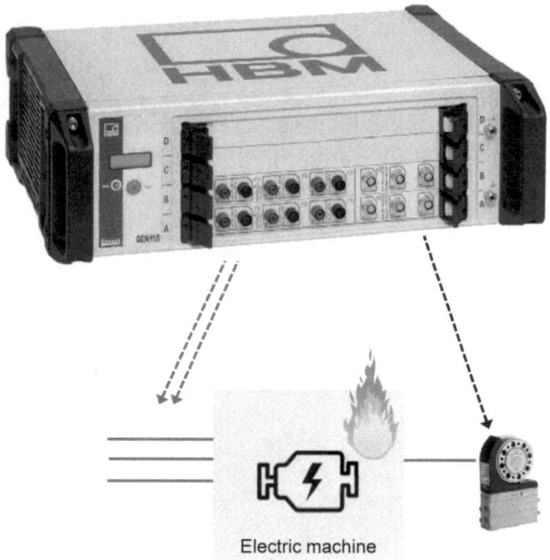

HBK
HOTTINGER BRÜEL & KJÆR

UNRESTRICTED

HBK
HOTTINGER BRÜEL & KJÆR

Measurement Uncertainty

Measuring Power Losses → A Differential Problem

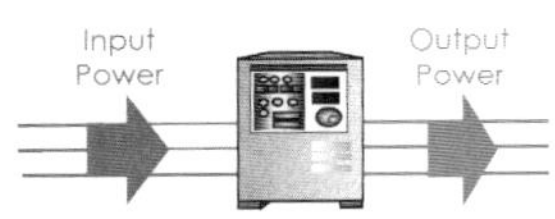

- 500 kW inverter
- 95% efficiency

	"Truth"	Measurement chain error @ 1% — Measured	Error	Measurement chain error @ 0,1% — Measured	Error
Input	500 kW	500 kW +/- 5 kW	1%	500 kW +/- 0.5 kW	0,1%
Output	475 kW	475 kW +/- 4.75 kW	1%	475 kW +/- 0.475 kW	0,1%
Losses	25 kW	25 kW +/- 9.75 kW	39,0%	25 kW +/- 0.975 kW	3,9%
Conduction	5 kW	5kW +/- 9.75 kW	😲	5 kW +/- .975 kW	19.5%

If you want to achieve **reasonable measurements** for derived values like **Power Loss** you need the **most accurate measurement** you can get

Measurement Uncertainty and Losses

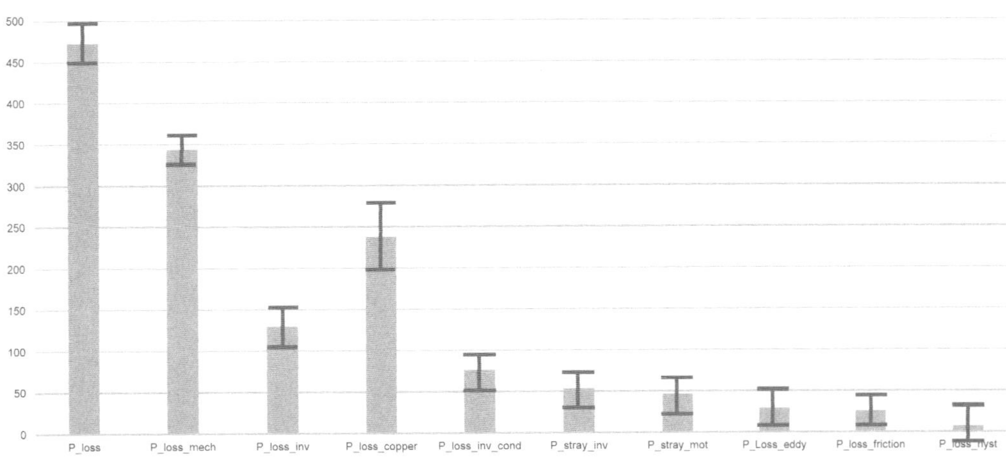

Real Example – Load Step

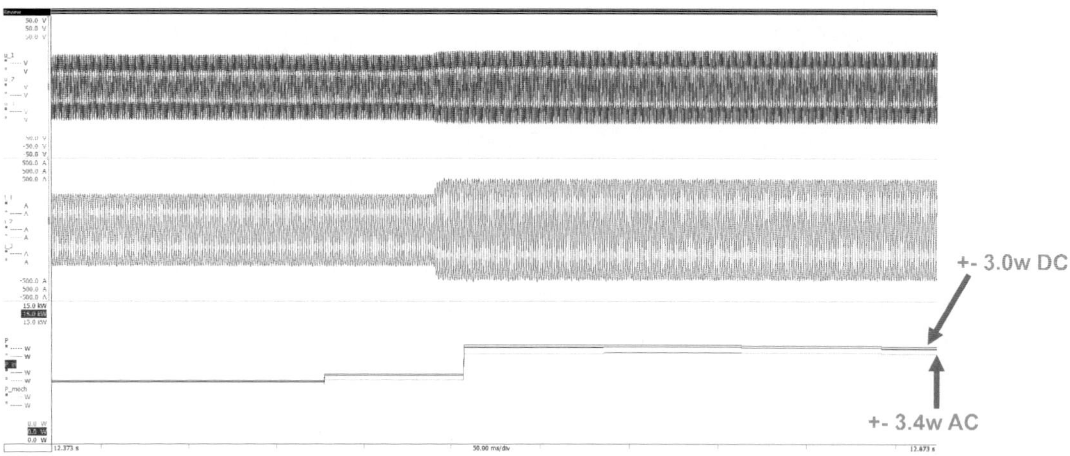

Measurements of raw signals

17 | PUBLIC

HBK
HOTTINGER BRÜEL & KJÆR

UNRESTRICTED

Example of Motor Losses

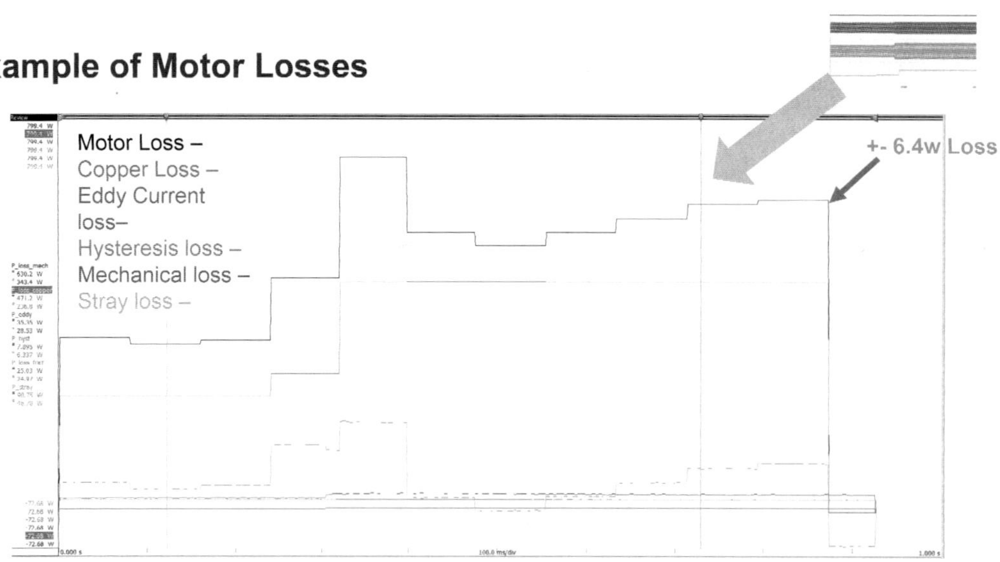

High accuracy measurement gives you ability to trust values

18 | PUBLIC

HBK
HOTTINGER BRÜEL & KJÆR

UNRESTRICTED

eDrive Value

- Simple data collection of electro-mechanical signals
- Fast and accurate Power Meausrements
  - **Lowest Measurement Uncertainty (MU)**
  - **Lowest MU across the frequency range**
  - **Lowest Torque MU**
- Custom Equations
- Recorded Data
  - Recorded data will allow you to refine models in post process with 1 test
- Local Support & Training

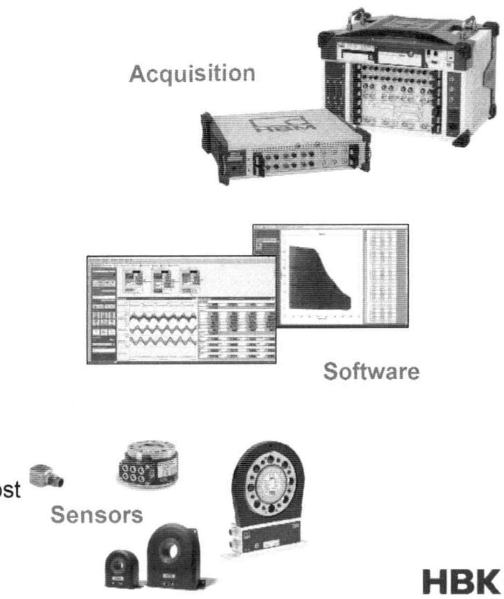

UNRESTRICTED

HBK HOTTINGER BRÜEL & KJÆR

HBK HOTTINGER BRÜEL & KJÆR

Thank You - Questions?

Mitch Marks
Business Development at HBK - Hottinger, Brüel & Kjær

HBM Brüel & Kjær

PUBLIC

File: HBM eDrive - Short Customer Introduction 2020 04 v03 en - public

TURNTIDE

How Intelligent Switched Reluctance Motor Systems Are Unlocking Our Sustainable Future

Piyush Desai
Vice President (Motor Design)
Turntide Technologies

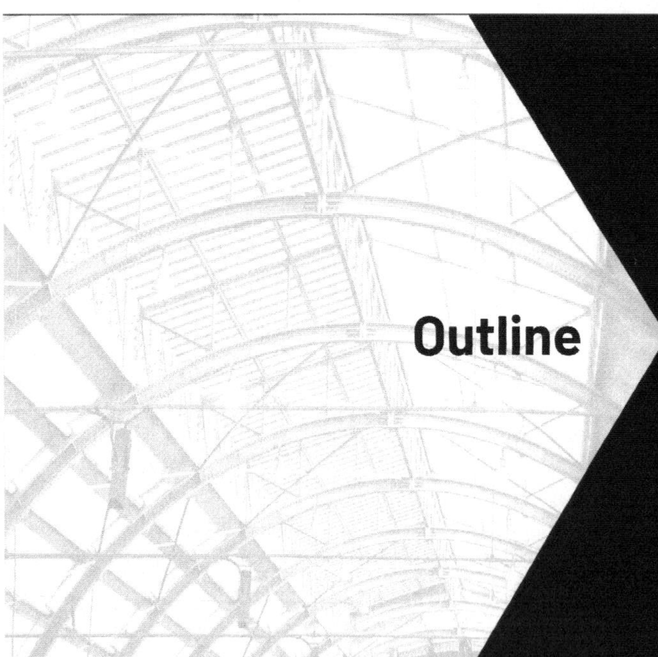

Outline

1. Introduction to Turntide
2. Overview of SRM technology & innovation
   a. Efficiency improvements
   b. Noise reduction
3. Impact and case studies

2021 Saw Record Breaking Climate Disasters
ROAD CLOSED
Image Credit: NOAA.gov

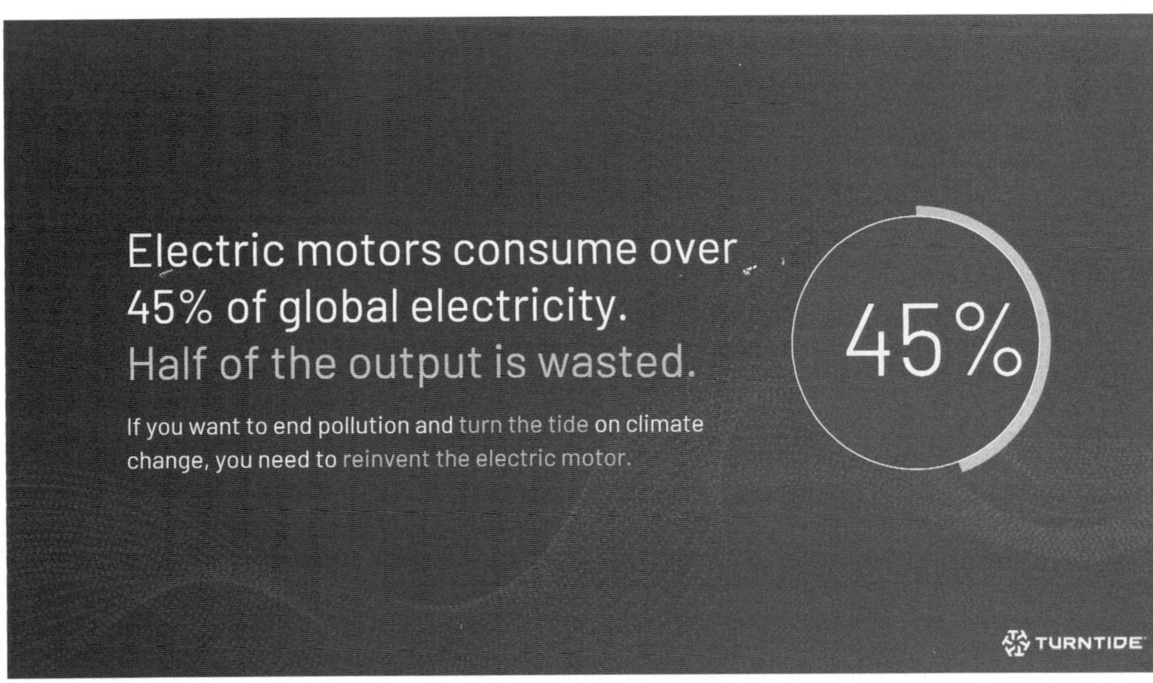
Electric motors consume over 45% of global electricity.
Half of the output is wasted.
If you want to end pollution and turn the tide on climate change, you need to reinvent the electric motor.
45%
TURNTIDE

Introduction to Turntide

OUR MISSION

Invent and scale breakthrough technologies to optimize how humanity uses energy

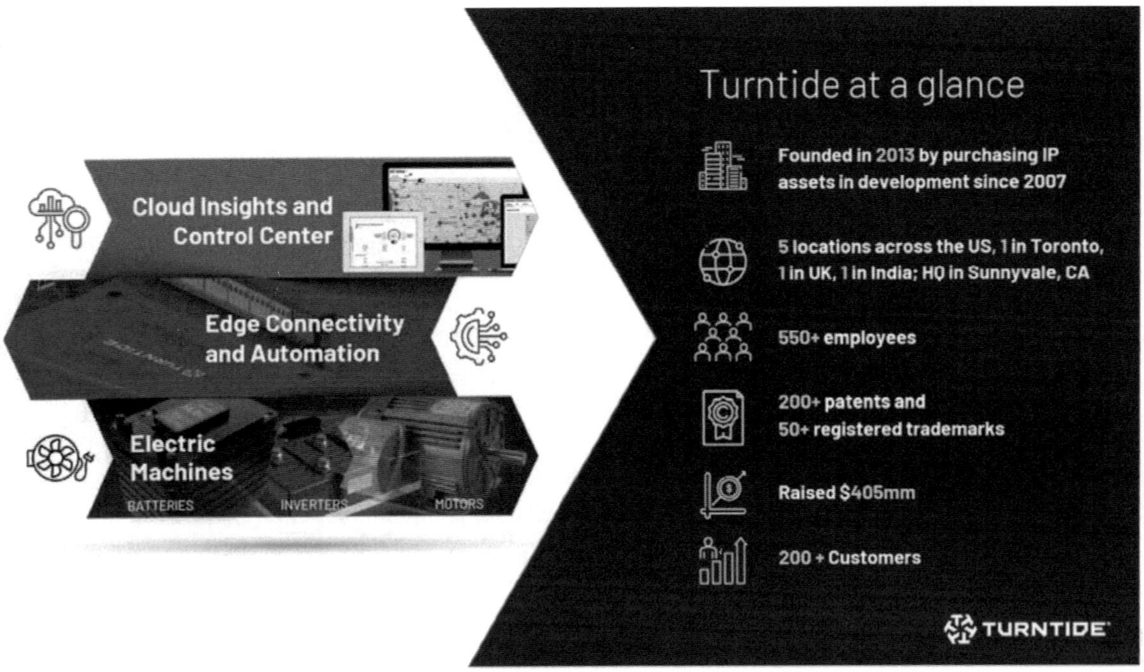
Turntide at a glance
Founded in 2013 by purchasing IP assets in development since 2007
5 locations across the US, 1 in Toronto, 1 in UK, 1 in India; HQ in Sunnyvale, CA
550+ employees
200+ patents and 50+ registered trademarks
Raised $405mm
200 + Customers
TURNTIDE
Cloud Insights and Control Center
Edge Connectivity and Automation
Electric Machines
BATTERIES
INVERTERS
MOTORS

Investors
BMW i Ventures
SAVEARTH
FOOTPRINT COALITION
$400M
raised to date
JLL
PeopleFund
WIND
copec
MESON CAPITAL
Breakthrough Energy
amazon
© Turntide Technologies. All rights reserved.

Overview of SRM Technology & Innovation

Early Motors From 1800's

The first real electric motor Moritz Jacobi, Königsberg, May 1834

Electromagnetic Engine
Gustav Froment
1848

DEMONSTRATION ELECTRO-MOTOR TRAIN
French, circa 1850-1860

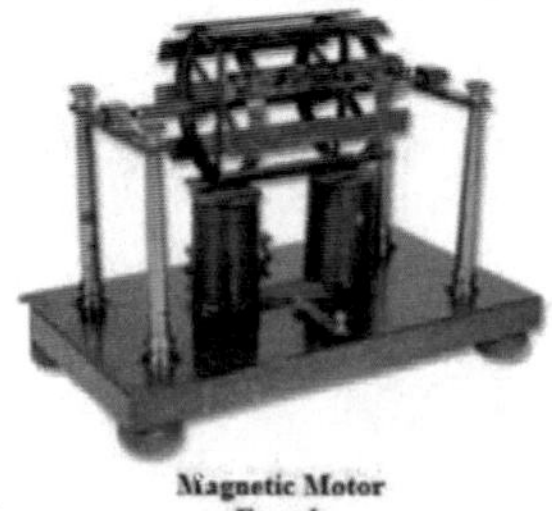

Magnetic Motor
French
1860's

AC Induction Motor
Nikola Tesla
1883

https://www.eti.kit.edu/english/1376.php

http://www.sparkmuseum.com/MOTORS.HTM

Switched Reluctance Is The Future

AC Induction:
Low cost, low efficiency

- Very mature design—invented 130+ years ago by Nikola Tesla
- Extremely iterated, now at physical limits of performance
- Inefficient outside narrow range
- Scalable to large size

Permanent Magnet:
High cost, high efficiency

- Can be more efficient than AC
- Best performance requires magnets—China controls 95% global supply of required rare earth materials
- Much higher cost
- Does not scale easily to larger sizes

Switched Reluctance (SRM):
Low cost, high efficiency

Superior physics
- No rotor current so no energy wasted in the rotor
- No expensive exotic materials required

Superior impact
- Simplest possible electric motor to manufacture
- Extremely reliable and durable to operate

SRM Advantages Too Compelling To Ignore

Extended constant power range
Optimal for traction drivetrain

Fault tolerant - limp home capable

Rare-earth free
Lower cost, cheaper to source and manufacture

Efficient where it matters the most

Reliability & longevity
Rugged -higher temperature capable, absence of usual failure modes (demagnetization, over-voltage during field weakening, insulation weakness, inverter shoot-through fault)

No magnet or winding on rotor
Lower inertia, cooler rotor, longer bearing life, higher speed capabilities, higher peak power, no magnets to overcome during deceleration & idling, free from cogging-torque

2014 DOE Report: SRM Outperforms Other Motor Designs

Table 7-2. Variable Speed Drive System Comparison. Source: Nidec Motor Corporation

Criteria	Induction	PM	SR
Maturity of technology	3	2	1
Power density	1	3	2
High starting torque	1	3	3
Cool rotor	1	3	3
Pancake profile capabilities	1	2	3
Maximum speed	2	1	3
Maximum speed range: base to top speed ratio	2	1	3
High peak efficiency	1	3	2
Flat efficiency over a wide speed range	1	2	3
Loss of controls/effect of back EMF	3	1	3
High temperature capability	3	1	3
Noise, vibration	3	3	2
Torque ripple	3	2	2
Robust, fault tolerance	1	1	3
Sensorless control capability	2	2	3
Low VA demand	1	2	3
	29	32	42

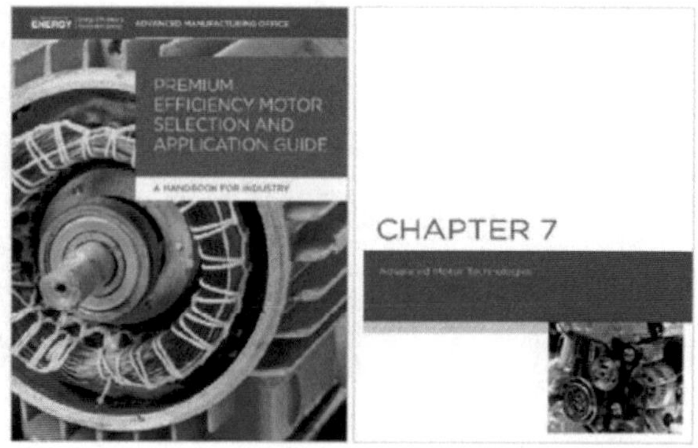

https://www.energy.gov/eere/amo/downloads/premium-efficiency-motor-selection-and-application-guide-handbook-industry

Five Key Technical Hurdles Blocked SRM From The Mass Market

- Maturity of technology
- Motor efficiency
- Power density
- Acoustic noise
- Torque ripple

High Rotor Pole SRM (HR-SRM): Better Efficiency & Higher Torque

Traditional SRM
(6 stator poles & 4 rotor poles)

Turntide HR-SRM
(6 stator poles & 10 rotor poles)

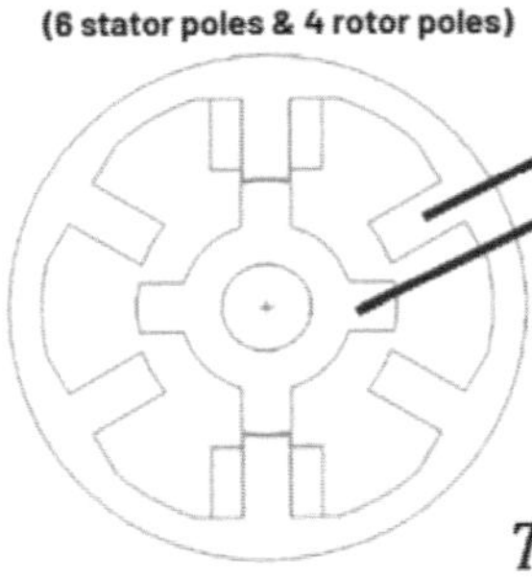

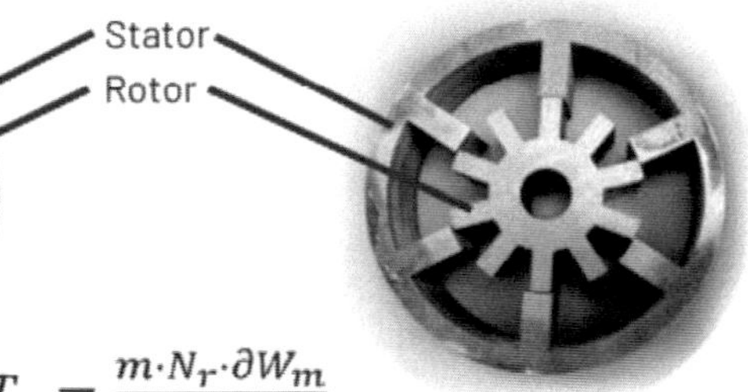

$$T_e = \frac{m \cdot N_r \cdot \partial W_m}{2\pi}$$

Average torque is proportional to the change in co-energy, number of phases, and _number of rotor poles_

HR-SRM benefits:

- ❑ Higher efficiency
- ❑ Higher torque
- ❑ Lower torque ripple
- ❑ Lower noise & vibrations

T_e = Average torque
∂W_m = Change in co-energy
N_r = Number of rotor poles
m = Number of phases

Comparison: 6/4 vs. 6/10

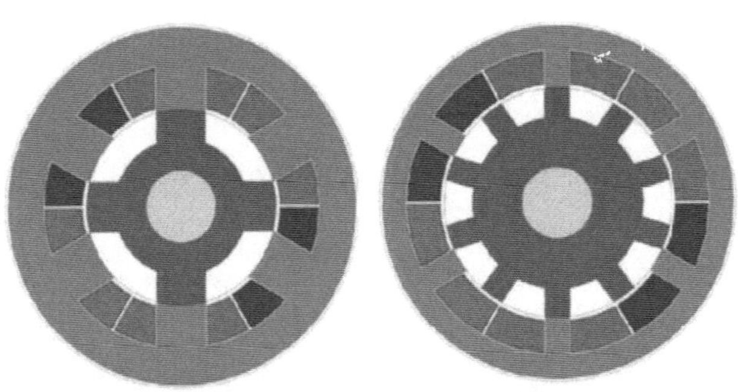

SRM: 6/4 **HR-SRM: 6/10**

Parameters	SRM 6/4	HR-SRM 6/10
Stator OD (mm)	247.40	247.40
Rotor OD (mm)	135	160
Stator pole arc angle (degree)	30	12
Coil area per slot (mm²)	662.72	909.32
Coil area comparison	100%	137.21%
Ratio of stator back-iron to stator pole width ratio	0.71	0.98
Ratio of rotor OD to stator OD	0.546	0.647

Noise - Fundamental SRM Challenge

High radial to tangential force ratio leads to high stator vibration & motor noise

Understand it better

Minimize the noise generation

- Low noise motor designs (multi-physics optimization)
- Current/waveform shaping

Minimize the noise propagation

- Q-series motors
- Damping and isolation (multi-physics optimization)

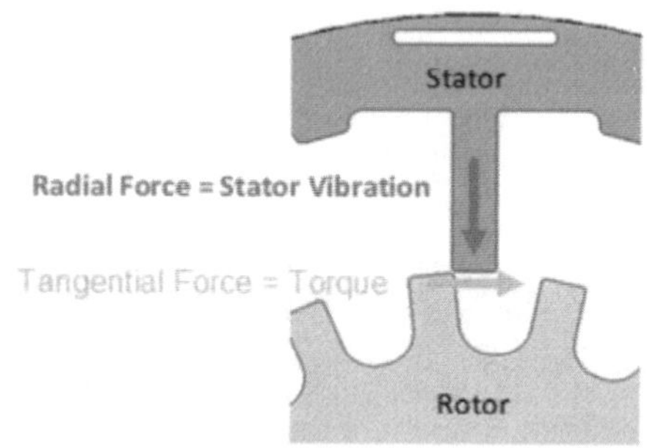

Understanding Noise

Noise is complicated, with many factors:

- Level → sound pressure level, loudness
- Speech → articulation index, speed Interference level
- Annoyance → sharpness
- Tonality → tone-to-noise ratio, prominence ratio
- Modulation → roughness and fluctuation strength
- "Prominence" in environmental context

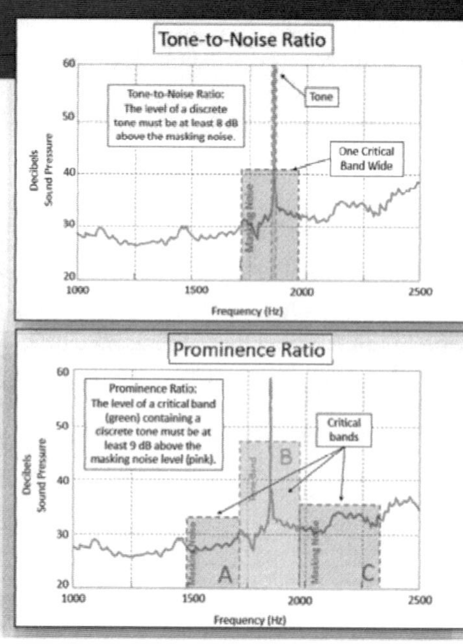

Basics of Waveform Shaping

SR motors are usually driven by a "square wave" current, which can induce stronger vibrations. →

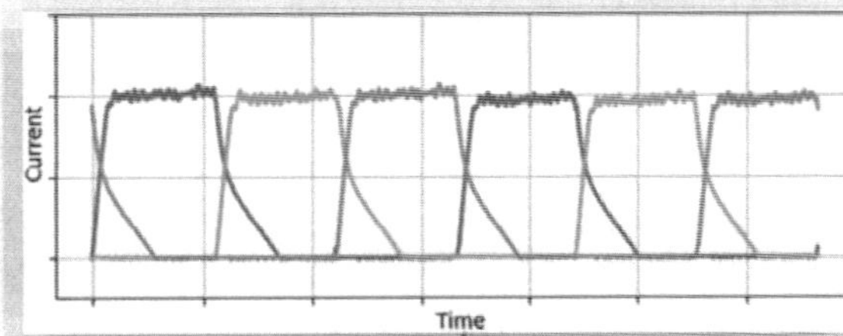

We can reshape the current that induces weaker vibrations while maintaining torque & efficiency. →

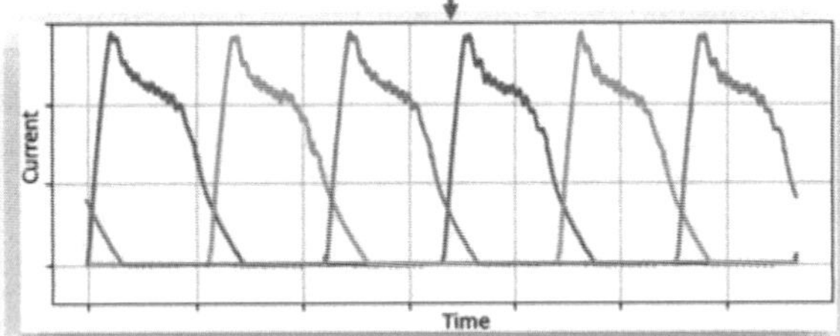

Family of Coefficients & Waveform Shapes

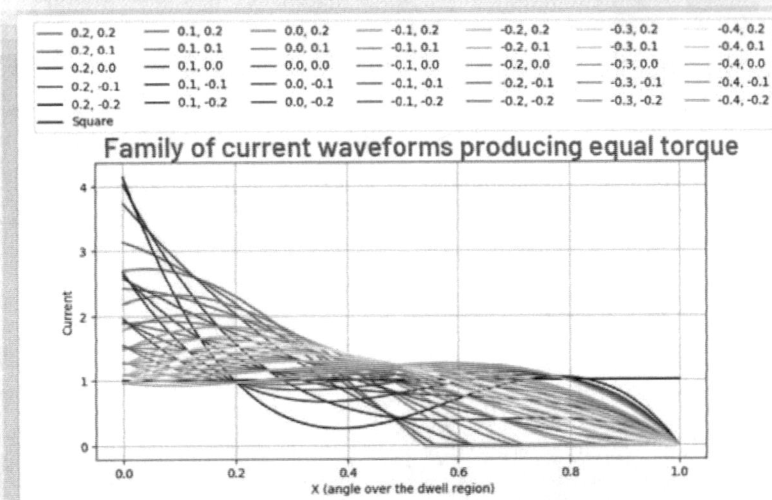

Noise Reduction With Waveform Shaping

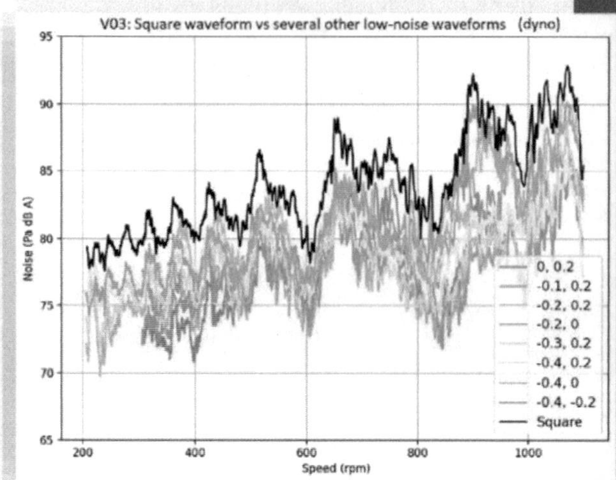

- Noise depends on waveform shape
- Waveform shape depends on some coefficients
- Software can intelligently adjust the coefficients on-the-fly to lock on to an "optimal" waveform
- Up to 10dB noise reduction without loss of torque and efficiency!!!

Impact

TURNTIDE

Proven Saving by Third-Party Validation

NREL
NATIONAL RENEWABLE ENERGY LABORATORY

29% to 71% Energy savings in condenser fan applications (1.5HP)

Fixed speed	29%
Variable speed	33%

LINK TO NREL REPORT

SOUTHERN CALIFORNIA **EDISON**
Energy for What's Ahead®

11% to 57% Energy savings in RTU fan applications (3.0HP)

Variable speed	11%

LINK TO REPORT   LINK TO WEBINAR

EnergyTrust of Oregon

24% to 31% Energy savings in freezer fan application (3HP)

Fixed speed (condenser fans)	24%
Fixed speed (evaporator fans)	31%

LINK TO REPORT

Case Study - Automotive Manufacturing Plant

GOAL: control energy consumption to help achieve net zero 2050 esure employee comfort & safety.

+ 4 Smart Motor Systems deployed in a 2 million sq ft plant
+ Energy monitoring kits installed before motors for M&V

Business Impact:

- $2.8K ANNUAL SAVINGS
- 75% ENERGY REDUCTION IN HVAC SUPPLY FAN
- 42.8 MWH IN ANNUAL ENERGY SAVINGS

Environmental Impact:

- 3,414 GALLONS OF GAS
- 37.2 ACRES OF FOREST
- 30.4 METRIC TON OF CO_2

Case Study: Major Chain Store Retailer

2,584 Motors

662* Sites

26 States

Total estimated yearly $ savings: $518,296*

Total estimated yearly kWh savings: 4,038,130*

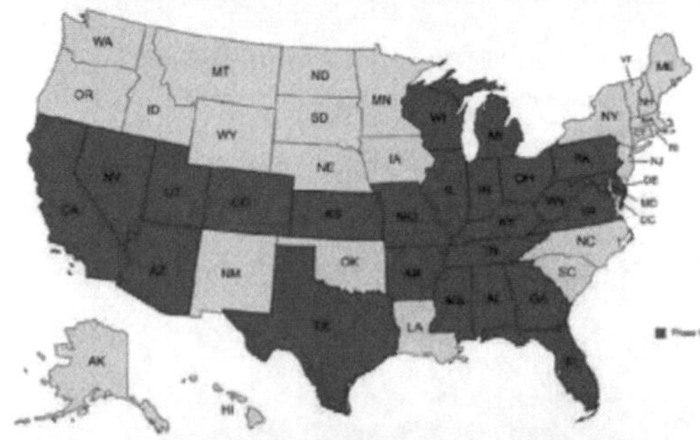

ENVIRONMENTAL IMPACT

2,862 Metric Tons of CO2

322,016 Gallons of Gas Consumed

345 Homes' Energy Use

*Total estimated savings adjusted for completed stores with data runtime data (provided by Venstar) and actual utility rates (provided by customer)

Potential Savings If We Were To Upgrade All Motors In Buildings

Energy Saving	Domestic (USA)		Global	
	tWh	Co2 mTons	tWh	Co2 mTons
10%	198	96	1,384	672
20%	395	192	2,768	1,343
30%	593	287	4,152	2,015
64%	1,265	614	8,857	4,299

The net carbon capture of the Amazon rainforest is **300 mTons** (30% row)

64% is our average customer energy savings from HVAC (64% row)

TURNTIDE

The Future is Exciting

- Amorphous and nanocrystalline material with superior magnetic properties
- 3D printed or injection moldable steel with nanocarbon infused metals
- Superconductors for windings like copper with nanotubes
- Utilizing motor magnetic structure for suspended bearings
- Next generation cooling technologies
- And lot more....

TURNTIDE

Q&A

Piyush Desai
Email: piyush@turntide.com
Phone: +1 312 505 7805
https://www.linkedin.com/in/drpiyushdesai

ARNOLD®
MAGNETIC TECHNOLOGIES
ENGINEERING SOLUTIONS TOGETHER
Auto, Aero and Defense Electrification: Optimizing Induction and PM Motor Design for Manufacturing
Aaron Williams
Director of Strategic Technologies
awilliams@arnoldmagnetics.com
2022
1

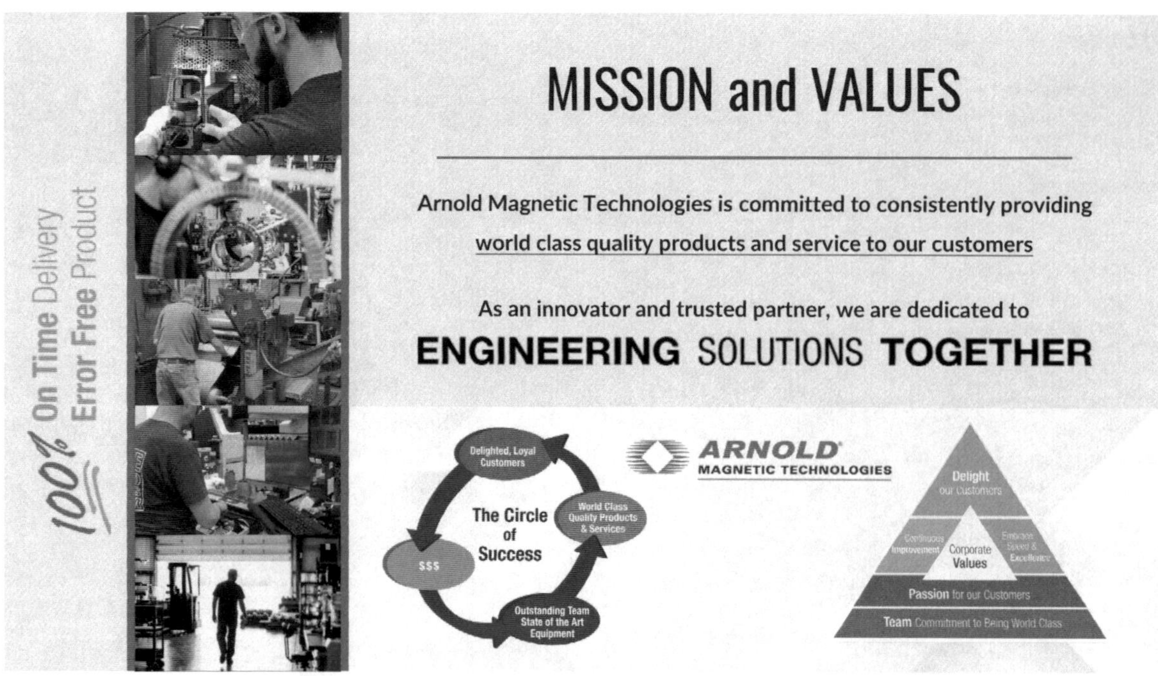
MISSION and VALUES
Arnold Magnetic Technologies is committed to consistently providing world class quality products and service to our customers
As an innovator and trusted partner, we are dedicated to
ENGINEERING SOLUTIONS TOGETHER
100% On Time Delivery
Error Free Product
Delighted, Loyal Customers
World Class Quality Products & Services
Outstanding Team State of the Art Equipment
$$$
The Circle of Success
ARNOLD
MAGNETIC TECHNOLOGIES
Delight our Customers
Corporate Values
Passion for our Customers
Team Commitment to Being World Class

GLOBAL SUPPLY CHAIN

With a Local Presence

ARNOLD MAGNETIC TECHNOLOGIES

FULLY INTEGRATED SUPPLY CHAIN

Security of Supply Chain is Ensured, Mine to Motor

Mining & Processing	Magnet Production	Magnet Fabrication	Magnetic Assemblies	Rotors and Stators	System Integration

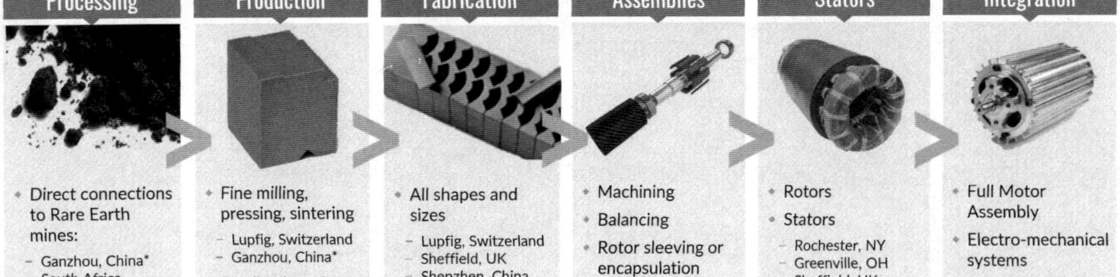

Mining & Processing	Magnet Production	Magnet Fabrication	Magnetic Assemblies	Rotors and Stators	System Integration
• Direct connections to Rare Earth mines: – Ganzhou, China* – South Africa • Multiple sources of supply secure raw material	• Fine milling, pressing, sintering – Lupfig, Switzerland – Ganzhou, China* • Duplication of production ensures global access	• All shapes and sizes – Lupfig, Switzerland – Sheffield, UK – Shenzhen, China – Rochester, NY – Marengo, IL – Ogallala, NE	• Machining • Balancing • Rotor sleeving or encapsulation – Rochester, NY – Marengo, IL – Sheffield, UK – Shenzhen, China	• Rotors • Stators – Rochester, NY – Greenville, OH – Sheffield, UK – Shenzhen, China	• Full Motor Assembly • Electro-mechanical systems – Greenville, OH – Ogallala, NE

SUPPORTED BY ENGINEERING & PROTOYPING AT TECH CENTER

*JV with rare earth producer

ARNOLD MAGNETIC TECHNOLOGIES

INDUSTRIES

Advancing Materials and Motor Technologies Since 1895

AEROSPACE & DEFENSE
- Every commercial plane in the sky
- Original NASA partner
- Many satellites
- Mars rovers
- Missile guidance

ELECTRIC & HYBRID
- Manned and unmanned Electric Vertical Take-Off and Landing (E-VTOL)
- Energy storage systems – lithium ion batteries and hydrogen fuel cell

OIL & GAS
- Downhole drilling
- Pipeline inspection
- Electric submersible pumps

MOTORSPORT
- Open-wheel racers – combustion and electric
- Moto-E
- Luxury performance vehicles

CONSUMER & INDUSTRIAL
- Motors
- Pumps
- Sensors
- Security
- Speakers
- Microphones

MEDICAL
- Implantable – motorized and stationery
- Diagnostics
- Radiation and laser focusing
- Shielding

SUPPORTED BY ENGINEERING & PROTOYPING AT TECH CENTER

ARNOLD MAGNETIC TECHNOLOGIES

INDUSTRY CERTIFICATIONS

When Quality Matters

ISO 9001:2015 — IATF 16949 — AS 9100 Rev D — Nadcap Administered by PRI ACCREDITED HEAT TREATING

TRUSTED PARTNER FOR AEROSPACE & DEFENSE

ITAR — Arnold is a US-based corporation with several ITAR locations complying with DFARS throughout our supply chain. — DFAR

ARNOLD MAGNETIC TECHNOLOGIES

ABSTRACT

As the demand for electrification continues to grow globally, the automotive, aerospace, and defense markets face unprecedented challenges. New technologies are placing greater demands on motors in terms of operating speeds, temperatures, and efficiencies. For example, very large turbine generators are needed to power multiple-wing propellers used on hybrid and electric aircraft. The presentation will examine the importance of optimizing induction and permanent magnet motor design for manufacturing. Also discussed are manufacturability pros and cons within the stator and rotor, as well as all the materials and processes that go into making a highly efficient, quality motor, adding in more background on die-cast induction machines and novel PM rotor topologies.

CURRENT AEROSPACE ELECTRIFICATION

Many electrical motor/generator technologies already in place on airframes

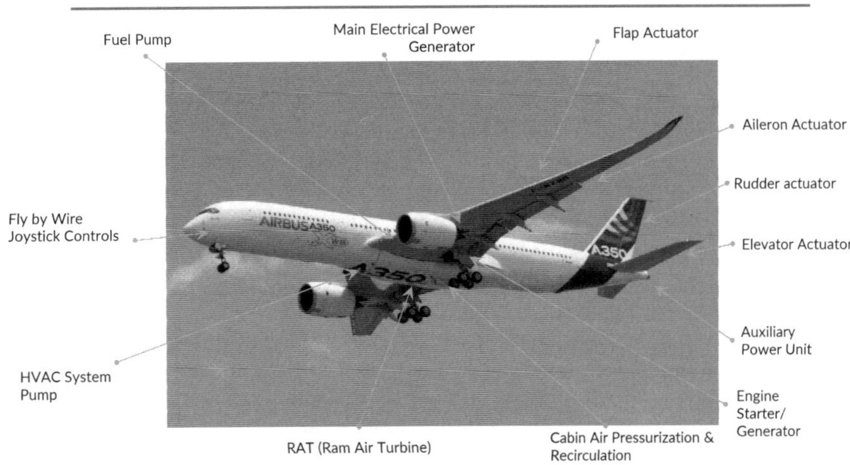

Image used for demonstration purposes only

ARNOLD MAGNETIC TECHNOLOGIES

CURRENT DEFENSE ELECTRIFICATION

Many electrical motor/generator technologies already in place on Ground Vehicles

Image used for demonstration purposes only

ARNOLD MAGNETIC TECHNOLOGIES

FUTURE ELECTRIC MOTOR CHALLANGES

- Thermal Management
- Power Density
- Higher Electrical Frequencies
- Weight Reduction
- Manufacturability
- SIZE, WEIGHT, POWER
- Secure Supply Chain
- Cost

ARNOLD MAGNETIC TECHNOLOGIES

WHAT TOPLOLOGY IS THE BEST SOLUTION?

Induction Machine

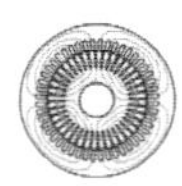

Permanent Magnet

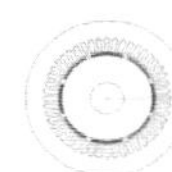

Switched Reluctance

There are manufacturing cost and performance tradeoffs

ARNOLD MAGNETIC TECHNOLOGIES

MOTOR TOPOLOGIES COMPARISON

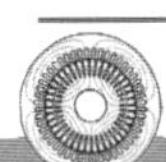  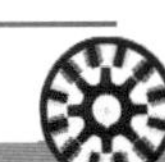

Induction Machine		Surface PM		Switched Reluctance	
Advantages	Disadvantages	Advantages	Disadvantages	Advantages	Disadvantages
High speeds	Rotor losses (cooling)	***Energy efficiency***	Permanent magnet temp. effects	High speeds	Acoustic noise
Simple construction	Less constant power speed range	Highest torque/inertia ratio	Magnet retention	Simple rotor construction	Complex control
High torque/inertia ratio	Low power density	Highest torque density	Iron Losses	Low rotor losses at low speeds	Rotor position sensor required
High torque density	Lower efficiency over op range	Good torque control	Magnet costs	Low cost	Small air gap
Low cost		Very low rotor losses	Excitation during a winding fault	No permanent excitation	Special drive topology
No permanent excitation		Common drive topology			Motor/drive control match required
Common drive topology		Simple construction			High windage

ARNOLD MAGNETIC TECHNOLOGIES

STARTS WITH DESIGN

The First Step

- Items needed to optimize your design
  - Machine Voltage
  - Power requirements
  - Speeds
  - Housing sizing
  - Cooling options
  - Efficiency requirements
  - End use platforms
- Design must fit your end use market and needs.

DESIGN

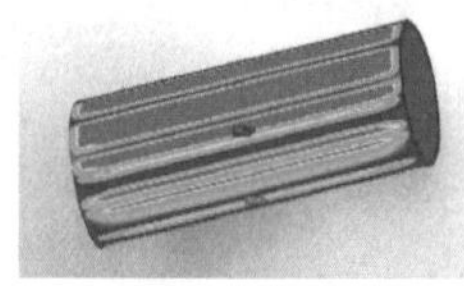

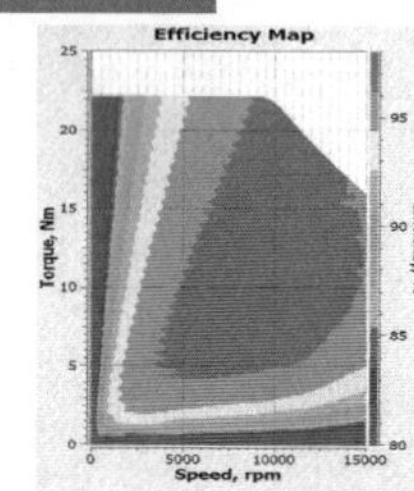

ARNOLD MAGNETIC TECHNOLOGIES

PM ROTOR DESIGN CONSIDERATIONS

MAGNETS

- High temp/coercivity needs – SmCo
- Best power density – Neo
- High temp and power density – Dy Diffused Neo
- High frequency application – Laminated magnets
- Lower cost – simple shapes like rectangles
- Better topology fit – complex shapes

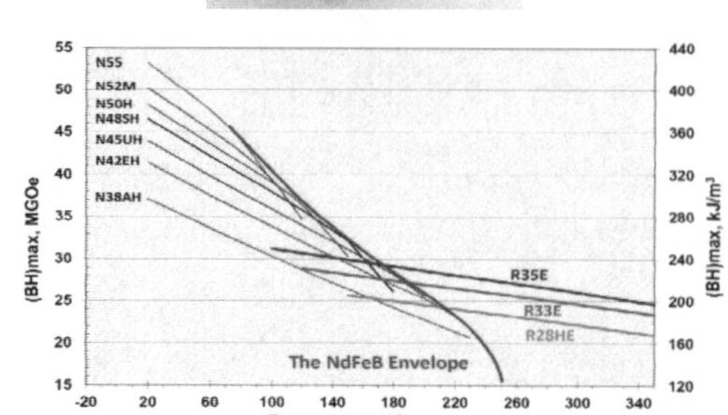

ARNOLD MAGNETIC TECHNOLOGIES

15

PM ROTOR DESIGN CONSIDERATIONS

SHAFTS

- Corrosion Resistance
  - Passivation needs
  - Type of steel used
- High Speeds?
  - Tolerances and bearing journal placement
  - Balancing plane locations

- High frequencies?
  - Solid shaft - lower
  - Laminated core - higher
- Temperature considerations
  - Cooling paths

ARNOLD MAGNETIC TECHNOLOGIES

16

PM ROTOR DESIGN CONSIDERATIONS

MAGNET RETENTION WITH METALS

- On a surface mounted magnet machine, the magnets will, as a result of centrifugal mass, try to escape the rotor assembly unless restrained. The faster the machine rotates, the greater these forces...and they multiply fast...

  mass x center of mass x speed^2
- Traditional materials include Inconel, Titanium, and Austenitic Stainless Steel
- Most commonly chosen is Inconel
- Coefficient of expansion is closest to the magnets being retained and Martensitic steels typically within the rotor assembly
- Non-magnetic
- Higher price point

PROS	CONS
Measurable interference and hence calculable stress	Dense, and hence self load (centrifugal) significant
Corrosion resistant	Regularly has differing temp, coeff. to content, resulting in differing interference, and hence stress across temp range
Approved for flight	Electrically conductive, so high losses (Eddy currents)

ARNOLD MAGNETIC TECHNOLOGIES

PM ROTOR DESIGN CONSIDERATIONS

MAGNET RETANTION WITH CARBON FIBER

- Light weight (low density)
- Reduced impact on the overall mass of the rotor, and hence it's inertia
- Reduced rotor mass = smaller bearings can be used
- Lowered self induced stresses at RPM, potentially enabling thinner sleeves
- It's strong….very strong….0.2% yield strength of Inconel (typically the strongest of sleeve materials used) is ~1100MPa….carbon fibre in some cases, is only limited by its UTS, which can be several times this.
- It is electrically conductive, but nothing like metals. Also, when sleeves are created by winding a tow of parallel fibres, it is conductive along the length of the fibre, but very little continuity from fibre to fibre (the epoxy binder isolates to a degree)
- Reduced losses in the sleeve

ARNOLD MAGNETIC TECHNOLOGIES

DIE CAST ROTOR SHAFTS

MULTIPLE OPTIONS

Machined Shafts can use multiple different materials and processes depending on the design and application.

- Turn/Lathe
- Mill
- Grind

Rotor Castings can use multiple different materials and processes depending on the design and application

Aluminum
- Cost - low
- Throughput - very high
- Design flexibility - high
- Performance - medium
- Bar retention - easy
- Porosity - medium-low

Copper Brazed
- Cost - very high
- Throughput - low
- Design flexibility - low
- Performance - high
- Bar retention - difficult
- Porosity - low

Copper
- Cost - high
- Throughput - medium
- Design flexibility - high
- Performance - high
- Bar retention - easy
- Porosity - very low

ARNOLD MAGNETIC TECHNOLOGIES

STATOR CONSIDERATIONS

LAMINATIONS

- Stator laminations can be produced in multiple ways
- They can be stamped using a stamping die - typically used in production. Usually requires higher tooling costs for a lower cost per lamination
- They can be laser cut - typically used for prototypes or sample parts. Higher cost per lamination
- Stator laminations can use many different types of materials such as M19 and Arnon™ silicon steel

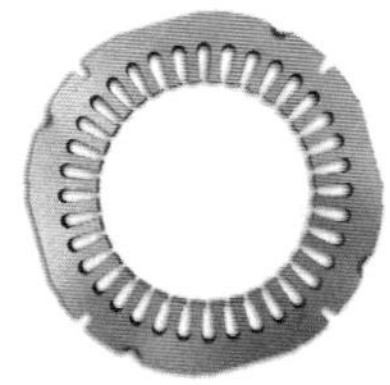

Stator Lamination

Stator Lamination Die

STATOR CONSIDERATIONS

LAMINATION MATERIAL

- Hi Cobalt Materials – Higher flux saturation but higher costs
- Regular Silicon Steels – Lowest Costs
- Very thin Silicon Steels – Lower Eddy Current Losses
  - Ultra thin 0.002" – 0.007" (0.051mm – 0.178mm)

21

STATOR CONSIDERATIONS

BULDING THE CORES

Bonded

- Using Materials such as:
  - Magna Tac E645
  - Scotchcast 265
- Higher cost, higher efficiency

Riveted

- Lower cost, less efficient

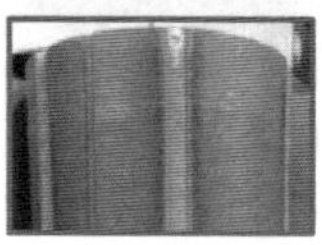

Welded

- Lower cost, less efficient

Clinched

- Clinched stack
- Moderate cost and efficiency
- Comes from Lamination manufacturer already stacked

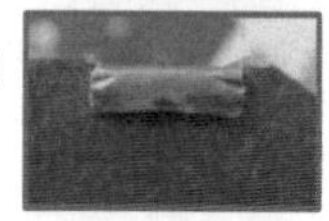

Interlocked

- Interlocked stack
- Moderate cost and efficiency
- Comes from Lamination manufacturer already stacked

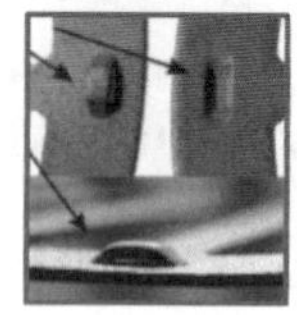

ARNOLD MAGNETIC TECHNOLOGIES

22

STATOR CONSIDERATIONS

INSULATORS

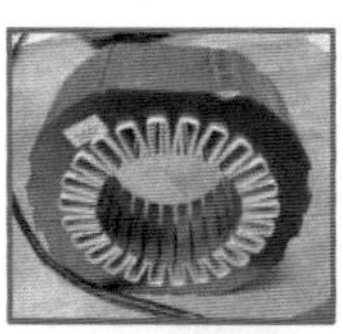

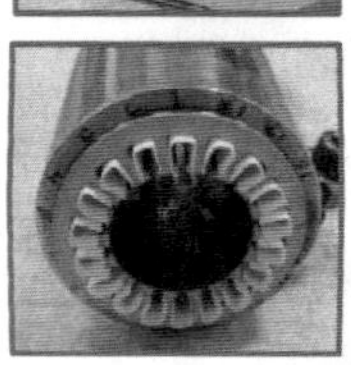

Epoxy (Powder Coat)

- Scotchcast 5230N

Slot Liners

- Nomex-Kapton-Nomex- For Class R (220*C) Motors
- Nomex- For class H (180*C) Motors
- Dacron-Mylar-Dacron for Class F(155*C) Motors

Middle Separator

- Mylar Class B (130*C)
- Dacron-Mylar-Dacron Class F (155*C)
- Nomex Class H (180*C)
- Nomex-Kapton-Nomex Class H (220*C)

Slot Wedge

- Mylar Class B (130*C)
- Dacron-Mylar-Dacron Class F (155*C)
- Nomex Class H (180*C)

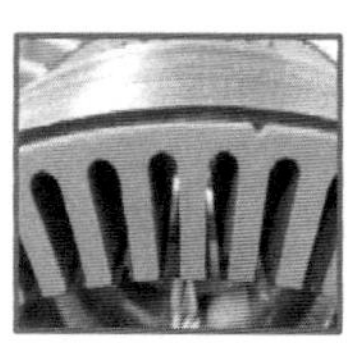

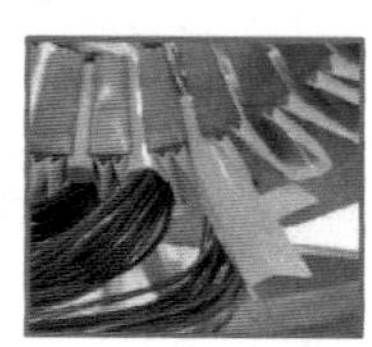

ARNOLD MAGNETIC TECHNOLOGIES

STATOR CONSIDERATIONS

MAGNET WIRE

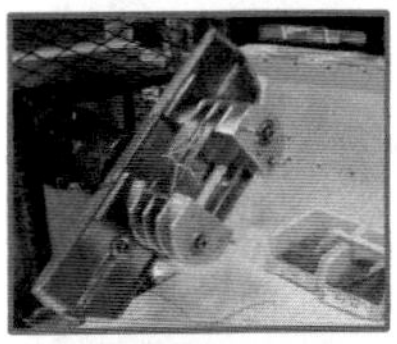

Magnet Wire used to form coils

- Heavy Build Coating: HML Class C (240°C)
- Coating: HTAIH Class K (200°C)
- Pulse Shield Plus and Ultra Shield Coating: Inverter-Duty Class C (240°C)
- Litz Wire Type 1-8

Turret Winder is used to form the coil groups to meet the motor design resistance.

Customer Specific tooling is needed for each application.

ARNOLD MAGNETIC TECHNOLOGIES

STATOR CONSIDERATIONS

INSERTED STATOR CONSIDERATIONS

Phase to Phase Insulation

Lead Wire

All inserted stators look similar but have a very custom design and used custom materials such as:

Sleeving

- Fiberglass
- Rubber
- Teflon
- Fiberglass/Rubber Composites
- Silicone Coated Fiberglass

Phase to Phase Insulation

- DMD
- Mylar
- Nomex
- NKN

Lead wire

Butt Connectors

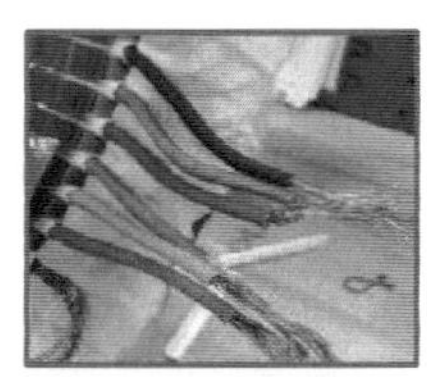

Sleeving

Butt Connectors

ARNOLD MAGNETIC TECHNOLOGIES

25

STATOR CONSIDERATIONS

LACING AND PHASE INSULATION

Tape with various widths and thicknesses

- Kapton
- Kevlar
- Fiberglass
- Teflon

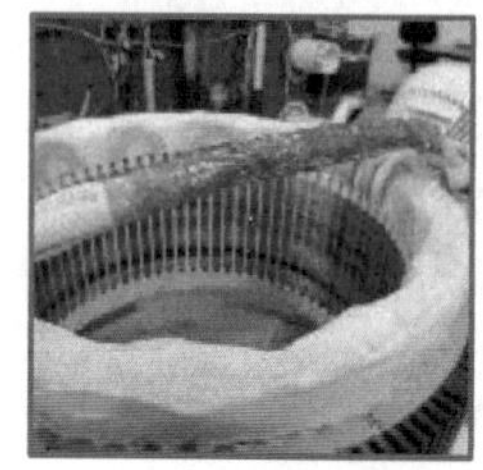

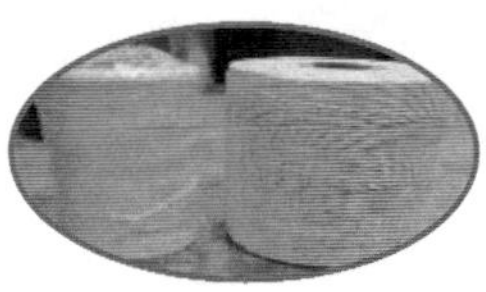

Lacing various coatings and shaping

- Teflon
- Polyurethane
- Synthetic Rubber
- Kevlar
- Polyester
- Fiberglass
- Nomex

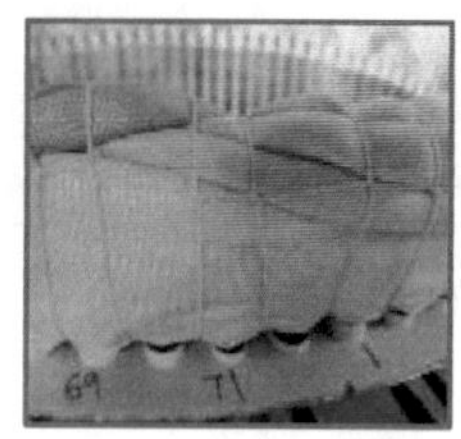

ARNOLD MAGNETIC TECHNOLOGIES

26

STATOR CONSIDERATIONS

VARNISHING

Dip and Bake

- 50 VTC Polyester
- Thinner- Vinyl Toluen
- Isonel 31-398
- Thinner-xyol

Trickle Varnishing

Vacuum Pressure Impregnation

- Epoxylite E-6001
- Thinner-Epoxy lite 6001S Reducer
- Pedigree 70 VTC
- Thinner- Vinyl toluene
- E478 Thixo VPI Resin

ARNOLD MAGNETIC TECHNOLOGIES

27

VALIDATION

Does it Perform as Intended?

- Arnold can test your system with:
  - Full CMM review
  - Back EMF Testing
  - Motor Test Stand Runs
  - Hi-POT equipment
  - Over speed testing
  - Environmental Testing
  - Etc

VALIDATE

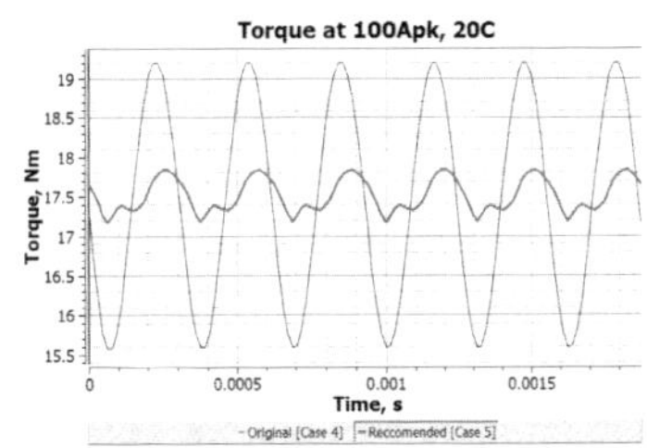

BUSINESS CONFIDENTIAL © Arnold Magnetic Technologies

ARNOLD MAGNETIC TECHNOLOGIES

28

COMMON MISTAKES

WHAT TO AVOID

- Laminations with excessively tight dimensional tolerances, which creates excessively short stamping die life and causes increased cost
- Shafts with precision features (splines, flats, etc.) meant to be case-hardened through carburization/austenitizing/quenching
- Inappropriate use of geometric dimensioning and tolerancing
- Assigning geometric tolerances that add little value or increase quality
- Inappropriate use of casting or porosity specifications
- Rotor and stator cores with dimensional and geometric tolerances suitable only for machined parts without providing the material allowances needed to machine the part
- Fabricated (brazed) rotors with the following features

BUSINESS CONFIDENTIAL © Arnold Magnetic Technologies

ARNOLD MAGNETIC TECHNOLOGIES

29

QUESTIONS?

infoNA@arnoldmagnetics.com
infoEU@arnoldmagnetics.com

arnoldmagnetics.com

/arnoldmagtech

ARNOLD
MAGNETIC TECHNOLOGIES

MAGNETICS 2022

AMERICAN
RARE EARTH

A subsidiary of American Resources Corporation (NASDAQ: AREC)

Creating an Efficient Rare Earth Element Circular Life Cycle
(Using Ligand Assisted Displacement Chromatography)

We all know rare earths are not rare, but the recycling of rare earths is not only rare but effectively nonexistent.

Demand for metals and magnets continue to see a strong demand profile.

The raw materials side of the business has been steady state with minimal supply growth.

2

AMERICAN
RARE EARTH, LLC

With the growth in demand we are seeing an influx of capital into the raw materials sector

---

We are at a rebirth of the industry and that rebirth has to start with innovation

---

Innovation must drive a process that is both cost competitive and environmentally safe

3 AMERICAN RARE EARTH, LLC

Supply Chain Challenges

Raw material	Process	Purification	Magnet producers
Ores, end of life products, waste streams	Concentrators, getting it to an economic state	Solvent based extraction, liquid to liquid solvent based extraction, Chromatography	Broader domestic manufacturing

4 AMERICAN RARE EARTH, LLC

The Supply Chain for Recycling Elements Starts with Collaboration

Over the last six years we have looked at multiple applications and technologies to produce concentrates and than ultimately purify the concentrates.

The US market or developed countries can't compete against China using same technology given labor costs, energy costs or environmental costs.

What is evident is that we can compete on innovation given rudimentary processes.

Creating the Most Environmentally-Conscious, Circular Economy for High-Value, End-of-Life Products

Over **$3 billion** worth of critical and REEs are landfilled or wasted from end-of-life products annually.

This figure is expanding rapidly based on the growth of electrification.

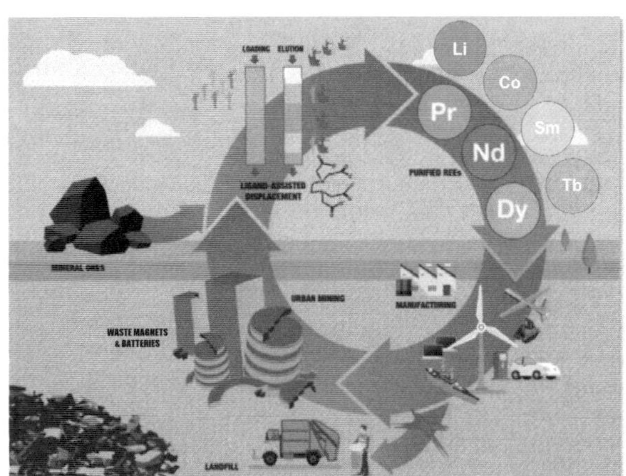

Process

Electrolysis produces monetizable products in the process

TEXAS TECH UNIVERSITY

OHIO UNIVERSITY

Process

Profitable	$$$
Environmental Impact (Positive)	+

Electrolysis Based Technology to Concentrate REE

Feedstock carbon wastes, Fly Ash and magnets

Electrolysis

Processed Rare Earth and Critical Elements Concentrate

Byproduct Economics:

Processing Fly Ash, Carbon and Hydrogen Create Monetizable Byproducts

Recycling fly ash from coal-based utilities while cleaning up legacy environmental liabilities

Electrolysis

- Rare Earth Elements
- Purified Carbon
- Concrete-Grade Fly Ash
- Hydrogen

7

AMERICAN RARE EARTH, LLC

Purify

PURDUE UNIVERSITY.

Purify

Cost (Low/Medium)	
Environmental Impact (Neutral)	=/+

The Most Environmentally-Safe Method for Creating Isolated & Pure Highly-Valuable REE

Concentrated REE

Purified REE Separated into Individual Elements

Ligand Assisted Displacement (LAD) Chromatography

Key Highlights:

$

Pure REE are more valuable than concentrate

Exclusive Technology to recycle permanent magnets and batteries

8

AMERICAN RARE EARTH, LLC

Partnerships that Matter

PURDUE UNIVERSITY	Davidson School of Chemical Engineering / Purdue Research Foundation - Science & Technology Expertise, Sponsored Research Partnership
TEXAS TECH UNIVERSITY	Edward E. Whitacre Jr. College of Engineering - Science & Technology Expertise, Sponsored Research Partnership
CMID ENGINEERS | ARCHITECTS | LAND SURVEYORS; Former executives at Lilly	Engineering, Design, Operational Expertise – Critical & REE Chromatography Isolation and Purification Facilities
The Heritage Group	The Heritage Group / HG Ventures – Upstream & Downstream partnership development, feedstock aggregation, materials science, environmental services
Institutionally Owned Wind Farms	Feedstock suppliers of end-of-life wind turbines / rare earth permanent magnets

9

AMERICAN RARE EARTH, LLC

LAD Chromatography Separation

A Much More Efficient & Safer Process to Isolate and Purify Critical and REEs

Current Method: Solvent Extraction requires > 1,000 mixer settlers with a large amount of waste discharged creating some of the most polluted sites in the world.

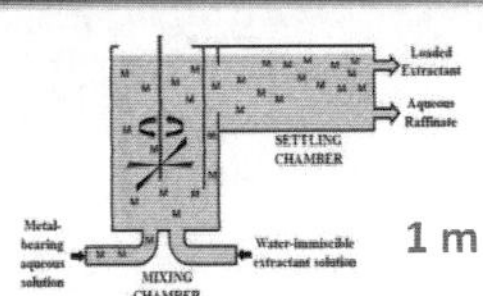

LAD Chromatography Separation's order of magnitude has a much higher interfacial area utilizing low-cost sorbents in a closed-loop, column-based system with little or no waste and with broad selectivity for critical & REEs.

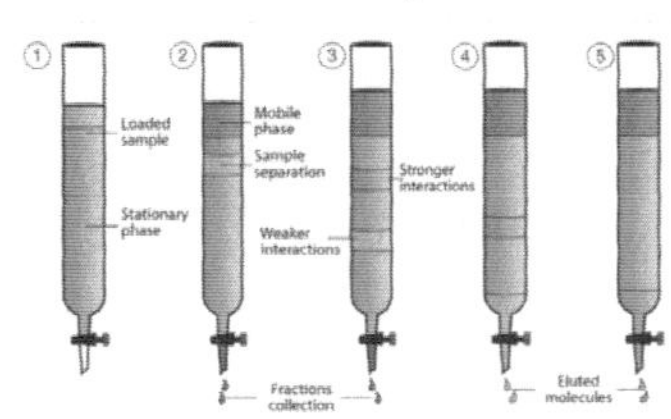

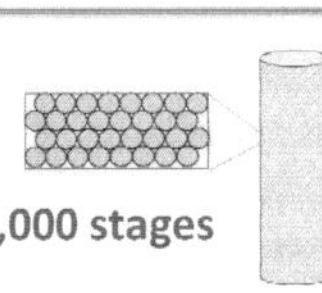

1 m ~ 1 stage ⟶ 1 m ~ 1,000 stages

10

AMERICAN RARE EARTH, LLC

Advantages to LAD Chromatography

	Solvent Extraction	ARE Chromatography	Advantages
Safety	• Flammable solvents • Toxic extractants • Harsh chemicals	• Aqueous solution • Dilute acid & base	Safer
Chemical cost	1	<0.5	Lower
Purity, Yield	99.5%, 88-90%	>99.5%, 99%	Higher
Productivity	1	10-100	Higher
Footprint	10-100	1	Smaller footprint
Start-up time	Months	Days	Shorter
Feedstocks and products	Specific	Flexible	More versatile
Separators	>1,000	5	Fewer
Initial investment	5	1	Lower
Waste	Acidic wastewater	Almost zero waste	Cleaner

11

AMERICAN RARE EARTH, LLC

Feedstocks for End of Life Products - Institutionally Owned Wind Farms, Metal Recyclers

Currently supplied from two Indiana based wind farms.

Expanded relationships to source end of life magnets, swarf and lithium-ion batteries / black mass.

- *Securing early feedstock for first rare earth magnet purification production line*
- *Securing early feedstock for first battery metals purification production line*

12

AMERICAN RARE EARTH, LLC

Success in Magnet Metal Isolation & Purification

Isolation and Purification of Rare Earth Magnet Metals to > 99.5% Purity and 99% Yield from End-of-Life Permanent Magnets from Wind Turbines and EVs

End-of-Life Permanent Magnets

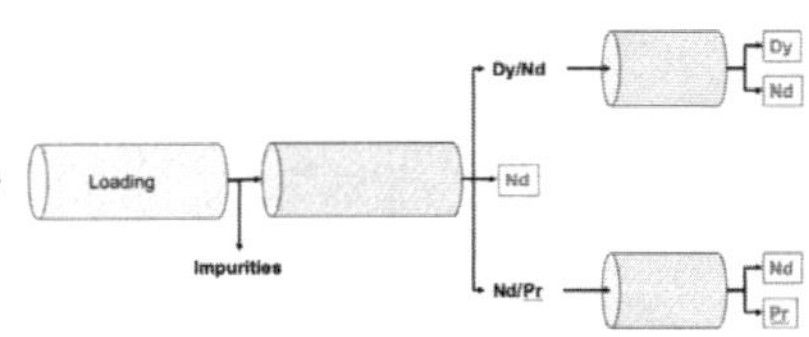

Two-Zone LAD Chromatography

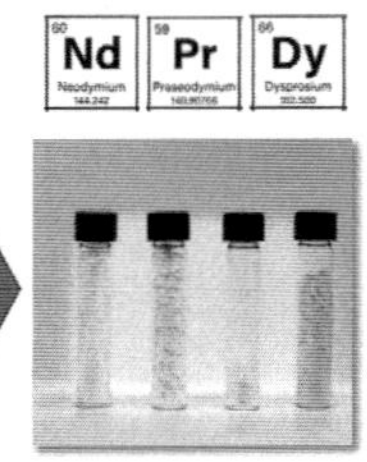

Isolated and Purified Magnet Metals

AMERICAN RARE EARTH, LLC

Success in Battery Metal Isolation & Purification

Isolation and Purification of Battery Metals to > 99.5% Purity from End-of-Life Lithium-Ion Batteries from EVs

Single EnerDel Waste Lithium-Ion Battery from EV

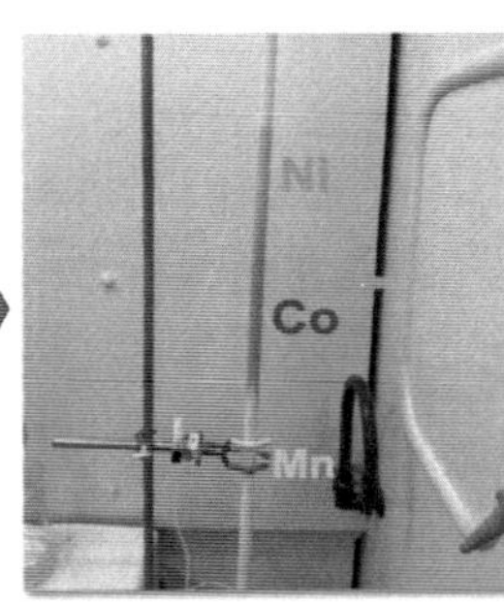

Chromatography Separation

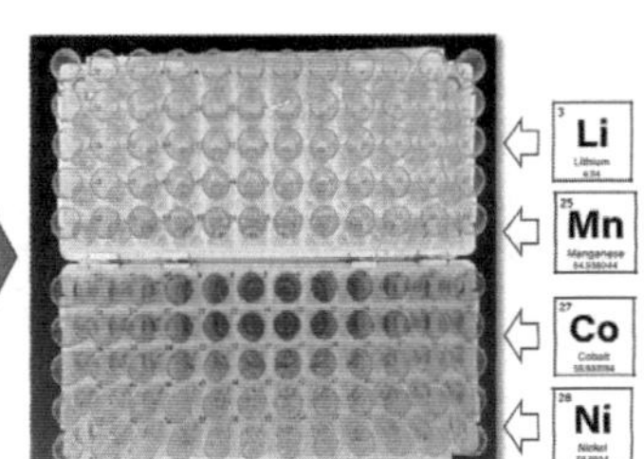

Isolated and Purified Battery Metals

AMERICAN RARE EARTH, LLC

Scalable – Our Facility

Our current facility in the final stages of completion is capable of generating north of $5 million of revenues producing 56,000 kgs of 99%+ purity of sellable rare earth and critical elements.

We are currently in the design and build phase of our full-scale commercial facility to isolate and purify rare earth and critical elements (permanent magnet and battery metals) capable of producing over 3.0 million kgs of rare earth and critical elements.

We are currently in the permitting phase of our selected 7.5 acre site located in southern Noblesville, IN

Current Production Train Schematics

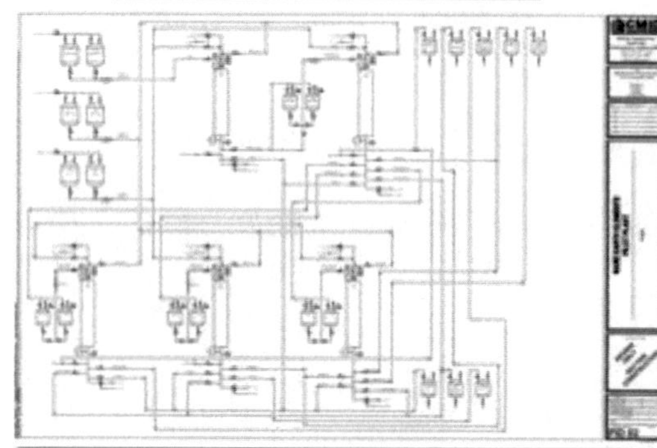

Rare Earth and Battery Metal Product Mix

In 2022 the Company will have the following products available for sale.

Element	Form	Purity
Neodymium (Nd)	Oxide	99.5% to 99.99%
Praseodymium (Pr)	Oxide	99.5% to 99.99%
Nd / Pr Mixed Oxide	Oxide	99.5% to 99.99%
Dysprosium (Dy)	Oxide	99.5% to 99.99%
Cobalt (Co)	Oxide	99.5% to 99.99%
Lithium (Li)	Oxide	99.5% to 99.99%
Nickle (Ni)	Oxide	99.5% to 99.99%
Manganese (Mn)	Oxide	99.5% to 99.99%
Co/Li/Ni/Mn Mixed Solution	Sulfate Solution	99.5% to 99.99%
Co/Li/Ni/Mn Mixed Solution	Nitrate salts or solutions	99.5% to 99.99%

What is needed

- Further Collaboration.
- Supply chain developments – We need it to progress logistically.
- We need domestic magnet producers to sell our products.

17

AMERICAN
RARE EARTH, LLC

AMERICAN

RESOURCES CORPORATION

Supporting Global Infrastructure

Motor and Drive Systems 2022

ASD Control Methods – Creating a flatter motor efficiency curve for more energy savings

Allen Neciosup, PhD
LV Drives / Application Engineering
Houston, Texas

TOSHIBA

Toshiba International Corporation
2022.02.08

Contents

01

Introduction

 2

Energy Savings

INDUSTRIAL MARKETS AND APPLICATIONS

HVAC

Mining /
Aggregate

Material Handling

Refrigeration & Chillers

Compressors,
Pumps & Fans

Conveyors

 3

Energy Savings

The need for higher efficiency is being approached by:

- Improved Induction Motors / New designs of Synchronous motors

IE3 → IE4 IE4 → IE5

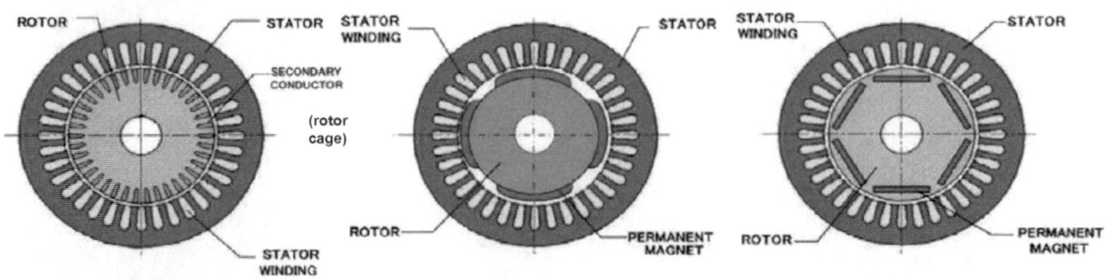

Induction Motor **SPM Motor** **IPM Motor**

All new Synchronous Motors need ASDs to operate

They can't start directly from the power line

(except hybrid cage designs)

 4

Controlling the power to the motor

ASDs are becoming "the future" of the electric motors

- **Three of five induction motors run on variable speed**
- **All new Synchronous Motors need ASDs to operate**

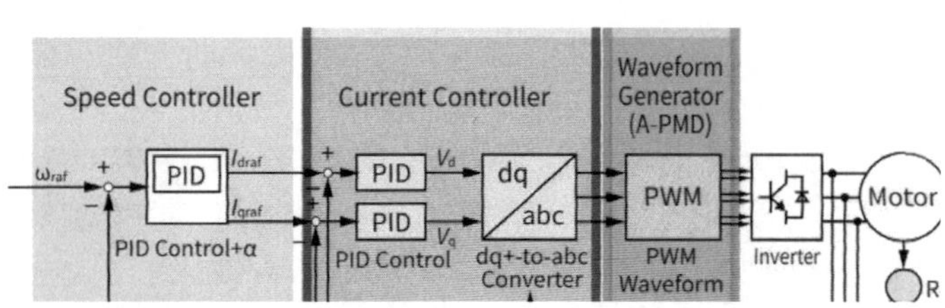

 5

Can ASDs make the induction motor efficiency curve flatter?

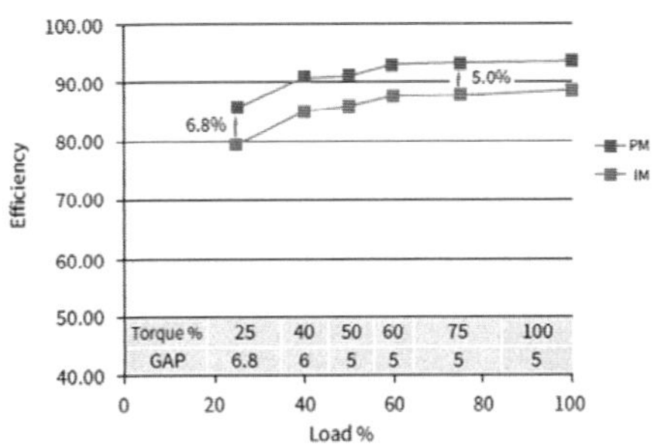

Motors Efficiency at Full Speed:
Induction Motor vs. Permanent Magnet Motor

5 to 7% less efficiency as the load decreases

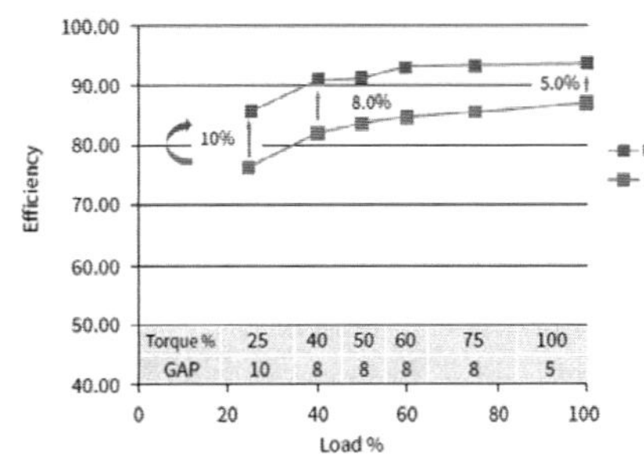

Motors Efficiency at Half Speed:
Induction Motor vs. Permanent Magnet Motor

Up to 10% less at half speed

Adjustable speed drives can make up for some of this difference

More modern ASD control algorithms can improve the reduced load/ speed performance of induction motors

02

Scalar Control Methods (Open Loop)

Scalar Control Methods

- Preset V/f ratios to match constant (CT) and variable torque (VT) load types.
- However V/f constant is applied to most motors indifferently.

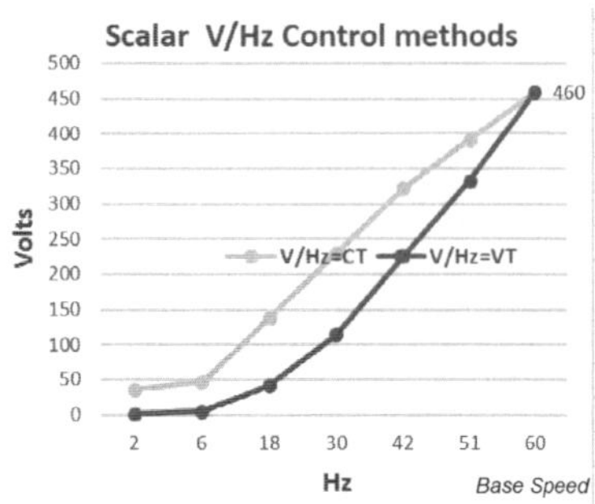

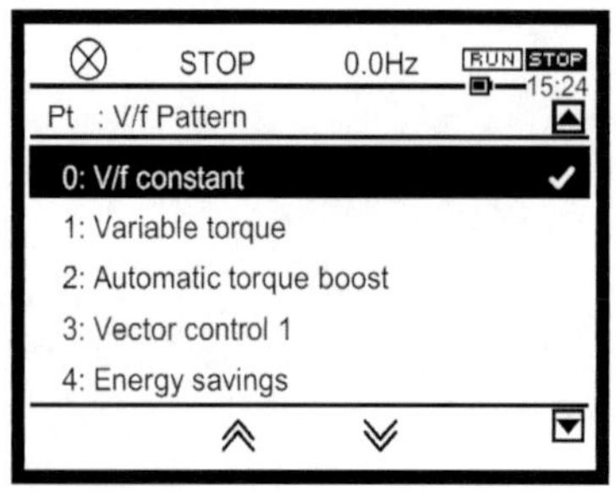

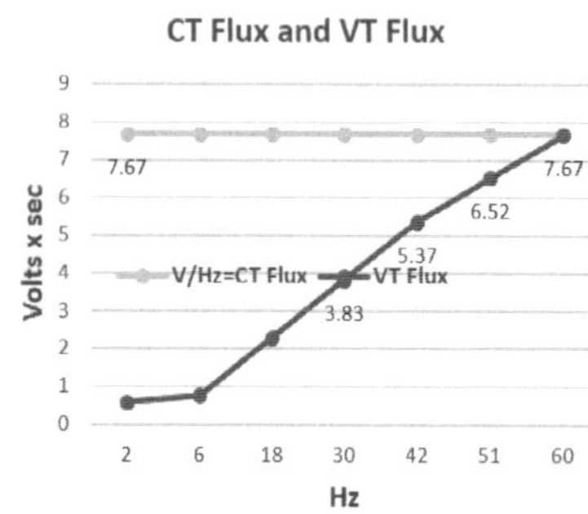

Scalar Control Methods

Challenges of preset V/F constant ratio

- *Poor efficiency at reduced load and or speed*
- *Poor torque capability at reduced speed*

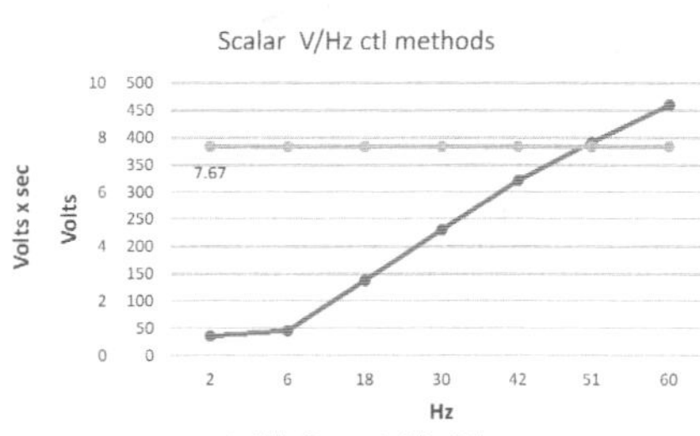

$$\phi_{ag} = \frac{E_1}{f} \neq \frac{V_s}{f}$$

$$\phi_{ag} = \frac{E_1}{f} \neq \frac{V_s}{f}$$

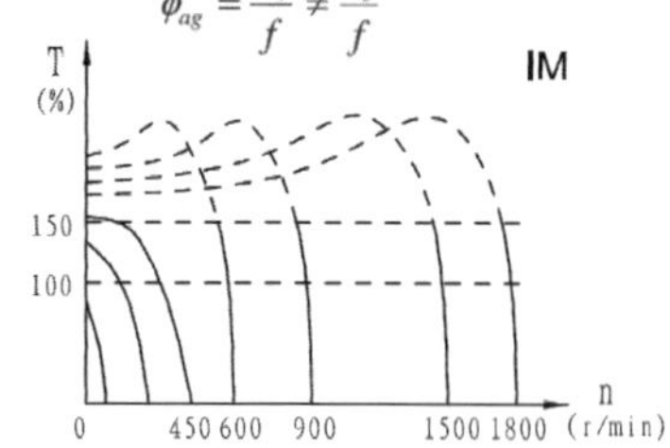

Scalar Control Methods

Operation challenges of preset VT control

Poor efficiency and torque capability if VT control is used for P2 and C3 curves

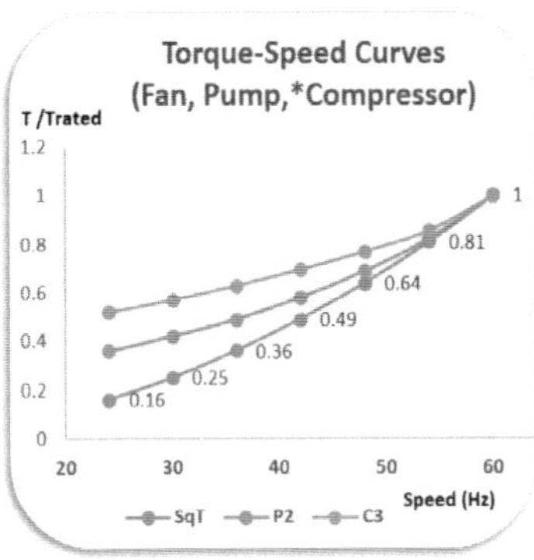

Custom VT Flux can solve both challenges but still may need manual adjustment

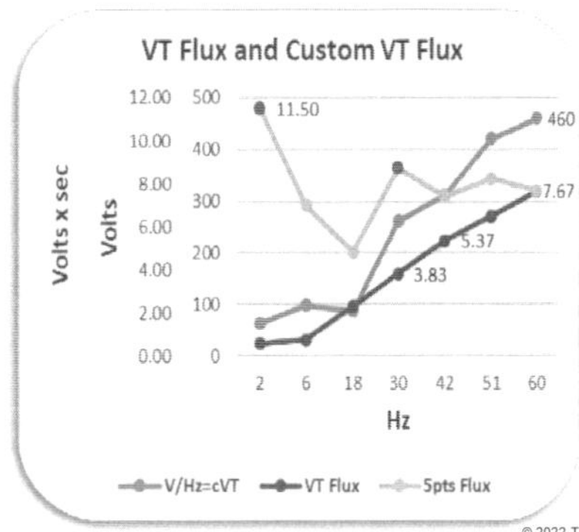

$$\phi_{ag} = \frac{E_1}{f} \neq \frac{V_s}{f}$$

 10

Scalar Control Methods

More challenges…

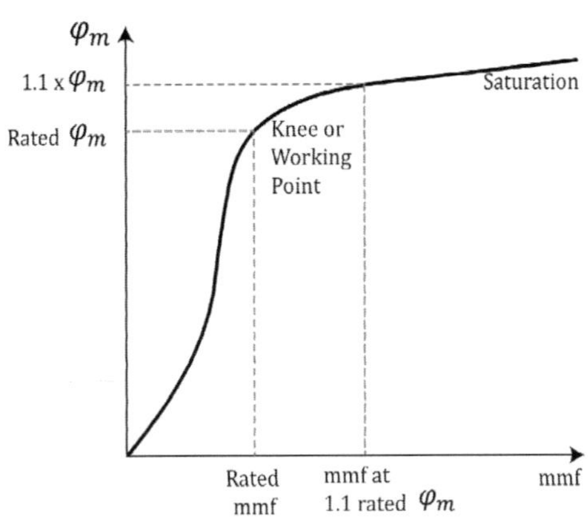

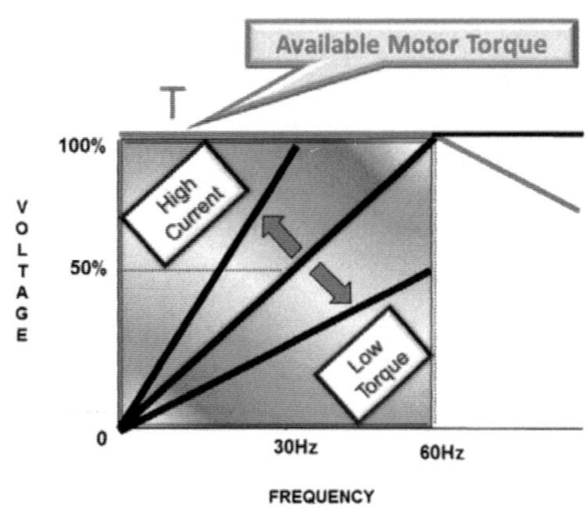

 11

Scalar Control Methods

And solutions.

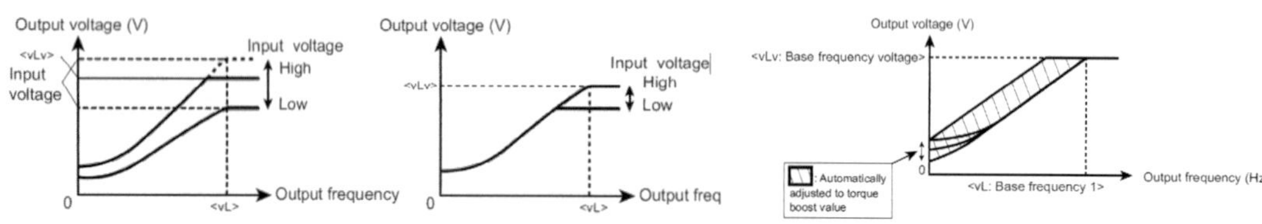

03

Vector and Advanced Control Strategies

"Close Loop", Sensor-less Vector, "self-sensing"

Vector (r-FOC) and Advanced Control Strategies

Vector Control principle - By using vector control, torque T can be expressed as the product of rotor flux Ψ_{dr} and motor current i_s in terms of d-q components as follows.

$$T = \frac{3}{2} P_n \frac{L_m}{L_r} \Psi_{dr} i_{qs}$$

where			
P_n	number of pole pairs	$\Psi\varphi_{dr}$	rotor flux ($\Psi_{dr} = L_m i_{ds}$)
L_m	mutual inductance	i_{ds}	d-axis stator current (**magnetizing**)
L_r	rotor winding self inductance	i_{qs}	q-axis stator current ("torque current")

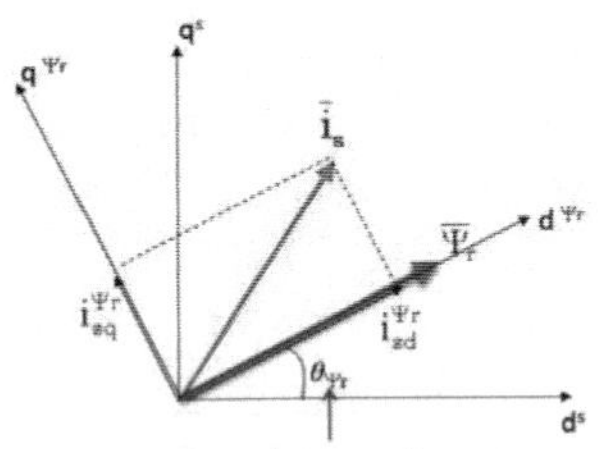

dq- reference frame
orientation angle

Vector control have decoupled i_s space vector into two components:

$$i_s = \sqrt{i_{ds}^2 + i_{qs}^2}$$

i_{ds}, i_{qs} can be used by vector and advanced control strategies to optimize efficiency (reduce the power loss)

$$p_{Cu} = \frac{3}{2} R_s (i_{ds}^2 + R_s i_{qs}^2)$$

$$p_{Fe} = c_1 \omega_e(i) \psi^2(i) + c_2 \omega_e^2(i) \psi^2(i)$$

 14

Vector and Advanced Control Strategies

Auto-tuning makes Setup easy - Inductances Ld, Lq, stator resistance and other values are obtained by drive auto-tuning and used for motor control.

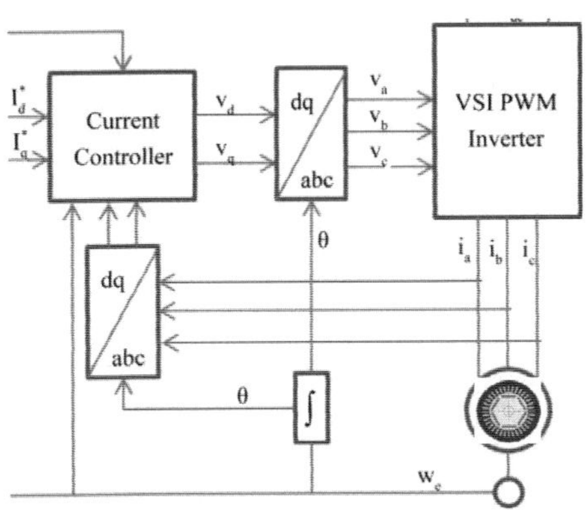

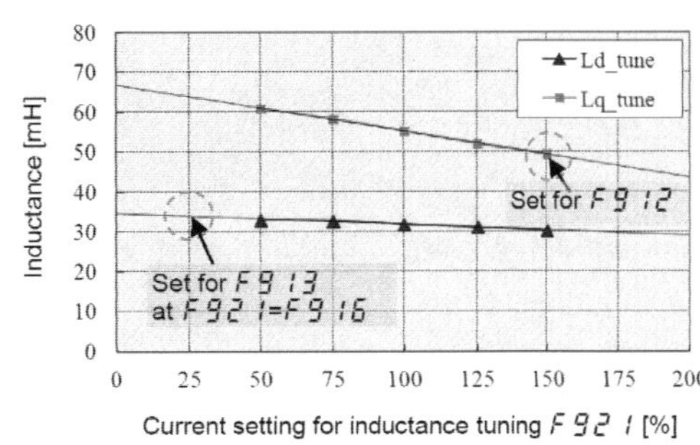

$$T_e = \frac{3p}{2} \left[\lambda_m i_q + (L_d - L_q) i_d i_q\right].$$

 15

Vector and Advanced Control Strategies

Advanced Energy Optimization strategies

$$p_{Cu} = \frac{3}{2}R_s(i_{ds}^2 + R_s i_{qs}^2)$$

$$p_{Fe} = c_1\omega_e(i)\psi^2(i) + c_2\omega_e^2(i)\psi^2(i)$$

i_{ds}	d-axis stator current (magnetizing)
i_{qs}	q-axis stator current ("torque current")
T	$\propto i_{ds}i_{qs}$ (~ area)

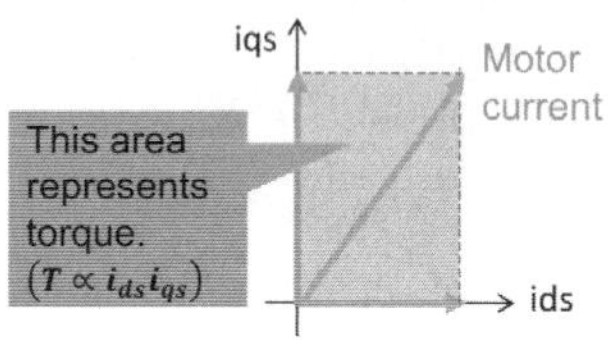

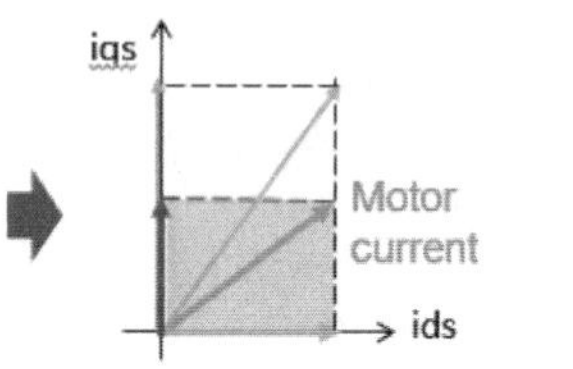

Vector Control (reduced iqs, constant ids)

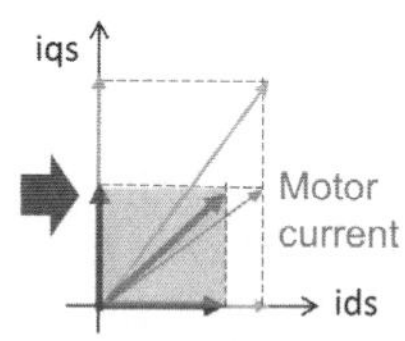

Advanced Energy Saving control (reduced iqs, ids)

Vector and Advanced Control Strategies

Traditional Field Oriented Control - T-FOC

$$i_{ds} + j\,i_{qs} = \boldsymbol{i}_s^s\, e^{-j\rho}$$

i_{ds} , i_{qs} -two degrees of freedom to produce torque

T-FOC choice is to constraint to one degree of freedom and achieve maximum flux for every speed up to base			
CT	Flux-Speed Law	$i_{mr,R}$	= constant = Rated
FW	Flux-Speed Law	$i_{mr,R}$	= field weakening (CPSR)
I_L^2	$i_{ds}^2 + i_{qs}^2 \le I_L^2$	$\le I_L^2$	Constraint due to motor current limit

$$T_{FOC,L} = k_t i_{mr,R}\sqrt{I_L^2 - i_{mr,R}^2}$$

$$T = \frac{3}{2}P_n\frac{L_m}{L_r}\Psi_{dr}i_{qs}$$

$$(\Psi_{dr} = L_m i_{ds})$$

$$T = \frac{3}{2}P_n\frac{(L_m)^2}{L_r}i_{ds}i_{qs}$$

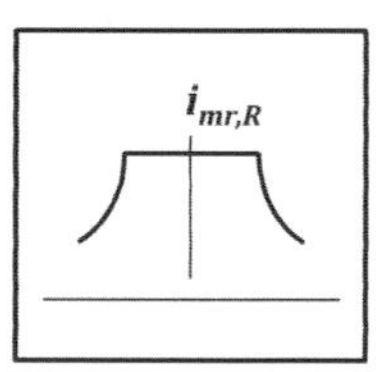

Flux-Speed Law

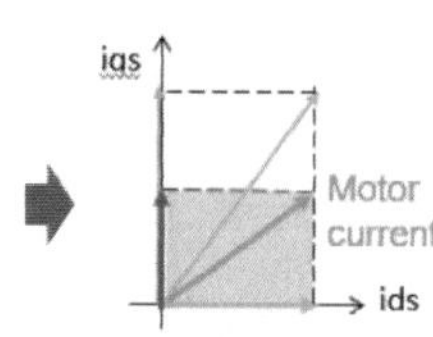

Vector Control (reduced iqs, constant ids)

T-FOC (room to improve efficiency)

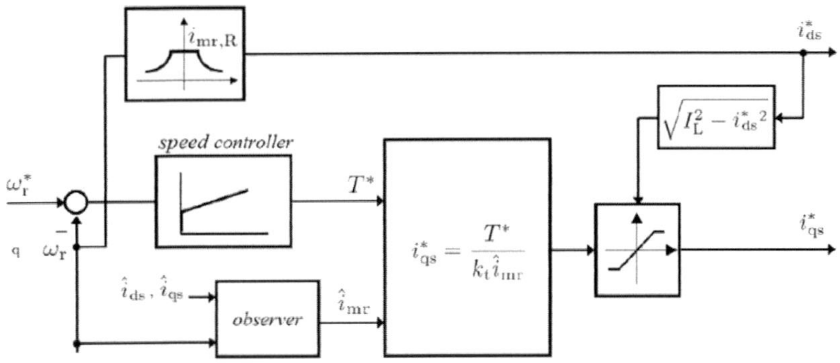

$$\begin{cases}\tau_r \frac{di_{mr}}{dt} + i_{mr} = i_{ds}\\ \frac{d\rho}{dt} = p\omega_r + \frac{i_{qs}}{\tau_r i_{mr}}\end{cases}$$

$$i_{ds}^2 + i_{qs}^2 \le I_L^2$$

$$T_{FOC,L} = k_t i_{mr,R}\sqrt{I_L^2 - i_{mr,R}^2}$$

Vector and Advanced Control Strategies

Loss distribution for the different control strategies

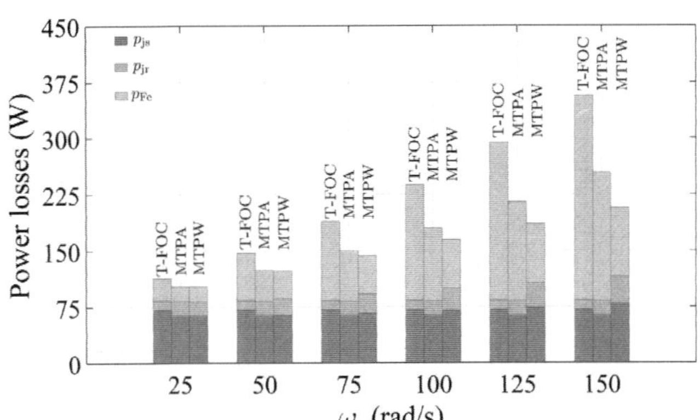

T_L = 3.5 N.m (1.1kw motor, 400V, 4 poles)

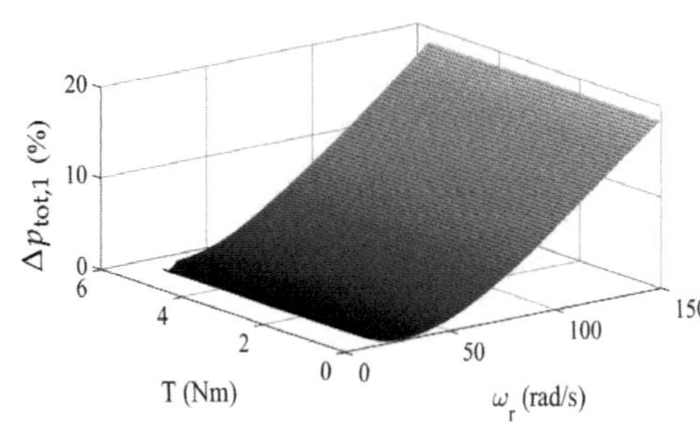

Loss reduction (%) over an Extended T_L range

https://doi.org/10.1007

04

Test Results

 20

Test Results

Test data of 200V-4P-2.2kW air handling fan motor

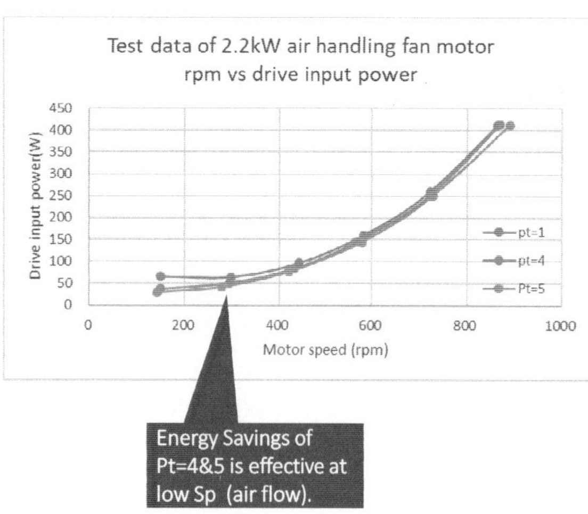

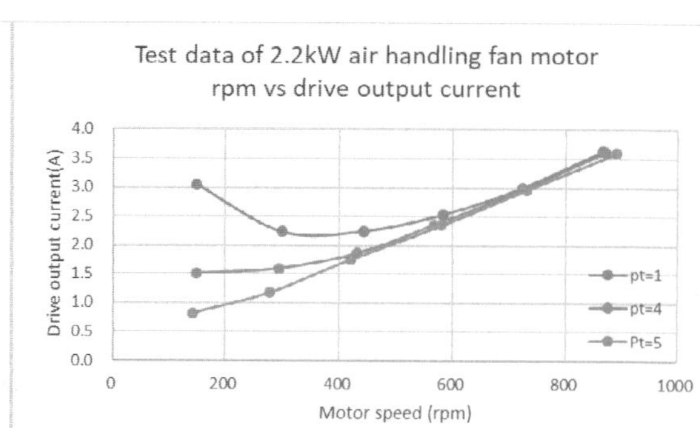

Energy Savings of Pt=4&5 is effective at low Sp (air flow).

 21

Test Results

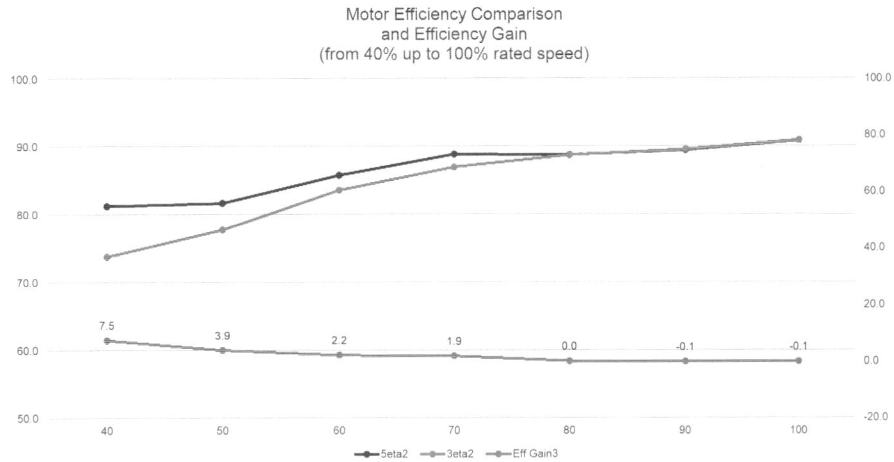

10HP, 4poles, NEMA Premium Efficiency induction motor

 22

Test Results

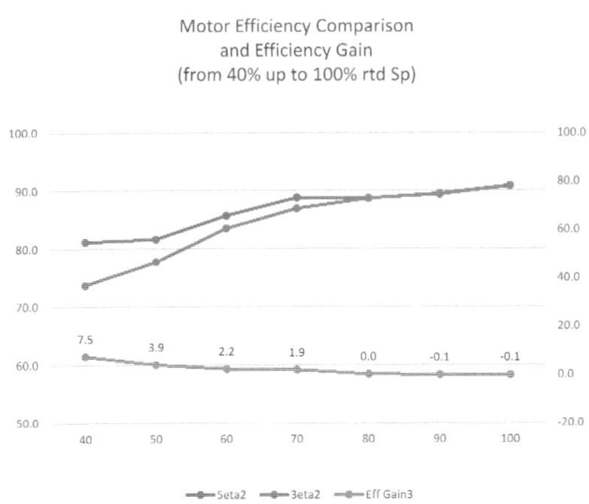

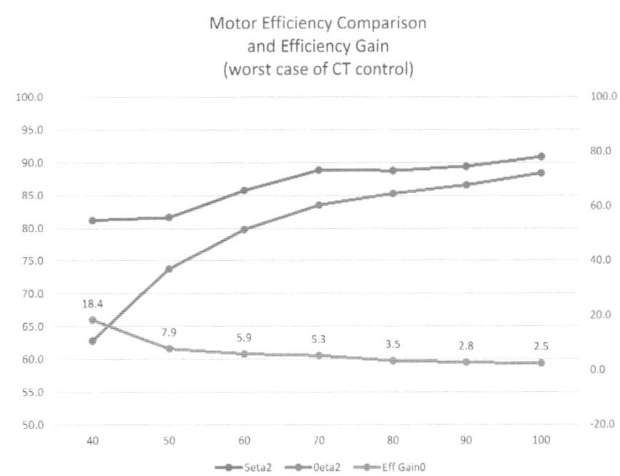

10HP, 4poles, NEMA Premium Efficiency induction motor

 23

Test Results

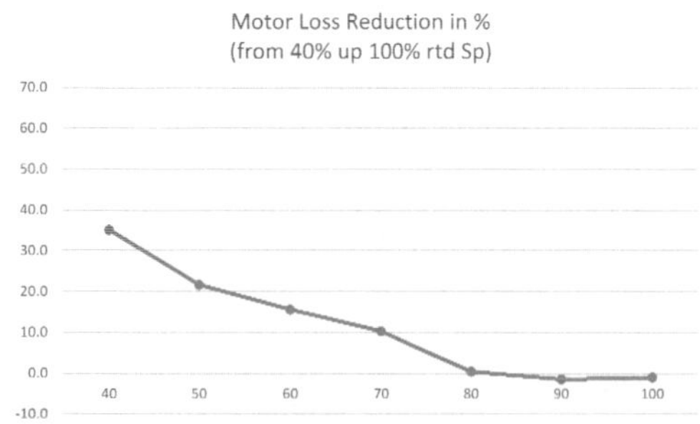

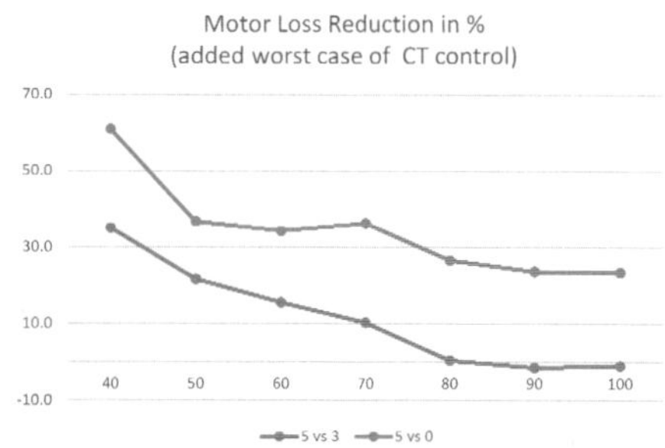

10HP, 4poles, NEMA Premium Efficiency induction motor

 24

Test Results

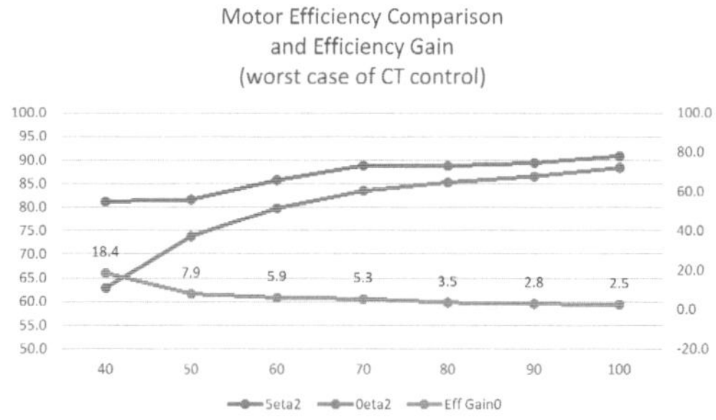

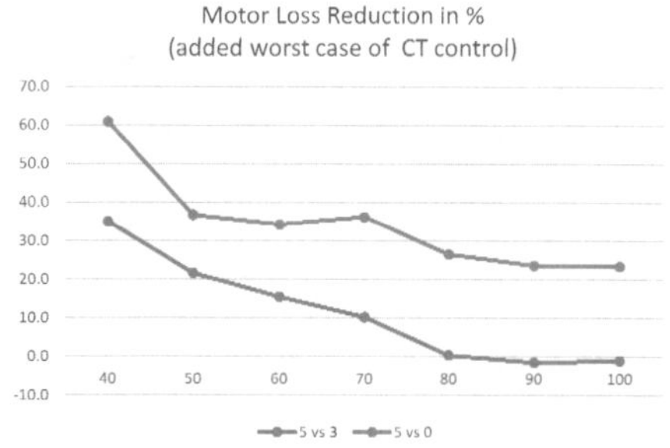

10HP, 4poles, NEMA Premium Efficiency induction motor

 25

05

Summary & Conclusion

Summary & Conclusion

- ASDs control methods can improve the efficiency of Induction and new Synchronous Motors
- We have focused in obtaining efficiency improvement results for fans and pumps and at this time we have presented the results in the low HP range
- Using an Induction motor with and off the shelf ASD with the proper control algorithm within drive system limitations can
  - Increase efficiency of the variable load/speed application.
  - At steady state, drives need to provide motor optimal air gap flux or the ids, iqs combination at each operating point for energy savings and the required dynamics for the application,
  - Minimize the motor current for less motor copper losses (MTPA), or
  - Maximize the efficiency (MTPW) for less input power consumption

Thank You

Presenter: Allen Neciosup, PhD.

To learn more about Toshiba, please visit our website at www.toshiba.com/tic.

TOSHIBA

- **Committed to People, Committed to the Future.**
- **Do the right thing.**
- **Look for a better way.**
- **Always consider the impact.**
- **Create together.**

Drew Horn – President and CEO
Greentech Minerals Holdings, Inc.

Magnet materials and critical minerals will define our future

Magnet materials are part of virtually every product we use, and demand is set to skyrocket:

- ❑ Emerging & consumer technologies
- ❑ Renewable energy platforms
- ❑ National defense needs

Rare Earth Demand will Double Over the Next 10 Years

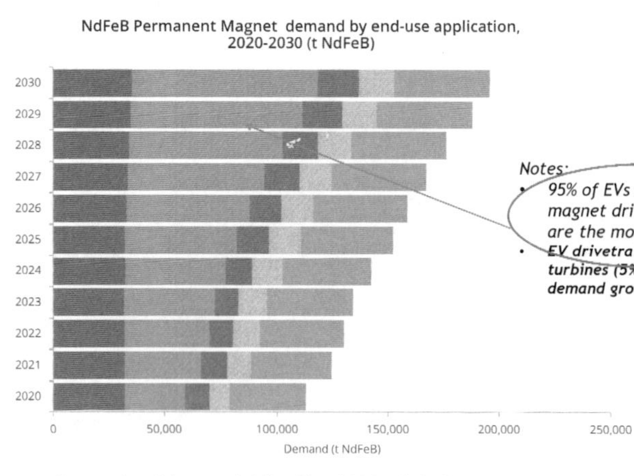

4

Rare Earths Demand Growth

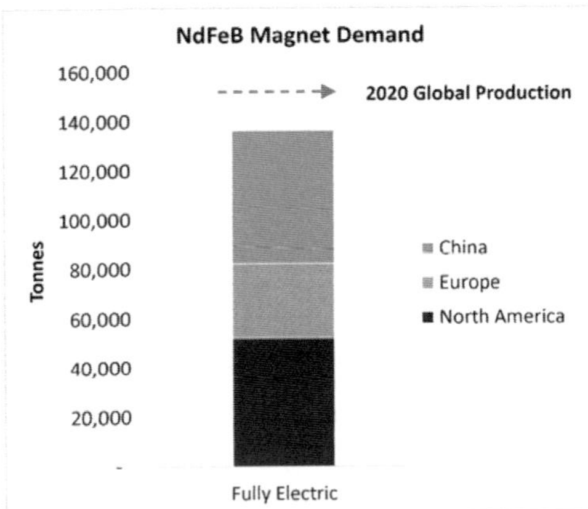

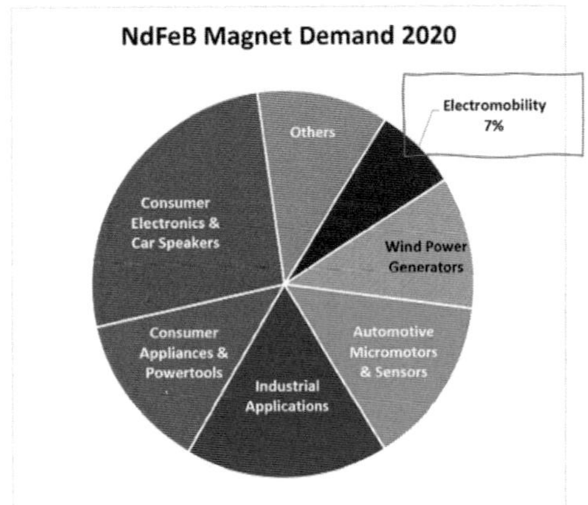

Adamas Intelligence

Source:

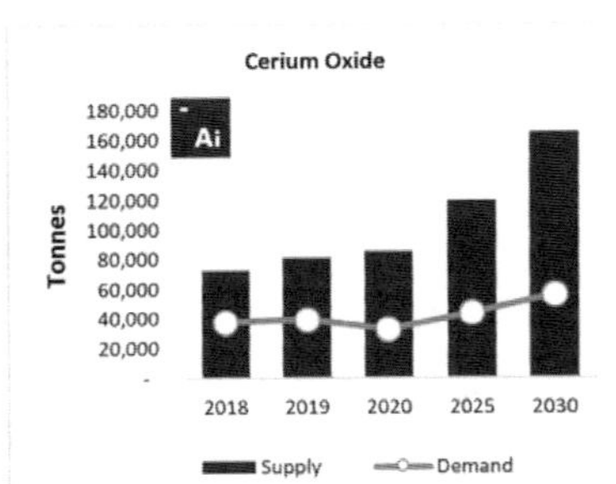

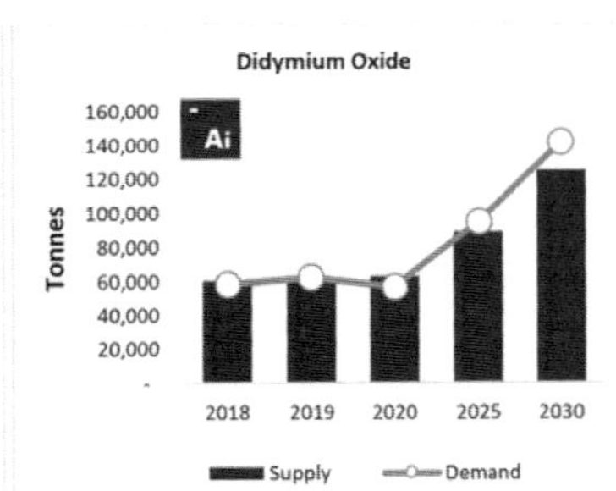

Adamas Intelligence

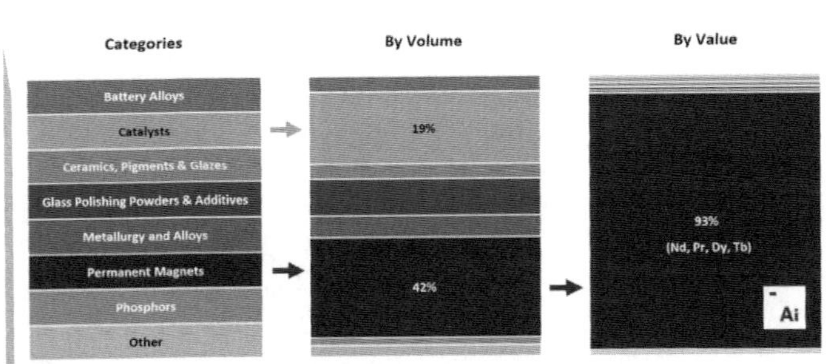

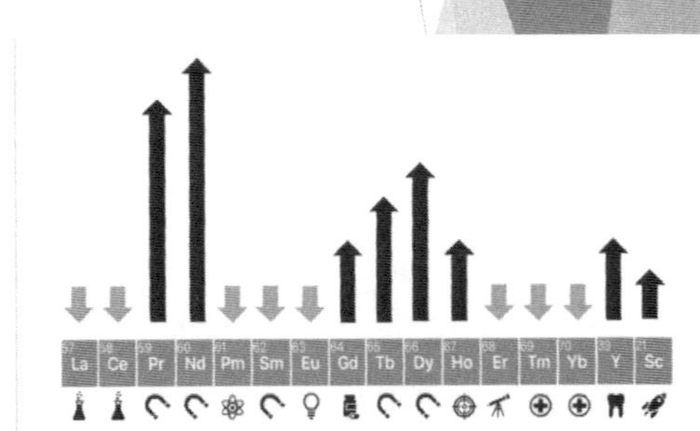

US National Security Implications

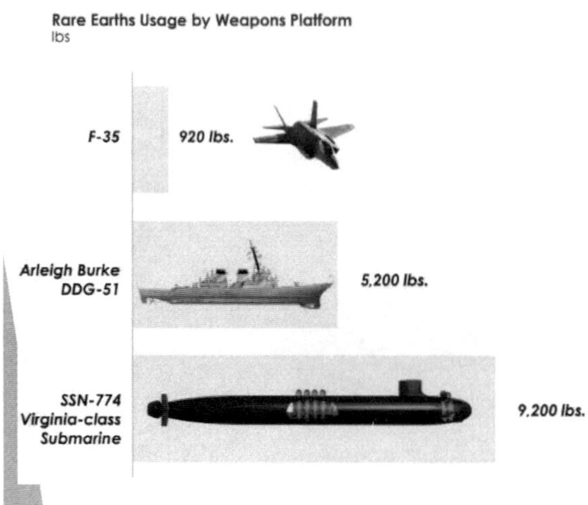

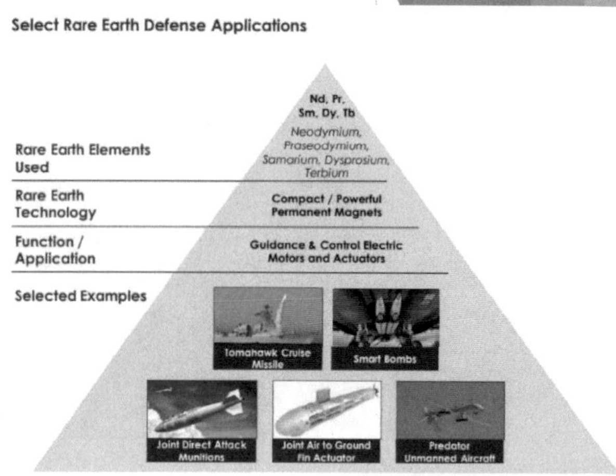

Source: Congressional Research Service

We must be dedicated to building a **secure, reliable supply chain**

- The vulnerabilities are very real
- Fair competition and free market principles cannot be sustained without access to reliable sources and capability

Turning the Corner: Increased Support for Supply Development and Value Creation

- Growing US Government Interest & Key Drivers
- Renewables and defense are the hook
- Policy and prioritization in support of US supply chain
- Project debt financing
- Credits and support for US domestic manufacturing
- Source Tracing Requirements are coming
- Commercial and Financial Markets ready to engage

A Vision and Path Forward

The Future is Bright!

- The US Government must transition from obstacle to enabler in the magnet materials sector
- Transparency, Environmental and Social Responsibility will drive substantive change in supply chain solutions

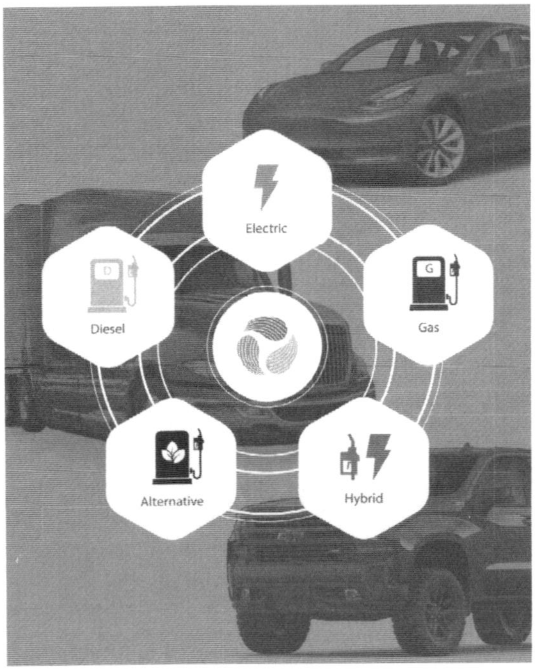

TULA

DYNAMIC MOTOR DRIVE

A STRATEGY OPTIMIZING ELECTRIC MOTOR EFFICIENCY

TULA TECHNOLOGY

TULA

Tula - Driving Towards the Future

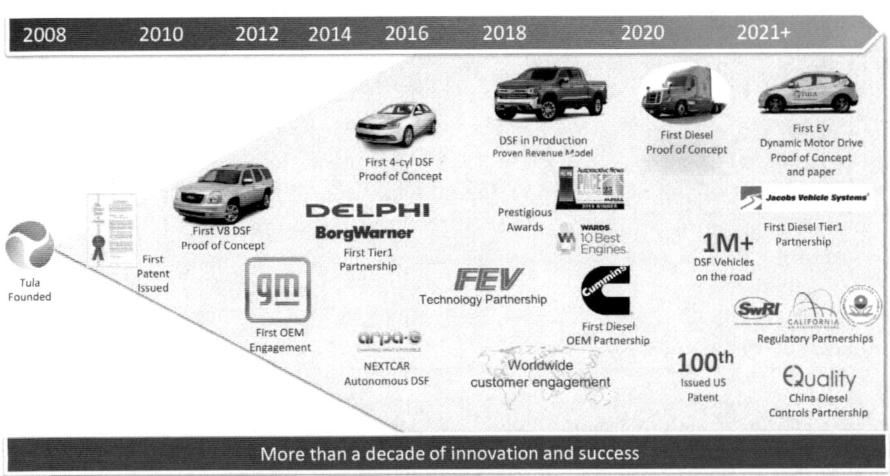

Confidential

Challenges of Climate Change

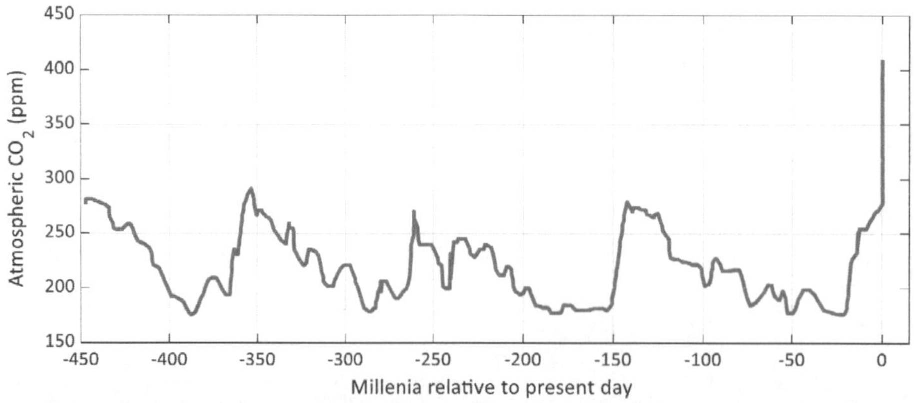

Greenhouse gas emission causes climate change. Automobiles are a major contributor

Confidential

Conventional Solutions Rely on Rare Materials

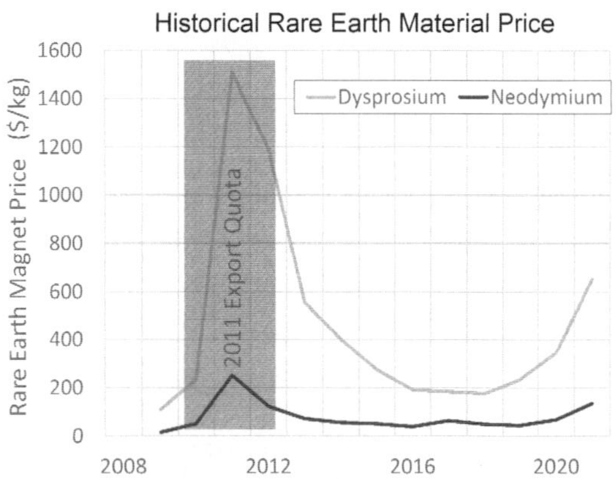

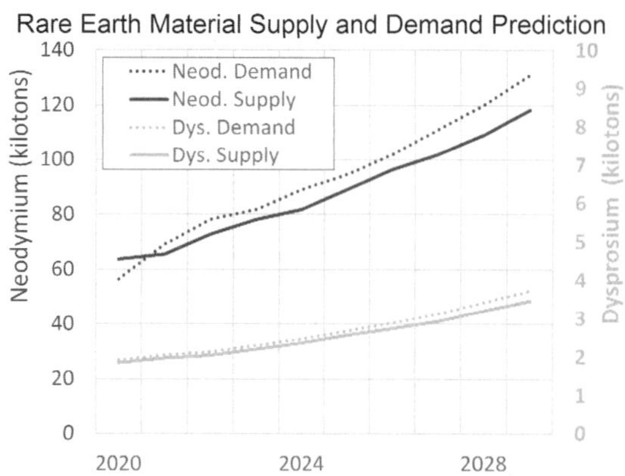

Heavy use of scarce materials can limit the implementation of permanent magnet EVs

Confidential

Dynamic Motor Drive (DMD) – The Concept

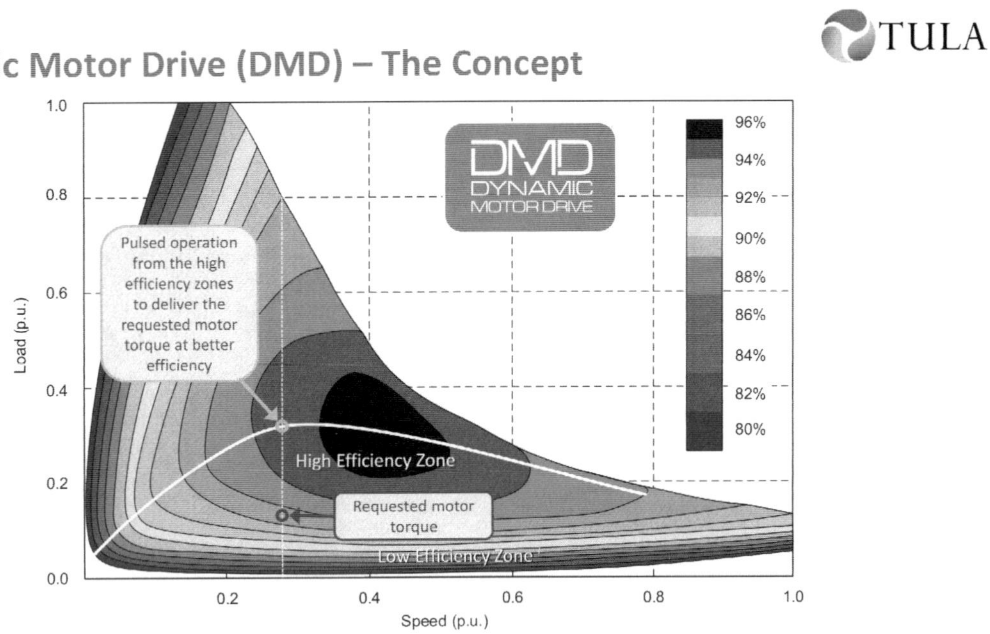

Dynamic Motor Drive (DMD) – The Concept

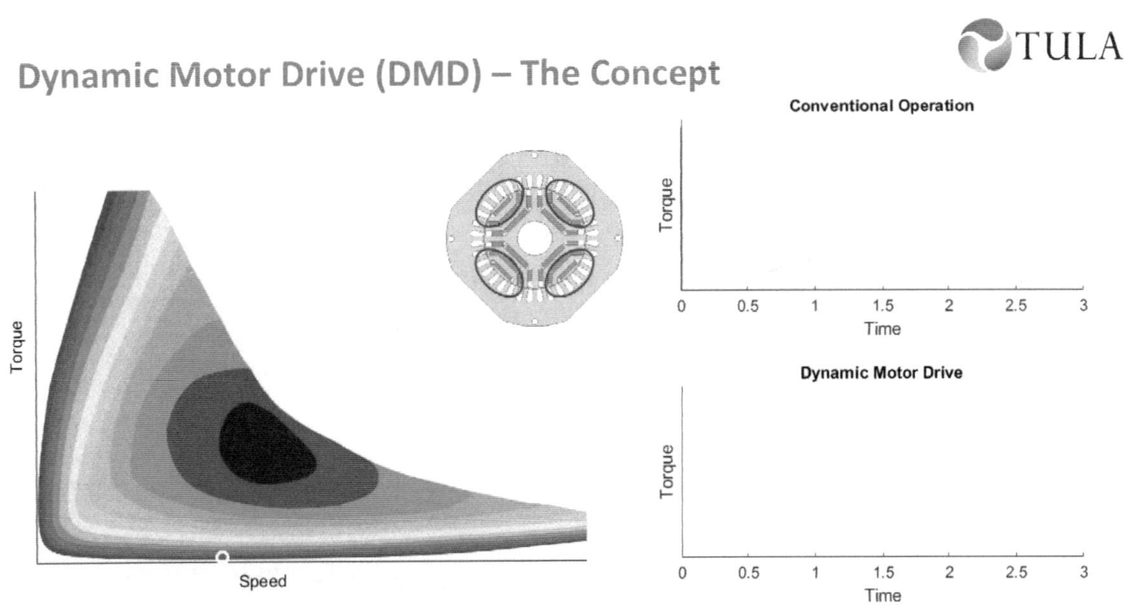

6

DMD Motor Architecture Selection

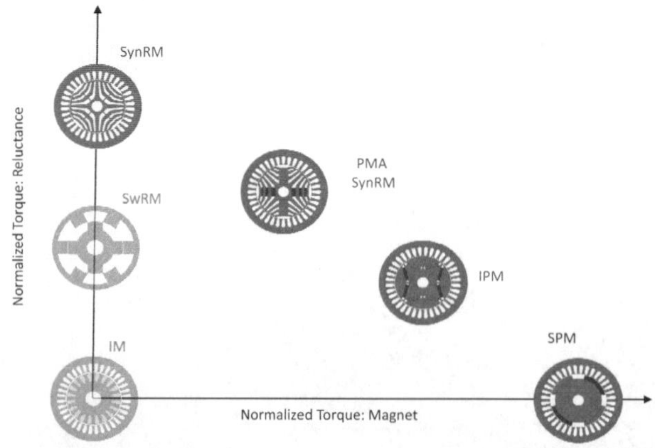

DMD is most effective for Synchronous Reluctance Motors (SynRM)

Confidential

Loss Improvement

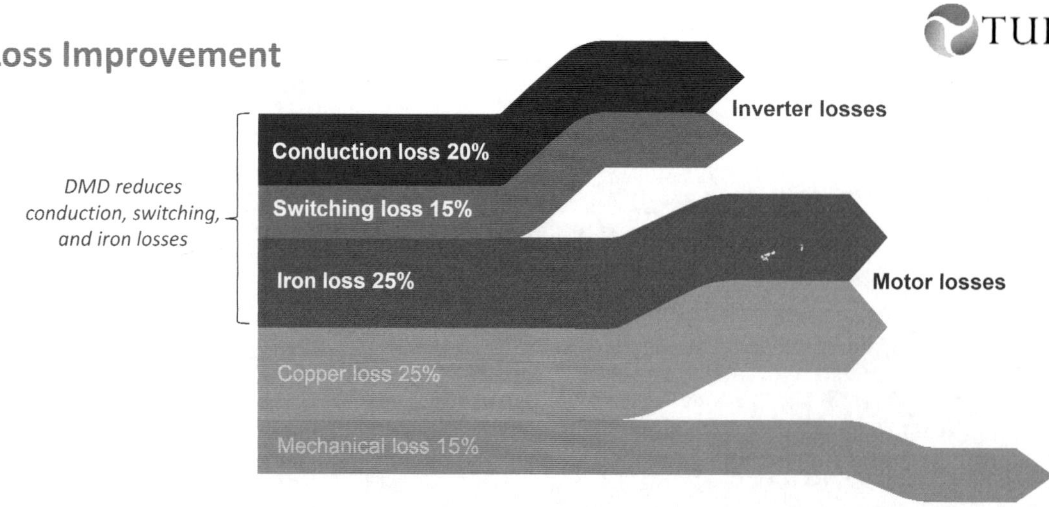

Optimizing these losses improves reluctance motor efficiency significantly

Confidential

TULA

Torque Production of Synchronous Reluctance Motor

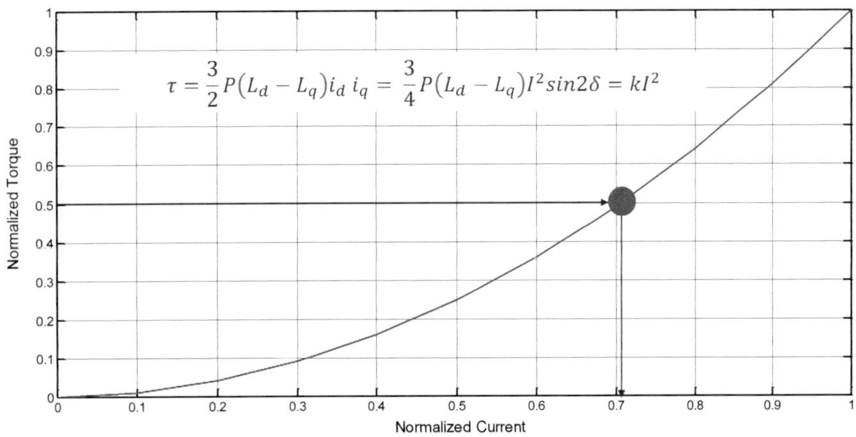

Torque is proportional to current² for SynRM's at moderate loads

Confidential

TULA

Optimization of Loss Tradeoffs

	Linear to Current	Quadratic to Current
Conduction Loss	$V_{ce0}\left(\frac{1}{2\pi} + \frac{m cos\theta}{8}\right)I$ DMD	$R_{ce}\left(\frac{1}{8} + \frac{m cos\theta}{3\pi}\right)I^2$ DMD
Switching Loss	$\frac{f_{sw}V_{dc}}{\pi I_{ref}V_{ref}}(E_{on} + E_{off} + E_{rr})I$ DMD	-
Copper Loss	-	RI^2 DMD
Hysteresis Loss	$k_h f B^{1.6} V$ DMD	
Eddy Current Loss	-	$k_w \delta^2 f^2 B^2 V$ DMD

Motors using reluctance torque are well suited for DMD

Confidential

DMD Motor Architecture Selection

TULA

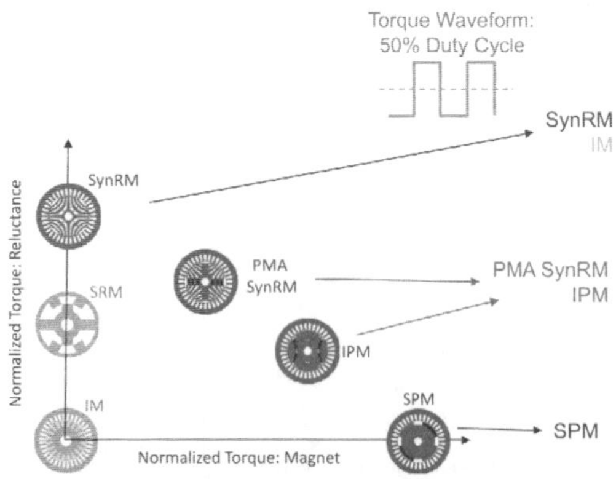

Current for 50% Duty Cycle	Losses I^2	Losses I	Losses Total	Impact of DMD
1.4x	1x	0.7x		Reduced Losses
1.4x – 2x	1x-2x	0.7x-1x		Implementation Specific
2x	2x	1x		Increased Losses

DMD is more effective for motors actively making use of reluctance torque

Tula Designed SynRM

TULA

No permanent magnets

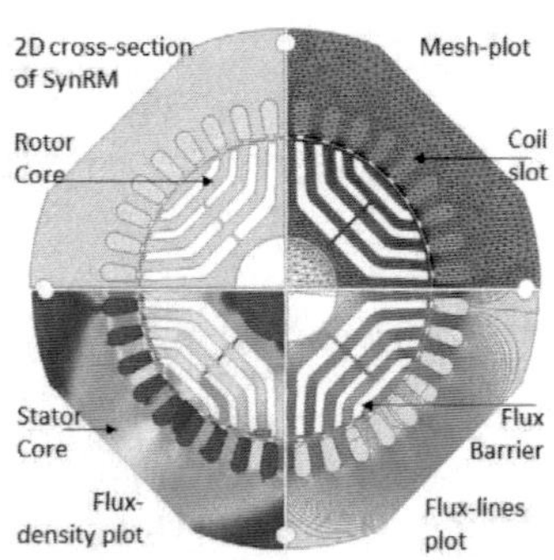

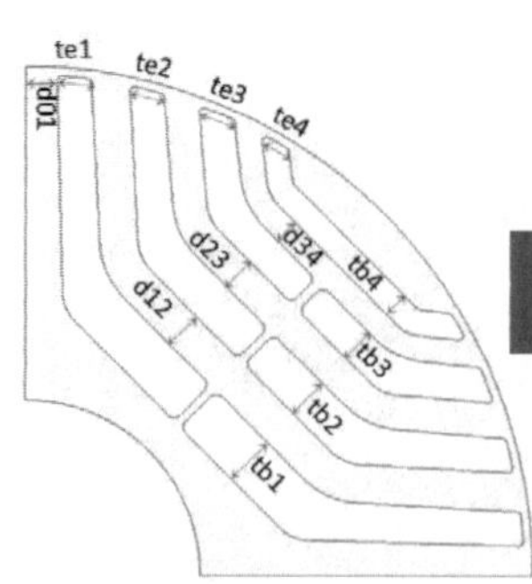

Flux barriers increase torque production

A proof-of-concept motor was designed and built by Tula to prove out DMD Strategy

Synchronous Reluctance Motor (SynRM) Design

TULA

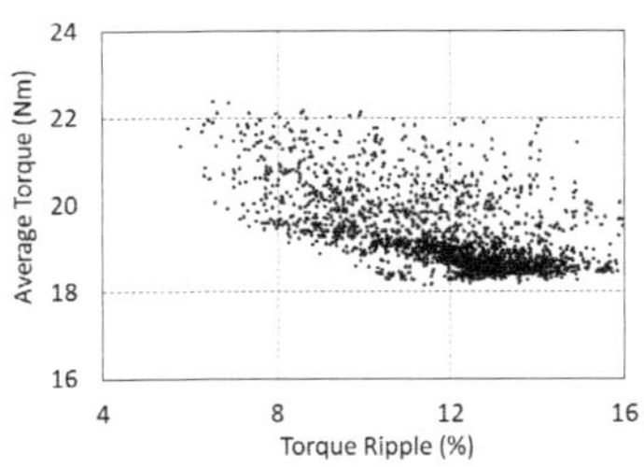

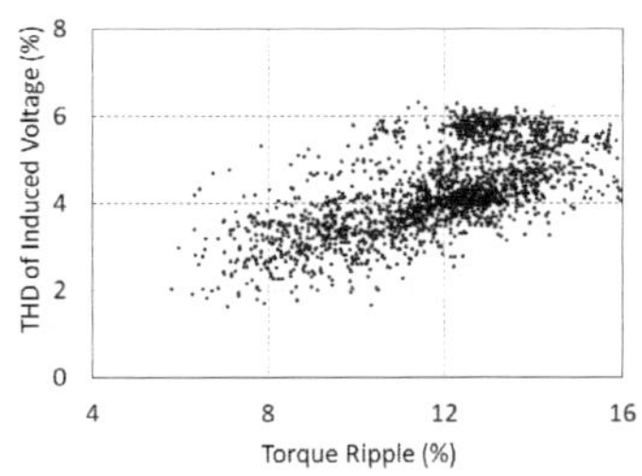

As a proof of concept, Tula has designed a 15kW SynRM using a multi-objective genetic algorithm (GA), optimizing torque, torque ripple, and harmonic distortions

Confidential

Control Optimation for DMD

TULA

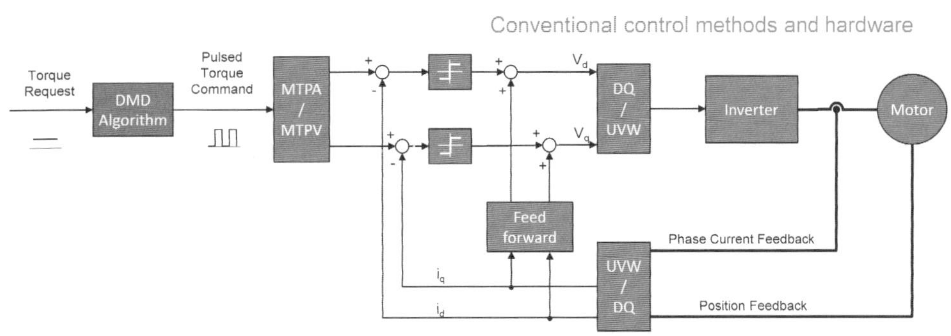

Tula's DMD algorithms were developed to allow implementation with conventional control algorithms

Time-optimized control methods optimize efficiency during transitions between high and low torque

Confidential

Torque Control Law

- Max torque per Ampere (MTPA) curve generated from Finite Element Analysis has around 1° error from test results
- This inaccuracy is corrected by compensating the iron loss model

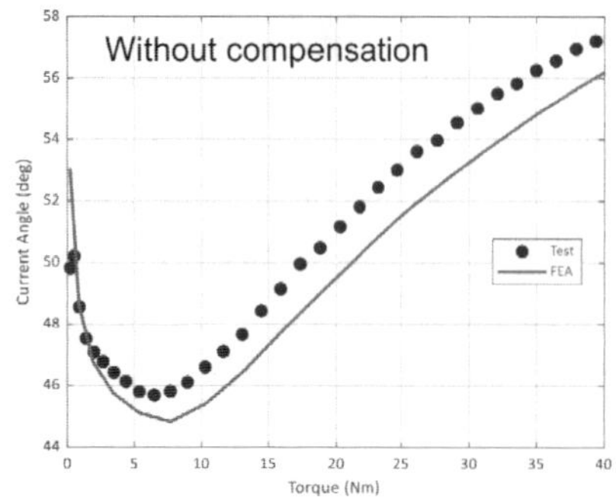

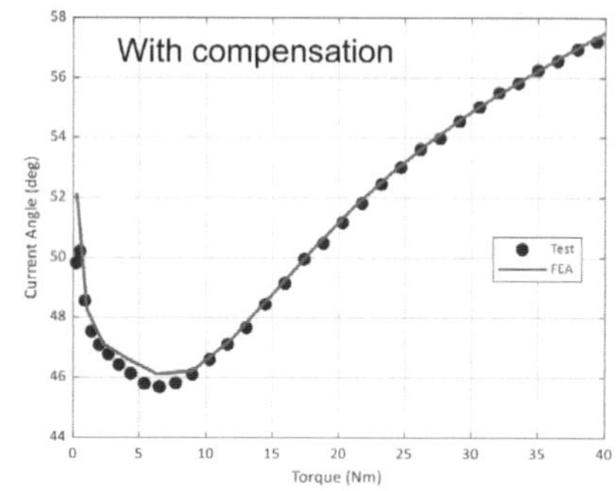

Confidential

Current Control Achieving Desired Response Speed

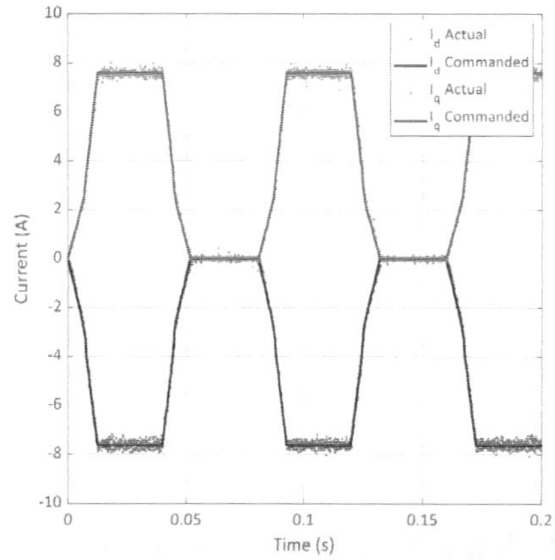

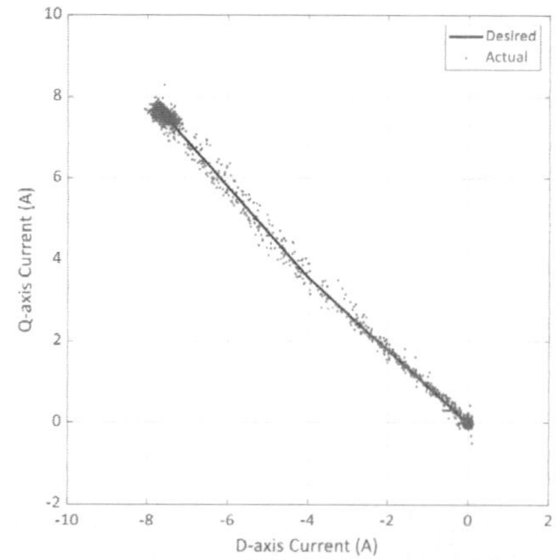

Excellent current tracking realized by deadbeat control

Confidential

Vehicle Sensitivity and Human Perception

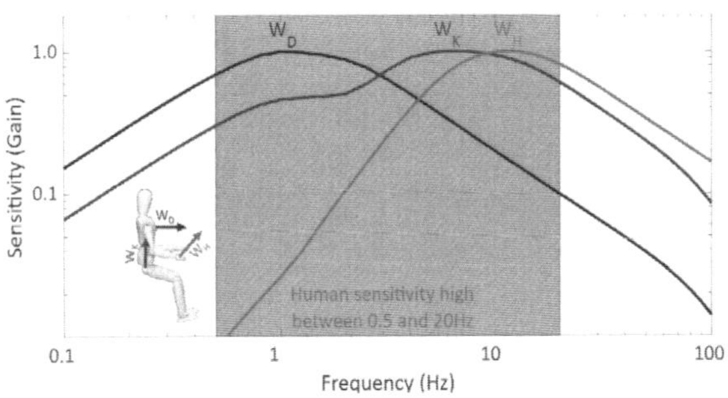

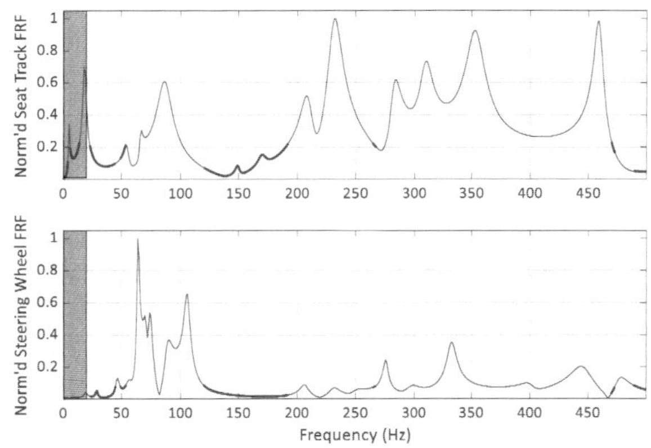

Torque modulation frequency selected has less human sensitivity

Confidential

Vibration Mitigation Strategies

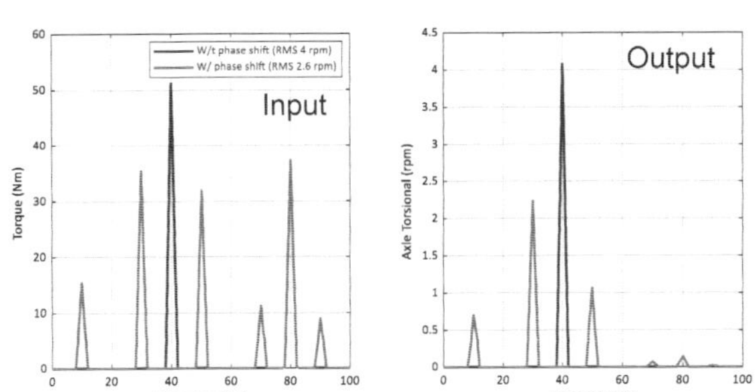

Switching modulation waveform phase between 0 and 180 degrees every 3 cycles

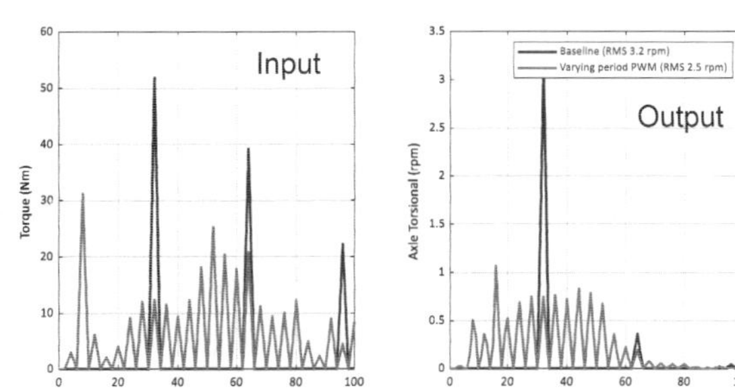

Changing torque modulation frequency randomly between 4 Hz and 40 Hz

Phase shifting and frequency changing are effective to lower and spread the vibration frequency

Confidential

Test Results of Efficiency Improvement of 15kW SynRM

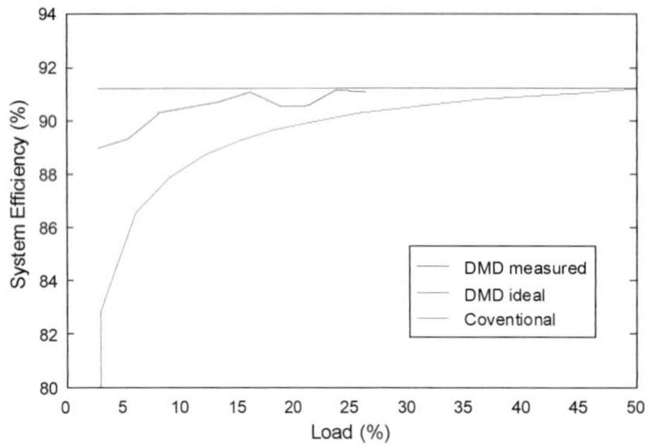

- Up to 7% efficiency improvement is verified at low loads with initial controller
- Advanced controller is under developing to narrow the gap to ideal values

Confidential

Simulation Results on Efficiency Improvement

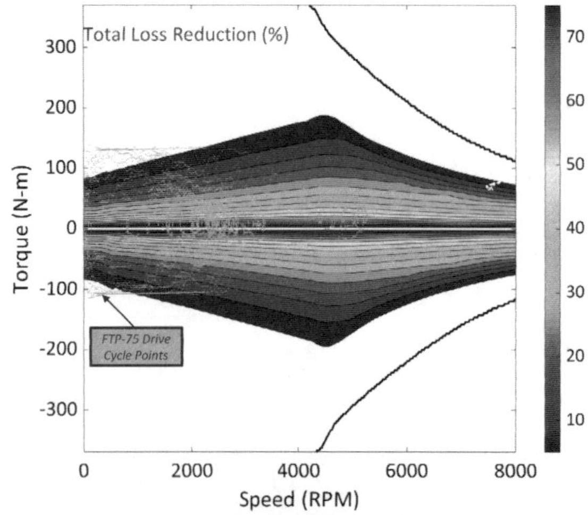

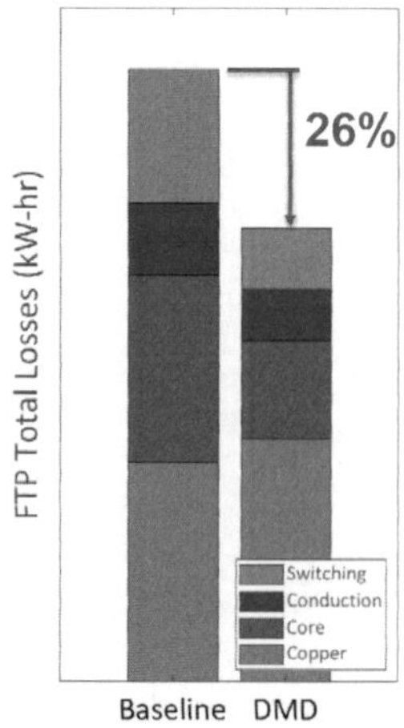

Drive cycle losses are reduced by 26%

Confidential

TULA

Simulation Results on Efficiency Improvement

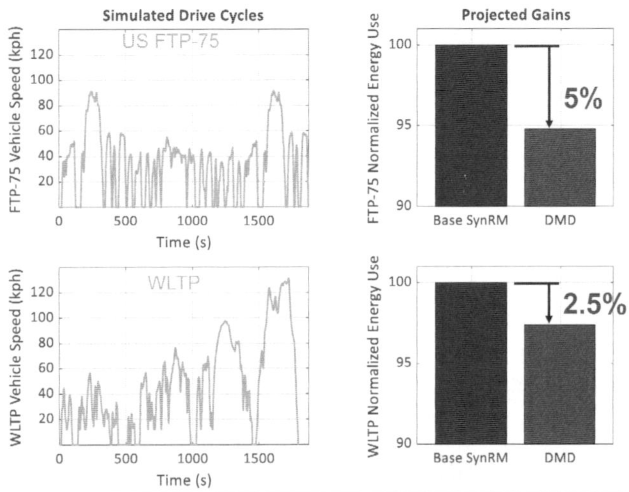

Substantial energy usage reduction of 2.5-5% for a 150kW application

TULA

Future Plan on Full-Sized Traction Motor Test

Our 150kW vehicle traction-motor development dyno is now operable and collecting initial data

We have implemented control on two demonstration Bolts

DMD Enables Better Efficiency

TULA

- Dynamic Motor Drive is a control strategy optimizing motor and inverter system efficiency
- It requires no additional hardware and is easy to implement in software with IP licensed from Tula
- Significant efficiency improvements on relevant drive cycles are achieved, helping to reduce or eliminate rare earth material dependence and downsize the battery capacity required
- The strategy makes use of a very fast response speed of the proposed current controller to realize optimal efficiency at both steady and transient states
- Vibration issues can be mitigated by using industry-proven techniques developed with Tula's Dynamic Skip Fire technology

PrNd secured supply

HANGZHOU PERMANENT MAGNET GROUP

Dual Design Idea

NdFeB or SmCo Magnet can be used (exchangeable)

- Same Geometry
- The decisive magnetic values are equivalent

2 great advantages

- Supply risk reduction
- Cost reduction, the cheaper raw material at each time can be used

Valid for any magnetic circuit like motors, generators, sensor systems,….

HANGZHOU PERMANENT MAGNET GROUP

PrNd supply gap – Motivation 1 for dual design

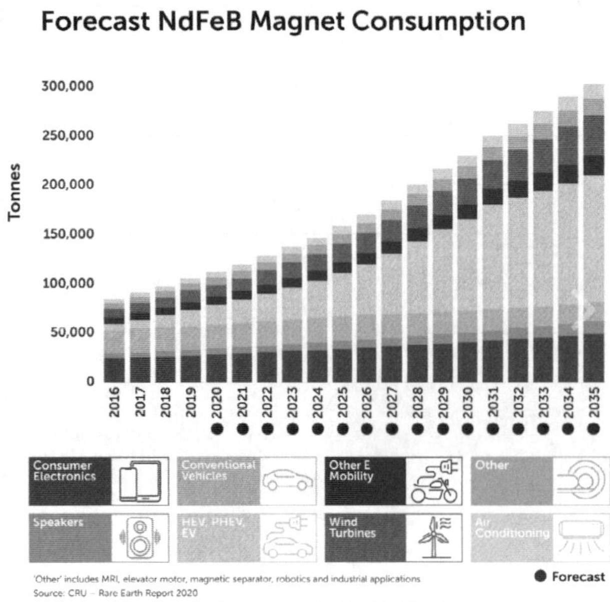

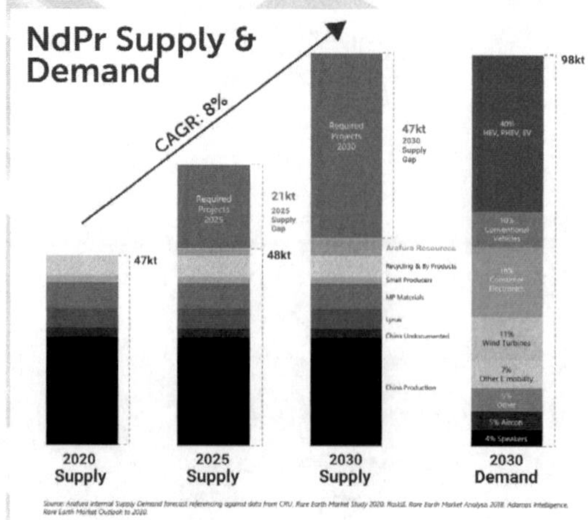

HANGZHOU PERMANENT MAGNET GROUP

SmCo raw materials

SmCo magnets raw material cost drivers are volatil and mostly independent from Nd price development

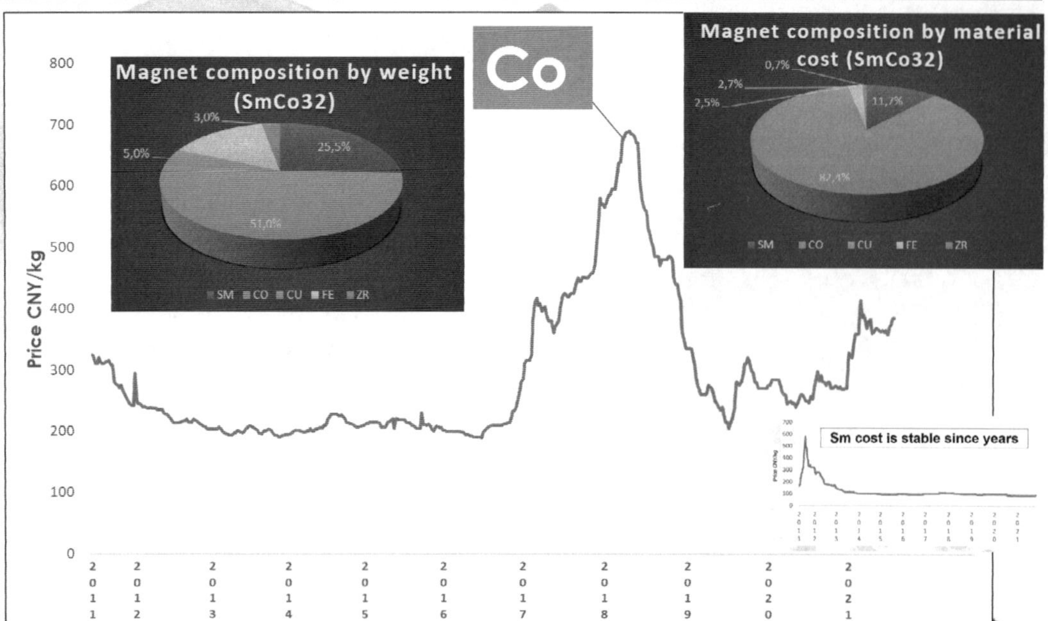

HANGZHOU PERMANENT MAGNET GROUP

NdFeB raw materials

Nd magnets raw material cost drivers are highly volatil

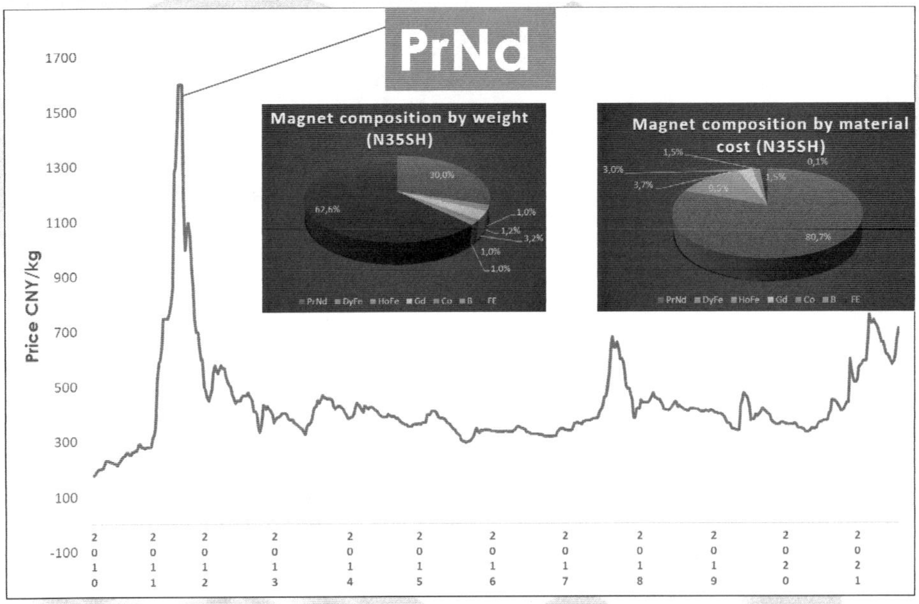

HANGZHOU PERMANENT MAGNET GROUP

Tb and Dy -> additional Cost Drivers for high Nd grades

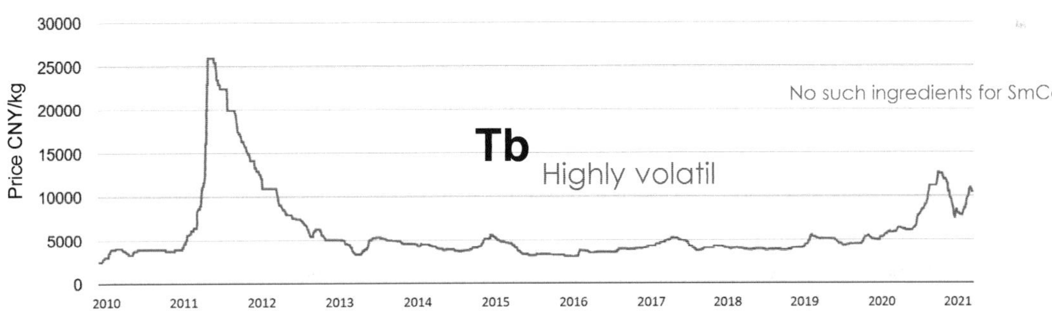

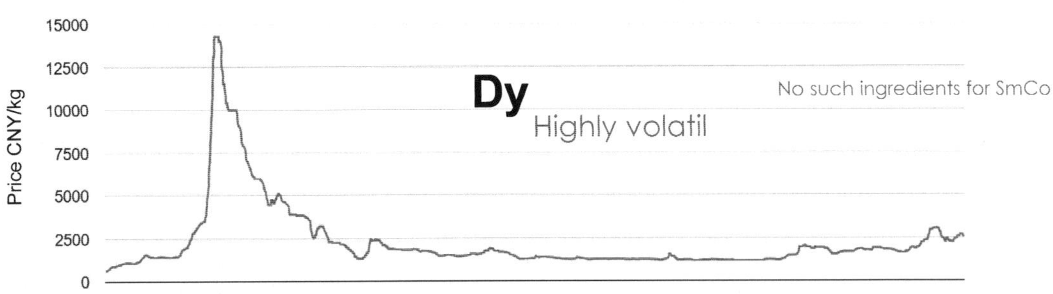

HANGZHOU PERMANENT MAGNET GROUP

Cost Drivers of Nd- and SmCo Magnets Motivation2

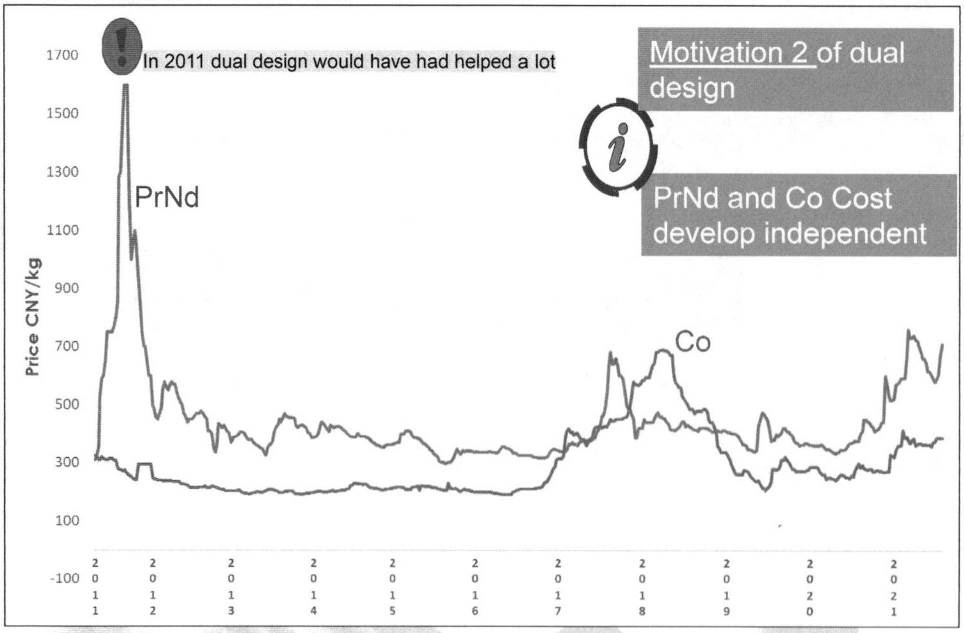

SmCo raw materials – Dual Design Motivation 3

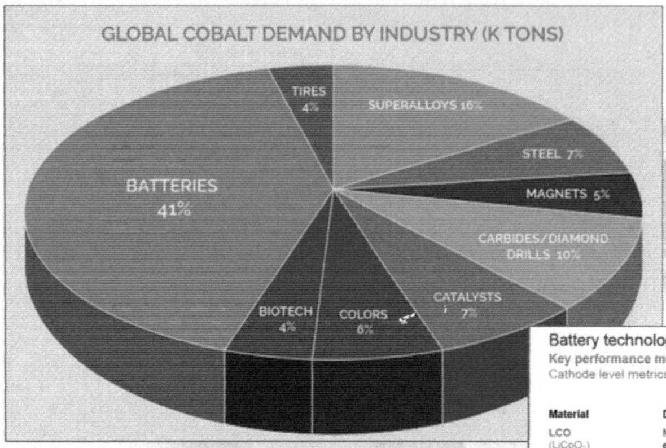

Cobalt demand is dominated by by batteries for electric vehicles

In other applications demand is stable

Battery manufacturers actively develop technologies with low or no Co-content

This reduces pressure on Co price

Battery technologies by chemistry with pros and cons

Key performance metrics of cathode chemistries

Cathode level metrics

Strong / Moderate / Weak

Material	Description	Safety	Cost USD/kWh	Energy density kWh/kg	Cycle life Times	Ni content Kg/kWh
LCO ($LiCoO_2$)	Mostly applied to consumer electronics. Limited application for xEVs (e.g., Tesla)	Low	Low	0.58	1,500 - 2,000	0
NMC1 ($LiNi_xCo_yMn_zO_2$)	Applied mainly in consumer electronics but increasing application for xEVs	Mid	Mid	0.60	2,000 - 3,000	0.69 (51 wt[2]%)
LMO ($LiMn_2O_4$)	Relatively mature technology. Applied in xEVs by Japanese OEMs (e.g., LEAF, iMiEV, Volt)	High	High	0.41	1,500 - 3,000	0
LFP ($LiFePO_4$)	Relatively new technology applied in xEVs and ESS. Driven by A123 and Chinese manufacturers (e.g., BYD, STL)	Very high	High	0.53	5,000-10,000	0
NCA ($LiNi_{0.8}Co_{0.15}Al_{0.05}O_2$)	Applied mostly in consumer electronics (often blended with other chemistries) and e-vehicles (e.g., Tesla)	Mid	Mid	0.72	NA	0.68 (49 wt[2]%)

1 For 811 configuration   2 By weight

Dual Design Magnets – Grade Pairs instead of 1 Grade

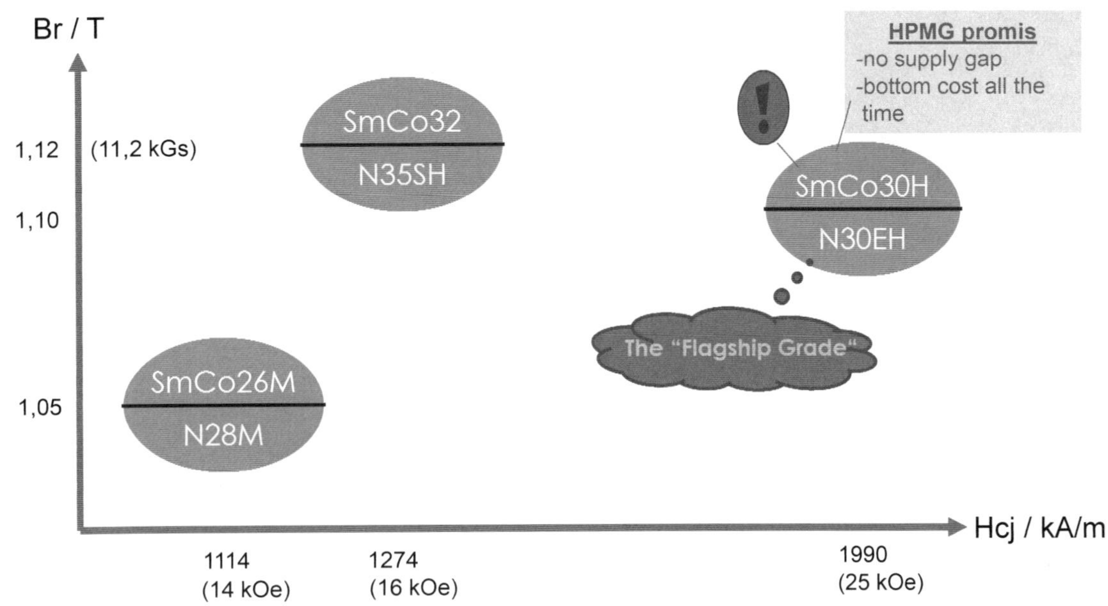

HANGZHOU PERMANENT MAGNET GROUP

Dual Design Magnets – Grade Pairs

HPMG Recommendation

Motor / Magnetic circuit design input data

Nomenclature 规定牌号	Grade 牌号	Parameters 性能: Br 剩磁感应强度 mT(kGs)	Hcb 矫顽力 kA/m(kOe)	Hcj 内禀矫顽力 kA/m(kOe)	(BH)max 最大磁能积 kJ/m3 (MGOe)	| Temperture Coefficient | 温度系数 |αBr| %/°C	|βHcj| %/°C	Tw 最高工作温度 °C	Br min @ Tw 剩磁感应强度 mT	Hcj min @ Tw 内禀矫顽力 kA/m
S-NdFeB 240/239	30EH	1080-1140 (10.8-11.4)	≥812 (≥10.2)	≥2388 (≥30)	223-247 (28-31)	0.095-0.11	0.42-0.50	200	866,16	238,8
RE2Co17 222/199	SmCo30H	1080-1100 (10.8-11)	≥788 (≥9.9)	≥1990 (≥25)	222-247 (28-31)	0.035	0.2	350	1011,96	1273,6
DDG 222/199	**D30EH**	**1080-1140 (10.8-11.4)**	**≥788 (≥9.9)**	**≥1990 (≥25)**	**222-247 (28-31)**	GBD		**200**	**866,16**	**238,8**
S-NdFeB 240/279	30TH	1080-1140 (10.8-11.4)	≥780 (≥9.8)	≥2785 (≥35)	223-247 (28-31)	0.095-0.11	0.40-0.48	240	818,64	334,2
RE2Co17 222/199	SmCo30H	1080-1100 (10.8-11)	≥788 (≥9.9)	≥1990 (≥25)	222-247 (28-31)	0.035	0.2	350	996,84	1114,4
DDG 222/199+	**D30TH**	**1080-1140 (10.8-11.4)**	**≥780 (≥9.8)**	**≥1990 (≥25)**	**222-247 (28-31)**	GBD		**240**	**818,64**	**334,2**
S-NdFeB 280/159	35SH	1180-1230 (11.8-12.3)	≥907 (≥11.4)	≥1600 (≥20)	263-287 (33-36)	0.11-0.12	0.50-0.60	150	1011,52	352
RE2Co17 230/127	SmCo32	1100-1140 (11-11.4)	≥796 (≥10)	≥1274 (≥16)	230-263 (29-33)	0.035	0.2	350	1049,95	942,76
DDG 230/127	**D35SH**	**1100-1230 (11-12.3)**	**≥796 (≥10)**	**≥1274 (≥16)**	**230-287 (29-36)**	HREE free		**150**	**1011,52**	**352**
S-NdFeB 220/111	28M	1040-1090 (10.4-10.9)	≥780 (≥9.8)	≥1114 (≥14)	218-230 (27-29)	0.11-0.13	0.60-0.70	100	931,84	490,16
RE2Co17 191/80	SmCo26M	1020-1060 (10.2-10.6)	≥637 (≥8)	≥637 (≥8)	191-215 (24-27)	0.03	0.2	250	995,52	668,64
DDG 191/80	**D28M**	**1020-1090 (10.4-10.9)**	**≥637 (≥8)**	**≥637 (≥8)**	**191-215 (24-27)**	HREE free		**100**	**931,84**	**490,16**

HANGZHOU PERMANENT MAGNET GROUP

NdFeB MATERIAL OVERVIEW

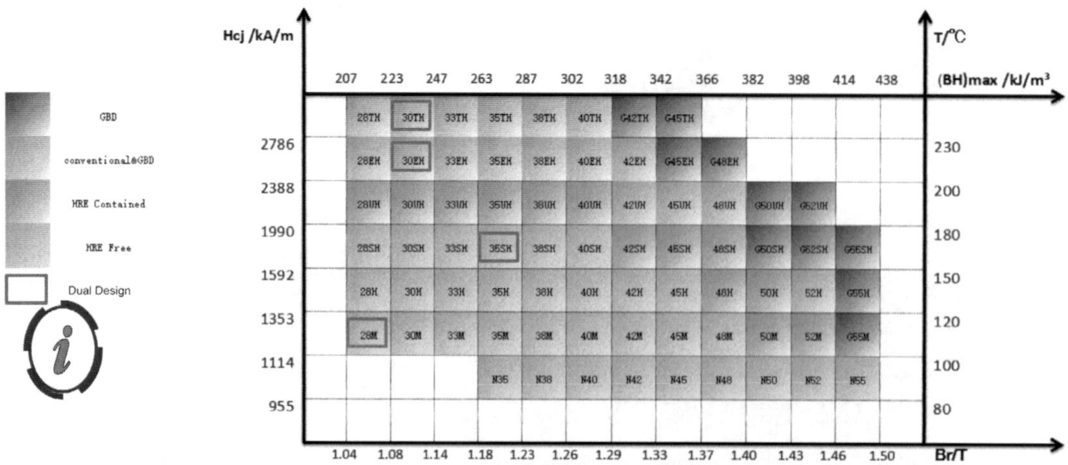

- No HRE in grade below N40SH
- G45TH,G48EH,G52UH,G55SH developed successfully
- (SmCo) Dual Design available for N30TH, N30EH, N35SH, N28M

HANGZHOU PERMANENT MAGNET GROUP

Dual Design – Material Cost comparison – July 21

The "Flagship Grade"

Material 1kg	Raw material	Amount	Total Weight (g)	Raw material cost(CNY/kg)	Material cost
SMCO 30H	SM	25,5%	255,00	86,00	¥21,9300
	CO	51,0%	510,00	385,00	¥196,3500
	CU	5,0%	70,00	48,00	¥3,3600
	FE	15,5%	155,00	5,40	¥0,8370
	ZR	3,0%	30,00	150,00	¥4,5000
Total:					¥226,9770

1 kg SmCo

Material 1kg	Raw material	Amount	Total Weight (g)	Raw material cost(CNY/kg)	Material cost
N30EH	PrNd	24%	240,00	710,00	¥170,4000
	DyFe	8%	80,00	2500,00	¥200,0000
	HoFe	5%	50,00	820,00	¥41,0000
	Co	1%	10,00	385,00	¥3,8500
	B	1%	10,00	27,50	¥0,2750
	FE	61%	610,00	6,50	¥3,9650
Total:					¥415,5250

+83%

1 kg NdFeB

Material 1kg	Raw material	Amount	Total Weight (g)	Raw material cost(CNY/kg)	Material cost
SMCO 32	SM	25,5%	255,00	86,00	¥21,9300
	CO	51,0%	510,00	385,00	¥196,3500
	CU	5,0%	70,00	48,00	¥3,3600
	FE	15,5%	155,00	5,40	¥0,8370
	ZR	3,0%	30,00	150,00	¥4,5000
Total:					¥226,9770

Material 1kg	Raw material	Amount	Total Weight (g)	Raw material cost(CNY/kg)	Material cost
N35SH	PrNd	30,0%	300,00	710,00	¥213,0000
	DyFe	1,0%	10,00	2500,00	¥25,0000
	HoFe	1,2%	12,00	820,00	¥9,8400
	Gd	3,2%	32,00	245,00	¥7,8400
	Co	1,0%	10,00	385,00	¥3,8500
	B	1,0%	10,00	27,50	¥0,2750
	FE	62,6%	626,00	6,50	¥4,0690
Total:					¥259,8050

Material 1kg	Raw material	Amount	Total Weight (g)	Raw material cost(CNY/kg)	Material cost
SMCO 26M	SM	26,3%	263,00	86,00	¥22,6180
	CO	49,7%	497,00	385,00	¥191,3450
	CU	6,0%	70,00	48,00	¥3,3600
	FE	15,0%	150,00	5,40	¥0,8100
	ZR	3,0%	30,00	150,00	¥4,5000
Total:					¥222,6330

Material 1kg	Raw material	Amount	Total Weight (g)	Raw material cost(CNY/kg)	Material cost
N28M	PrNd	25,0%	250,00	710,00	¥177,5000
	DyFe	0,0%	0,00	2500,00	¥0,0000
	HoFe	0,0%	0,00	820,00	¥0,0000
	Gd	7,5%	75,00	245,00	¥18,3750
	Co	0,0%	0,00	385,00	¥0,0000
	B	1,0%	10,00	27,50	¥0,2750
	FE	66,5%	665,00	6,50	¥4,3225
Total:					¥196,1500

HANGZHOU PERMANENT MAGNET GROUP

Dual Design – Material Index

Index < 1 -> SmCo is cheaper

Index > 1 -> NdFeB is cheaper

Nomenclature 规定牌号	Grade 牌号
S-NdFeB 240/239	30EH
RE2Co17 222/199	SmCo30H
DDG 222/199	D30EH

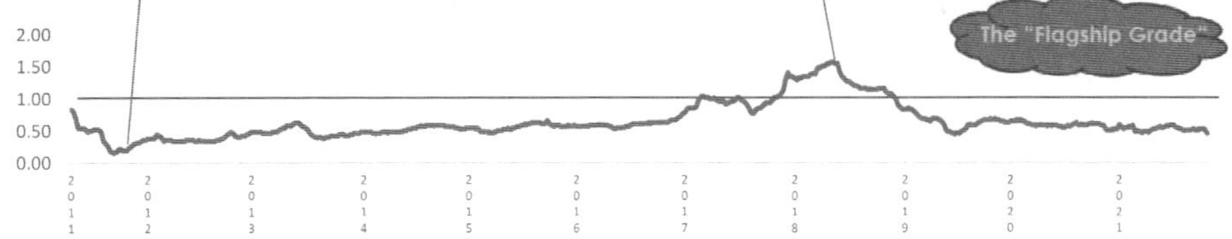

Nomenclature 规定牌号	Grade 牌号
S-NdFeB 280/159	35SH
RE2Co17 230/127	SmCo32
DDG 230/127	D35SH

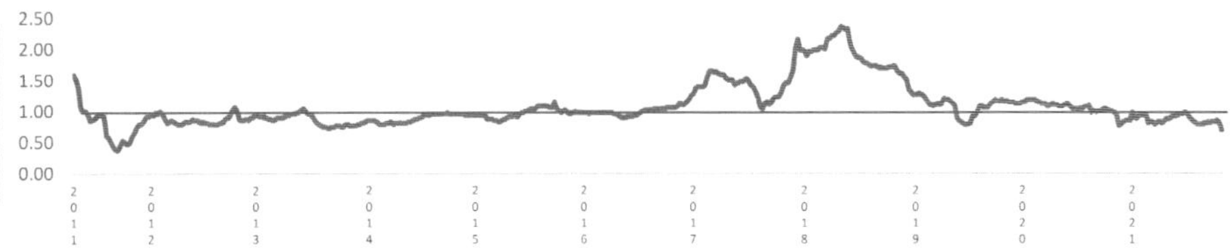

Nomenclature 规定牌号	Grade 牌号
S-NdFeB 220/111	28M
RE2Co17 191/80	SmCo26M
DDG 191/80	D28M

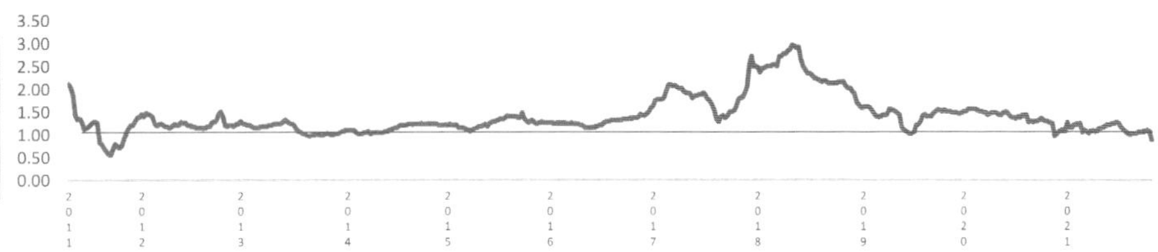

HANGZHOU PERMANENT MAGNET GROUP

Dual Design – realized examples

	Type	Dimensions [mm]	weight [g]	Grain boundary diffusion	Material	Grade	Cost Index [%]
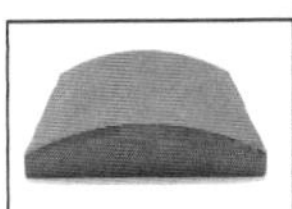	bread loaf	R95x120x100x24	1800	no	NdFeB	N30TH	100
			1960	no	SmCo	DDG 222/199+	**77**
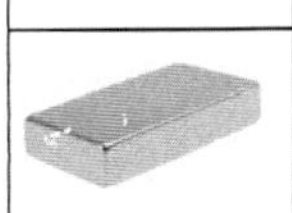	block	30x30X5	34,65	yes	NdFeB	N30TH	100
			37,8	no	SmCo	DDG 222/199+	**83**
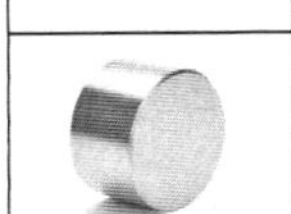	cylinder	25x20	76	no	NdFeB	N30EH	100
			82,91	no	SmCo	DDG 222/199	**92**
	Ring	40x23x6	39	yes	NdFeB	N30EH	100
			42,55	no	SmCo	DDG 222/199	**97**

HANGZHOU PERMANENT MAGNET GROUP

Dual Design Magnets – Cost Savings example

Dual design Cost savings 328.436 USD

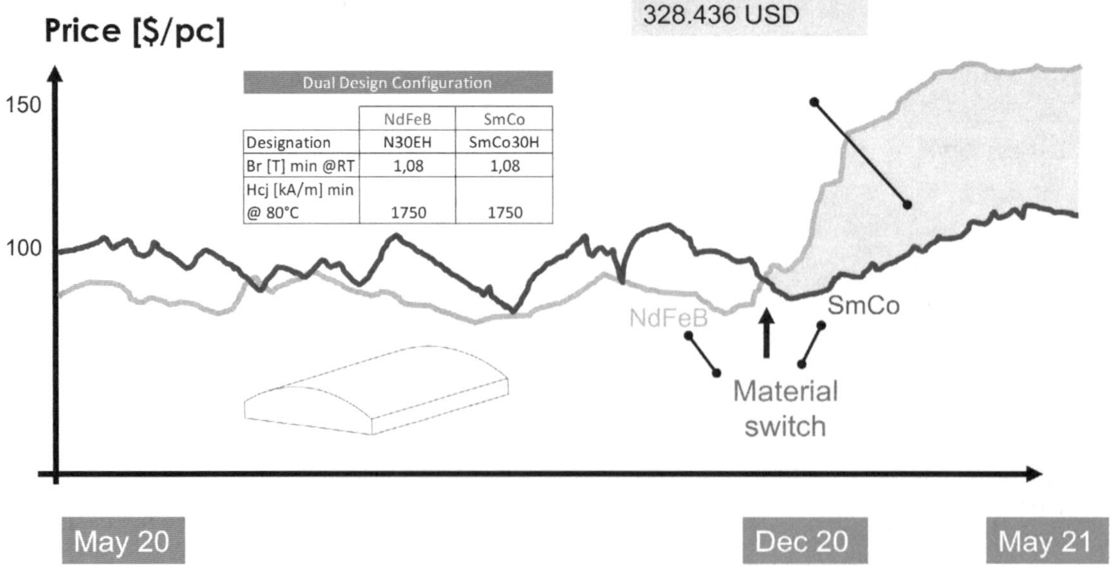

Dual Design Configuration

	NdFeB	SmCo
Designation	N30EH	SmCo30H
Br [T] min @RT	1,08	1,08
Hcj [kA/m] min @ 80°C	1750	1750

HANGZHOU PERMANENT MAGNET GROUP

Dual Design – HPMG flagship example

Application: Generator for temperature controlled truck trailors

Rotor: 4 poles

Dual design Cost savings in 2021 1.107.211 USD with SmCo

HANGZHOU PERMANENT MAGNET GROUP

Dual Design – GBD block shape example

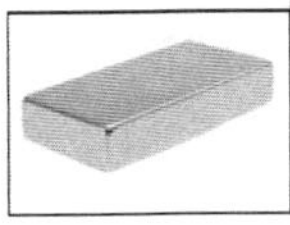

Type	Dimensions [mm]	weight [g]	Grain boundary diffusion	Material	Grade
block	30x30X5	34,65	yes	NdFeB	N30TH
		37,8	no	SmCo	DDG 222/199+

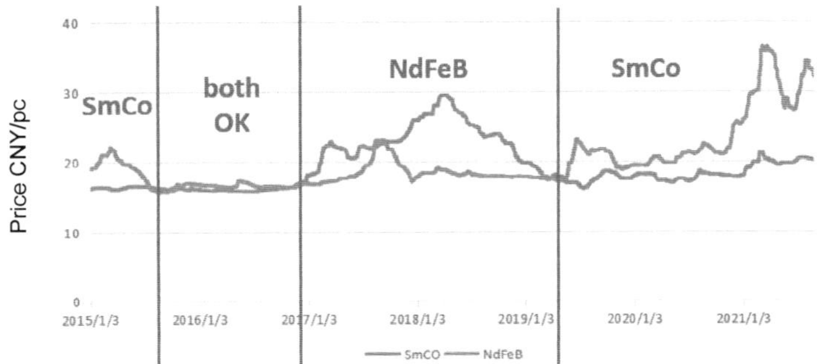

Each Magnet item to be considered individually

Procurement 4.0

Also for Nd -"mainstream shape magnet" with GBD -> SmCo can be more cost effective

HANGZHOU PERMANENT MAGNET GROUP

Dual Design recycling

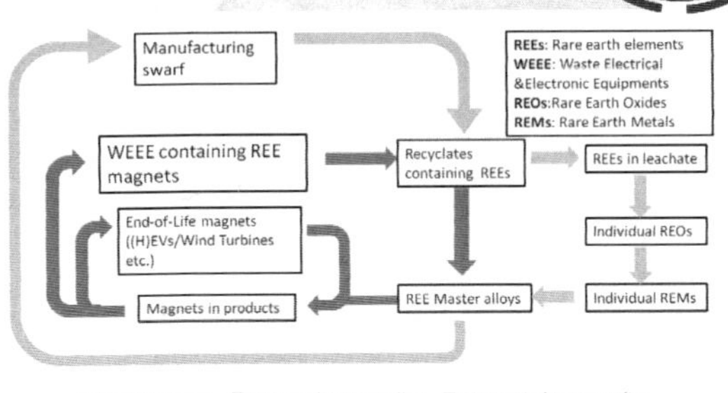

	NdFeB	SmCo
Magnet direct re-use	✓	✓
Magnet identification	✓	✓
Direct recycling	✓	✓
Element recycling	✓	✓
Produceable < 70% virgin material	✓	✓

HANGZHOU PERMANENT MAGNET GROUP

6 Steps Dual Design Circle

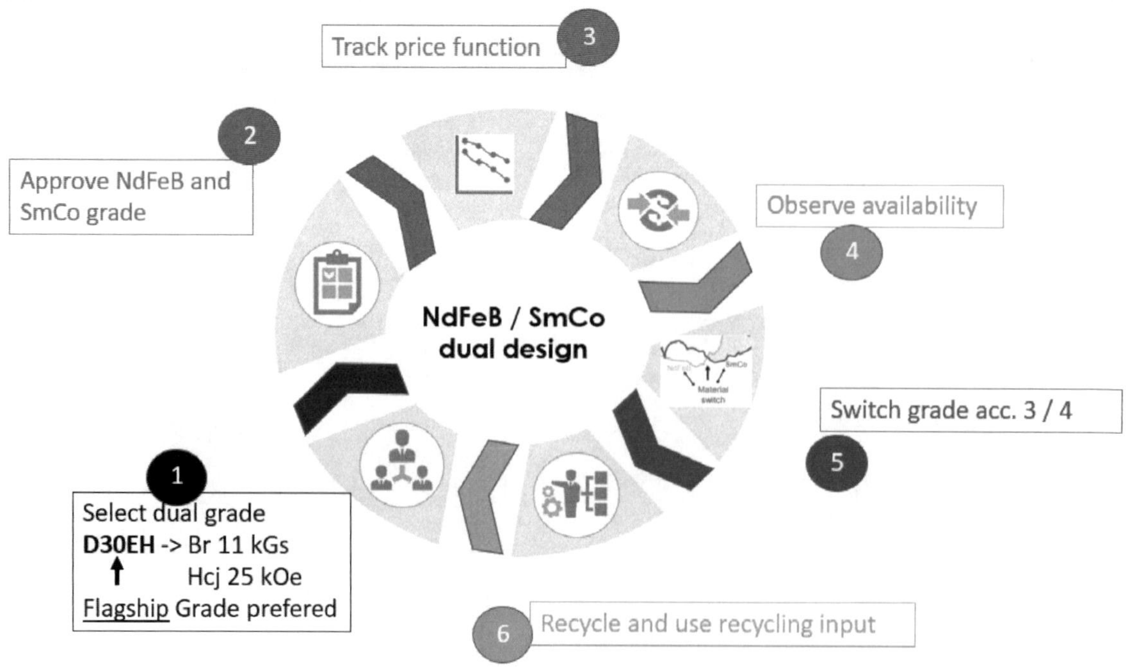

HANGZHOU PERMANENT MAGNET GROUP

Dual Design – the perfect puzzle of future design

bottom cost material stock exchange	One flagship grade for unified easy recycling	Option for low / high temperature application in one circuit	Easy recycling
End customer wants no Co -> NdFeB	Option for coating / no coating version in one circuit	Supply redundancy	Low virgin material input
Cost transparency	End customer wants no HREE -> SmCo	temperature robustness	Option for low / high temperature coeffcient application in one circuit

HANGZHOU PERMANENT MAGNET GROUP

The End

Thank you very much for

your attention!

HANGZHOU PERMANENT MAGNET GROUP

NdFeB / SmCo basic data comparison

Mechanical & Physical Performance Parameters	Units	NdFeB Parallel to Magnetized Direction C//	NdFeB Perpendicular to Magnetized Direction C⊥	SmCo5 Parallel to Magnetized Direction C//	SmCo5 Perpendicular to Magnetized Direction C⊥	Sm2Co17 Parallel to Magnetized Direction C//	Sm2Co17 Perpendicular to Magnetized Direction C⊥
Coefficient of Thermal Expansion	10^{-6}/K	4~9	-2~0	6~7	12~13	8~10	12~13
Curie Temperature, Tc	℃	~310		~820		~820	
Young Modulus	10^9 N/m²	150~200		180~220		180~220	
Flexural Strength	Mpa	150~400		≥90	≥100	≥80	≥100
Compressive Strength	Mpa	1000~1100		≥700		≥600	
Electrical Conductivity	μΩ.m	1.2~1.6		0.7~1		0.7~1	
Density	g/cm3	7.40~7.70		8.2~8.6		8.3~8.5	
Hardness, Vickers	HV	500~700		300~600		400~700	

HANGZHOU PERMANENT MAGNET GROUP

HPMG Co – where is mined - Backup

Word wide mining:

HPMG Sources:

	Mine production 2018	Mine production 2019[e]
United States	490	500
Australia	4,880	5,100
Canada	3,520	3,000
China	2,000	2,000
Congo (Kinshasa)	104,000	100,000
Cuba	3,500	3,500
Madagascar	3,300	3,300
Morocco	2,100	2,100
New Caledonia[8]	2,100	1,600
Papua New Guinea	3,280	3,100
Philippines	4,600	4,600
Russia	6,100	6,100
South Africa	2,300	2,400
Other countries	5,540	5,700
World total (rounded)	148,000	140,000

China → Jinchuan Group

Madagascar → Sumitomo Metal Mining Co., Ltd **Ambatovy Mine**

World total → HPMG 700 ton (0,5%)

- Appr. 95% by-product of Cu and/or Ni mining

HANGZHOU PERMANENT MAGNET GROUP

Cobalt – where is it refined - Backup

SmCo supply chain is different from Nd

Country	Mined	Refined	Refined Qty (mt)
Australia	×	×	3,200
Brazil	×	×	400
Belgium		×	6,329*
Canada/Norway (Glencore)	×	×	9,044
China	×	×	45,046 (mainly imported raw material)
Cuba	×		See Canada
France		×	119
Finland		×	11,187 (mainly imported raw material)
India		×	100
Japan		×	4,305
Madagascar	x	x	3,273
Morocco	×	×	1,568
New Caledonia	×		*To be updated*
Russia	×	×	3,092
South Africa	×	×	1,101
Uganda	×	×	0 (ceased operations 2014)
D.R.C.	×	×	400
Zambia	×	×	4,725
TOTAL			~93,889(Tonnes) **

China → Jinchuan Group

Madagascar → Sumitomo Metal Mining Co., Ltd

TOTAL → HPMG 465 ton (0,5%)

HANGZHOU PERMANENT MAGNET GROUP

Dual Design – HPMG flagship example - backup

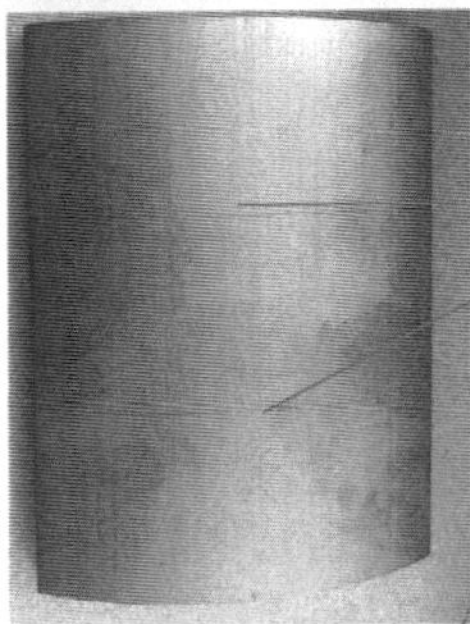

NdFeB magnet monolithic

SmCo magnet glued from 3 pieces

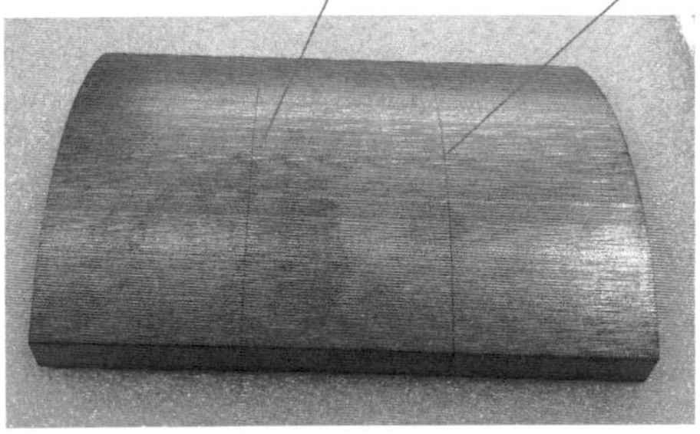

SmCo high temp. reserves

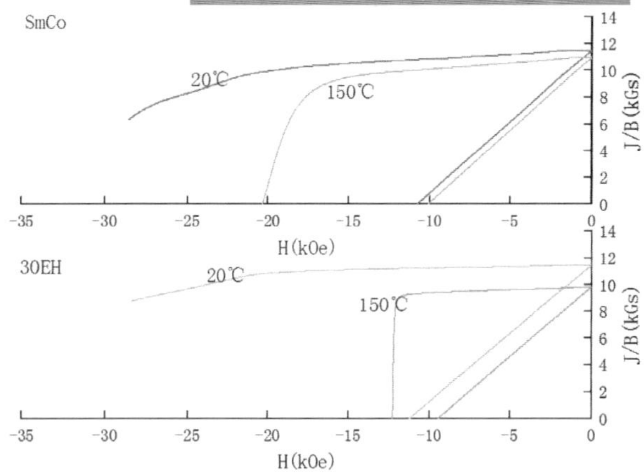

Dual Design – HPMG flagship example - backup

Flux specification with narrow tolerance is reached by NdFeB as well as by SmCo ->equivalency

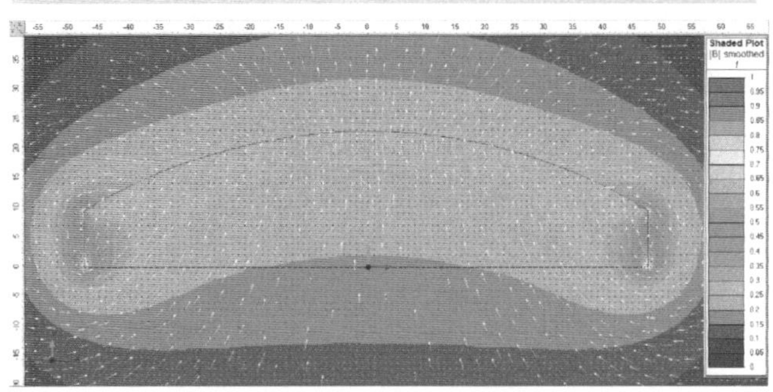

PrNd secured supply core statement - Backup

Do I need to invest in a mine?

Or can I go for dual design?

HANGZHOU PERMANENT MAGNET GROUP

Backup - SmCo raw materials

Sm cost is stable since years

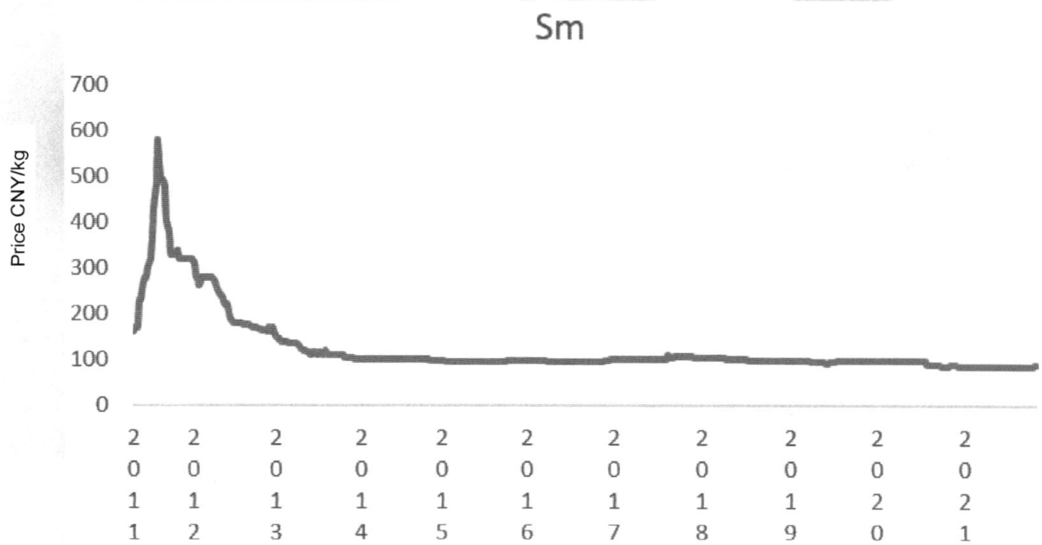

HANGZHOU PERMANENT MAGNET GROUP

Backup - Dual Design advantage summary

Summary:

- Clearly demand of NdFeb is growing related to E-moblity.
- Clearly PrNd, Tb, Dy are volatil on high price level.
- No shortage in the coming years for SmCo.
- Price of Sm, Co stable în the last 10 year, price peaks 2016/2018.
- New battery technologies using less Co.
- Dual Design promises low volatility.
- Dual Design is an “insurance“ for supply risk.

Challenges for permanent magnets in Hybrid vehicles

Sim Narasimhan
P2Ptechnologies

P2P technologies

P2P Technologies is a Division of CS 21 LLC, registered in NJ, USA.

Intellectual Property strategies; Business Strategies

- **Guidance in material selection and processing of metal powders**
- **Sales of Neo , rare earth, and Ferrite permanent magnets**
- **Seminars on Powder Metallurgy, Permanent magnets**

Outline of Presentation

- Rare earths and intermetallics
- Electric Vehicle Traction Motors
- Heavy rare earth usage dilemma and advances
- Newer magnets Scenario
- Conclusion

Which are the rare earths?

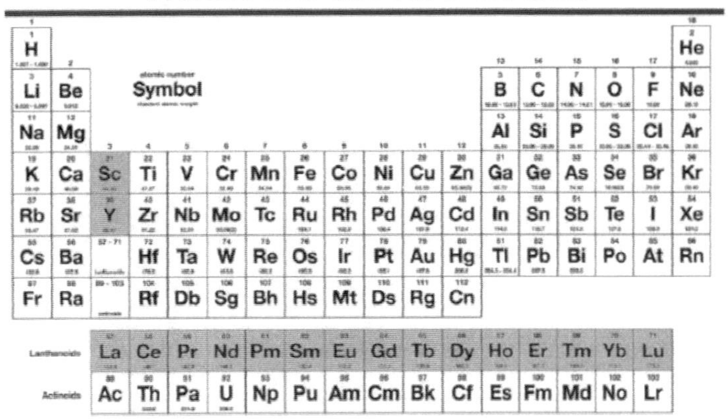

Rare earth elements: 17 chemical elements

5 are considered to be the most economically critical

Nd Y Eu Tb Dy

Rare earth deposits

- Rare earths are not concentrated in economic viable quantities
- Have similar Ionic radii making it to difficult to separate
- Occurs along with similar ionic radii Ca^{2+} ,Th^{4+} , U^{4+} creating a big environmental issues, mine tailings
- One ton of rare earth creates 12,000tons of waste water and 2,000 tons mine tailings

Global Distribution of Rare Earth Deposits

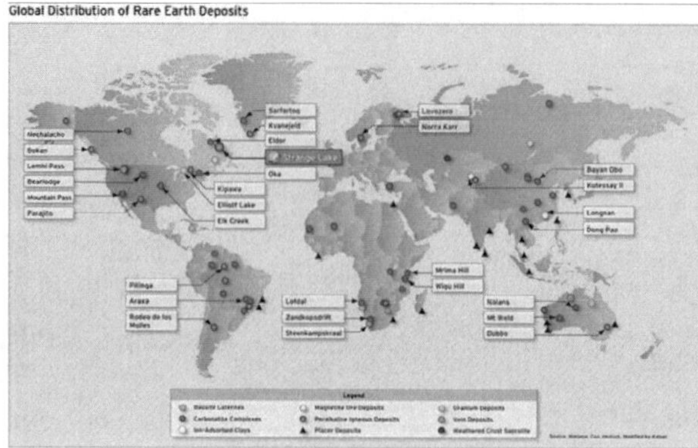

Light rare earths (La, Ce) are more abundant

Location	Mountain pass, CA, China, Vietnam	Australia, Fl Brazil, China	China, Malyasia	China	Saturation Induction of R2Fe14B phase T	Preferred Direction of Magnetiz ation At RT
Ore type	Bastnasite	Monazite	Xenotime	Laterite		
Y	trace	1.4-2.4%	59-61%	8-65%	1.3222	C-axis
La	23-33%	21-23%	1.24%	1.82-43%	1.271	-
Ce	49-50%	43-45%	3.13%	0.4-2.4%	1.1438	C-axis
Pr	4.3-6.2%	5-6%	0.5%	0.7-9.0%	1.6	C-axis
Nd	12-18%	17-18%	1.6-3.5%	3.0-31.7%	1.61	C-axis*
Sm	0.8	3-4.9%	1.1-2.2%	2.8-3.9%	1.4295	Plane
Gd			3.5-5.0%	3.0-6.9%	0.8037	C-axis
Tb			0.9-1.2%	0-1.3%	0.6359	C-axis
Dy	HRE		8.3-9.1%	0-6.7%	0.6381	C-axis
Ho			2-2.6%	0-1.6%	0.7532	C-axis*
Er			5.0-6.4%	0-4.9%	0.8456	C-axis*
Tu			1-1.1%	0-0.7%	1.0485	C-axis*
Yb			6-6.8%	0.3-2.5%	-	-
La+Ce	72-83%	64-68%				
Nd+Pr	16-24%	22-24%				
Dy			8.3-9.1%			

Rare earths form Intemetallics with 3d transitional elements

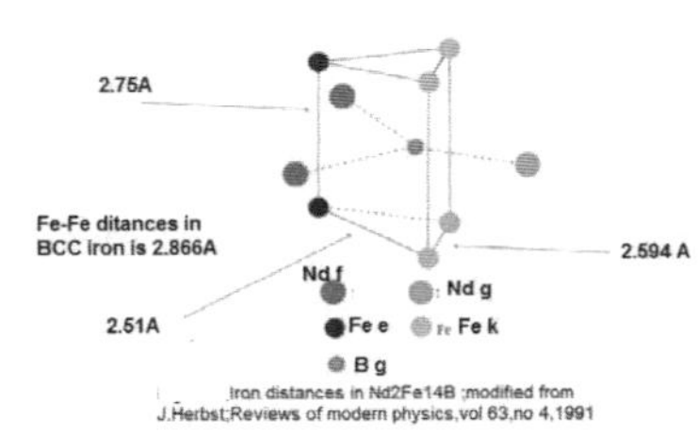

Iron distances in Nd2Fe14B ;modified from J.Herbst;Reviews of modern physics,vol 63,no 4,1991

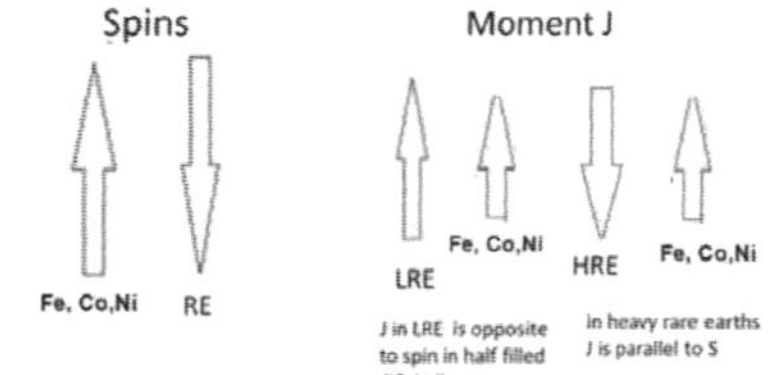

- Russel Saunders Coupling in the magnetically ordered State

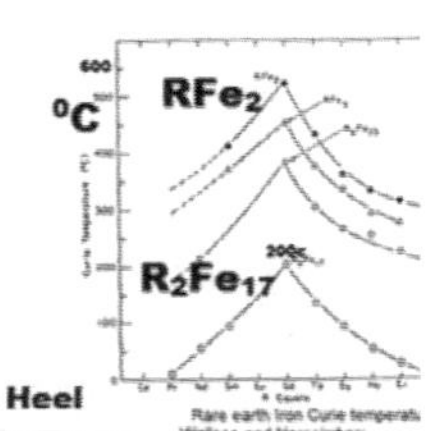

Rare earth Iron Curie temperatu Wallace and Narasimhan

Achilles Heel
Low Curie Temp
of NdFeB 312 C

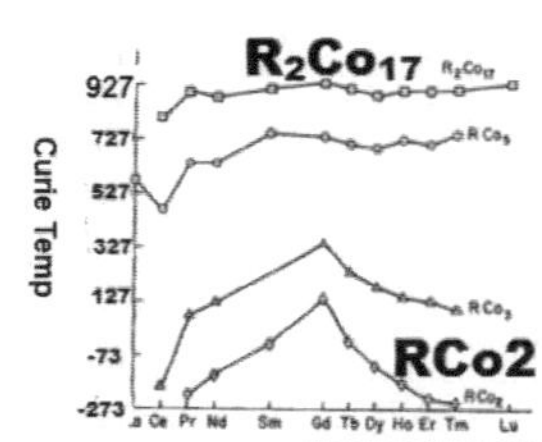

Rare Earth Cobalt alloys Curie temperature,Wallace

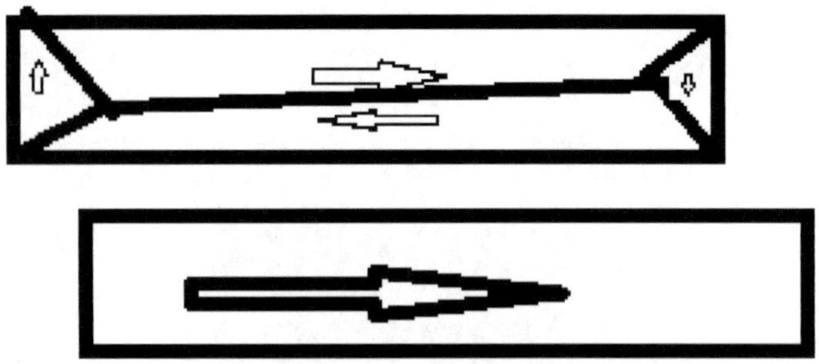

H

Small Magnetic Field moves the domain wall ;net magnetiztion positive

NdFeB

Anisotropic magnet

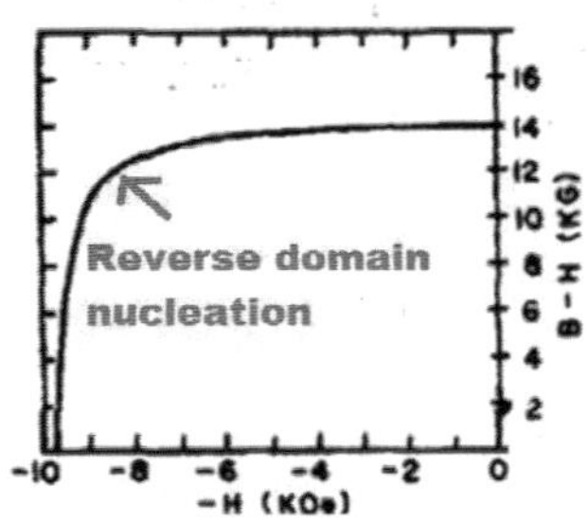

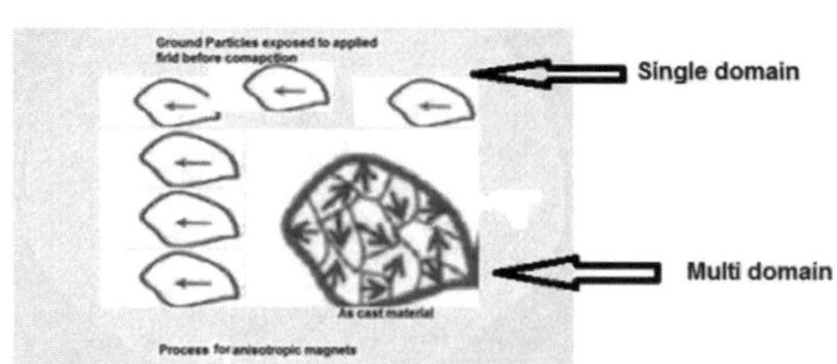

B_r=1.4T,H_c=736kA/m^3 , H_{ci}=787kA/m^3 ,BH_{max}=358kJ/m^3

made by low oxygen proces(1984)

Narasimhan, 1984

Anisotropic magnet ,crushing cast alloy and orienting in a mgnetic field and :**sintering**

Ansotropy field is about 7 T ,Intrinsic coercive force achieved is far below 7T,nucleation of reverse domains

2. $$V_m = \frac{B_g^2 A_g L_g \sigma_r}{BH}$$

V_m = Magnet Volume
B_g = Air Gap Flux Density
A_g = Air Gap Cross Sectional Area
σ_r = Leakage and Reluctance Factor

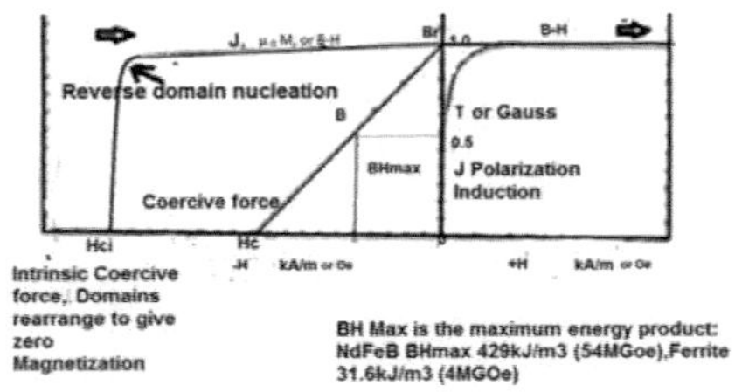

BH Max is the maximum energy product: NdFeB BHmax 429kJ/m3 (54MGoe),Ferrite 31.6kJ/m3 (4MGOe)

1.

BH_{max}; energy product defines the magnet volume in an application (Vol α 1/BHmax)

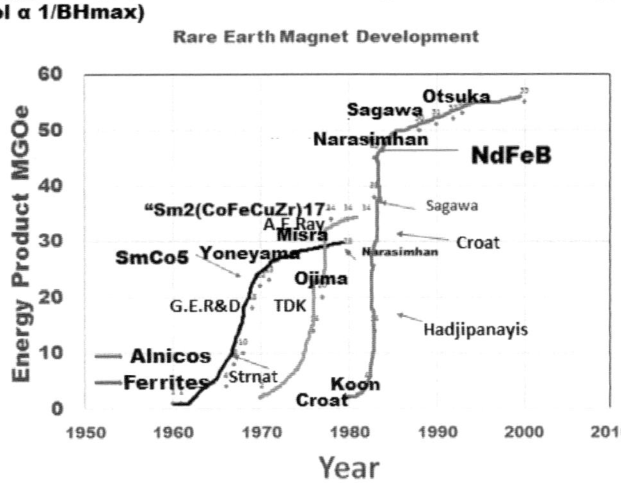

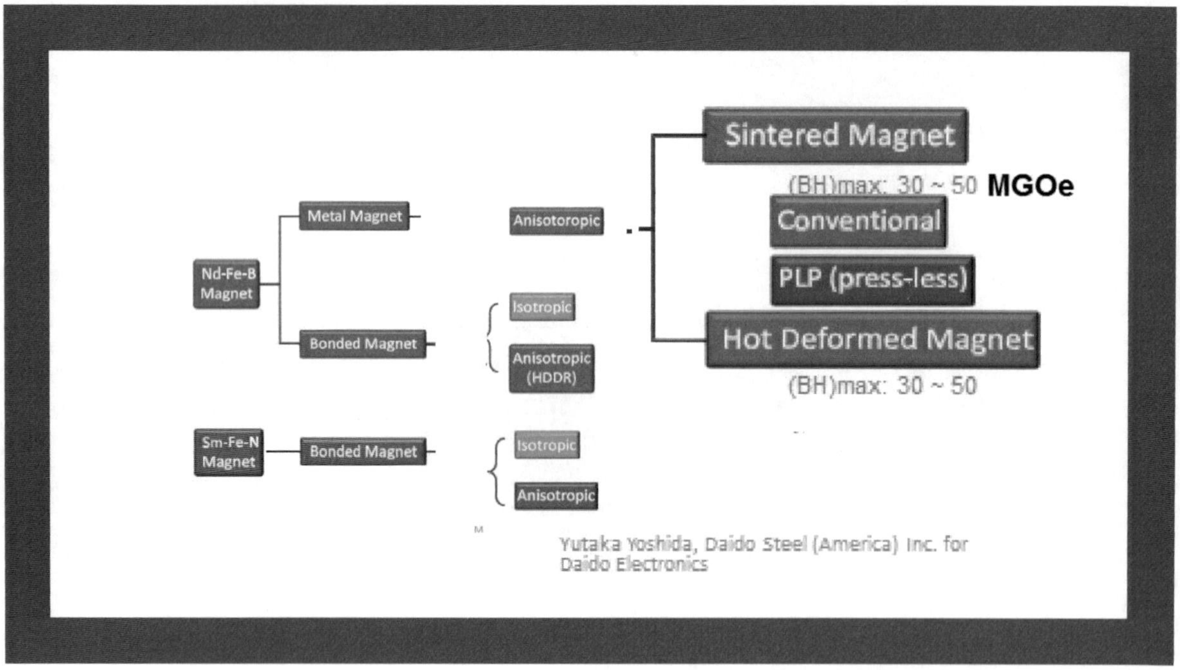

Nd-Fe-B Magnet
Metal Magnet
Bonded Magnet
Anisotoropic
Isotropic
Anisotropic (HDDR)
Sintered Magnet
(BH)max: 30 ~ 50 MGOe
Conventional
PLP (press-less)
Hot Deformed Magnet
(BH)max: 30 ~ 50
Sm-Fe-N Magnet
Bonded Magnet
Isotropic
Anisotropic
Yutaka Yoshida, Daido Steel (America) Inc. for Daido Electronics

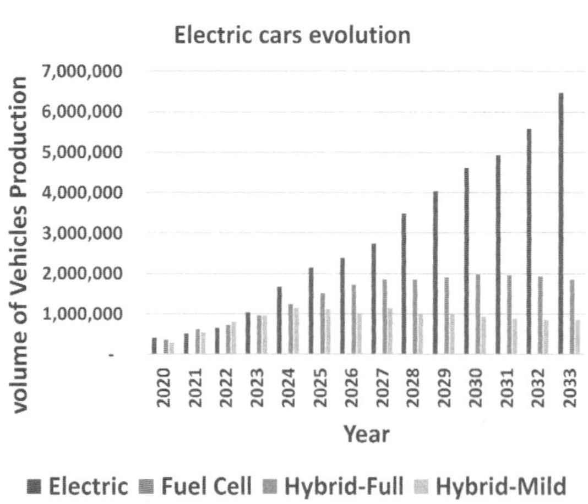

Electric cars evolution
volume of Vehicles Production
7,000,000
6,000,000
5,000,000
4,000,000
3,000,000
2,000,000
1,000,000
-
2020
2021
2022
2023
2024
2025
2026
2027
2028
2029
2030
2031
2032
2033
Year
Electric
Fuel Cell
Hybrid-Full
Hybrid-Mild

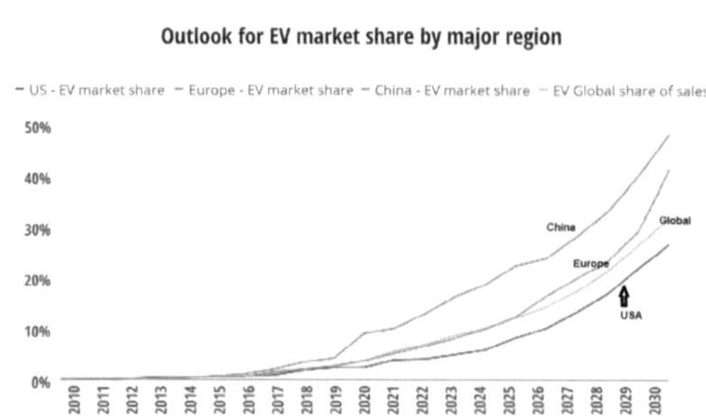

Outlook for EV market share by major region
US - EV market share
Europe - EV market share
China - EV market share
EV Global share of sales
50%
40%
30%
20%
10%
0%
China
Global
Europe
USA

RARE EARTH MAGNETS FOUND IN HYBRID AND ELECTRIC VEHICLES		
Hybrid & EV part	**Quantity**	**Type of RE Magnet**
HVAC systems	45-50 gr	Mostly Nd & Dy
Steering, transmission, braking systems	160-200 gr	Mostly NdFeB
Hybrid engine or electric motor compartment	800-5,000 gr	Mostly Nd, Dy
Various other items (secutiy, seats, cameras, etc.)	20-30 gr	Mostly Nd
Door & window systems	67-85 gr	Mostly NdFeB
Entertainment (speakers, radio,etc)	40-50 gr	Mostly NdFeB
EV Batteries	3,800-4,200 gr	Nd
Fuel and Exhaust system for Hybrids	70-80 gr	Mostly Ce

Types Of Traction Motors

- Induction - high efficiency, smoother torque, established technology(Longer drive looses about 4% efficiency)
- Permanent magnet - most efficient because does not require external field excitation.(Back EMF is a big issue at high speeds)
- Switched reluctance- lower cost, scalable power output , no back emf issues

- Switch Reluctance Motor

Preference for low reluctance state rotates the shaft

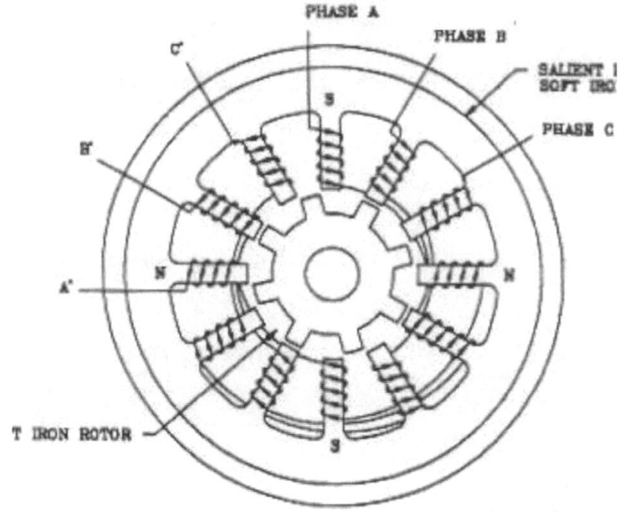

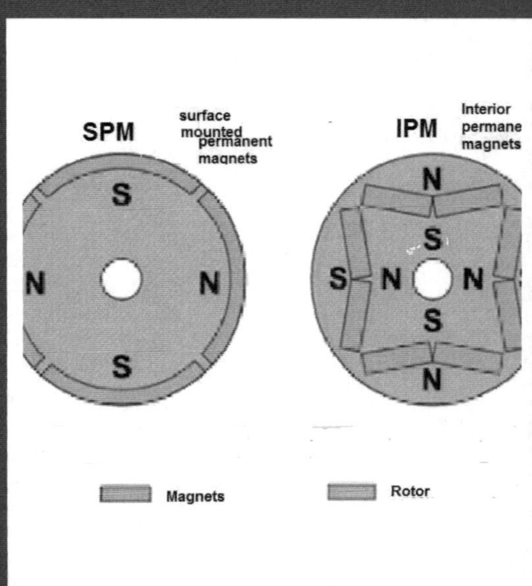

Neo Motor in IPM Motor

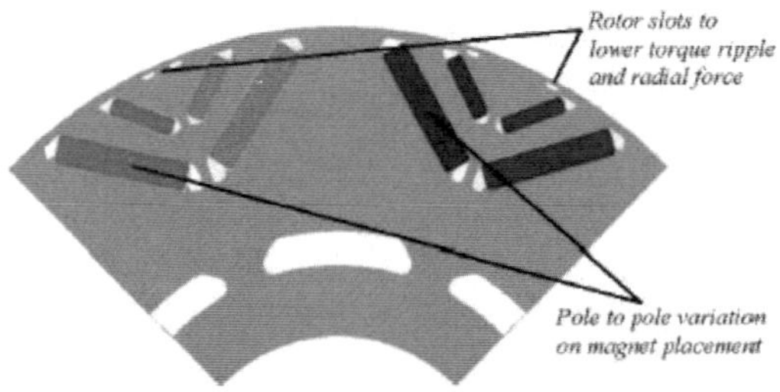

Figure 13. Rotor lamination geometry of the optimzed rotor

400 Neo magnets are used to fit V grooves in rotor IPM

P2PTech

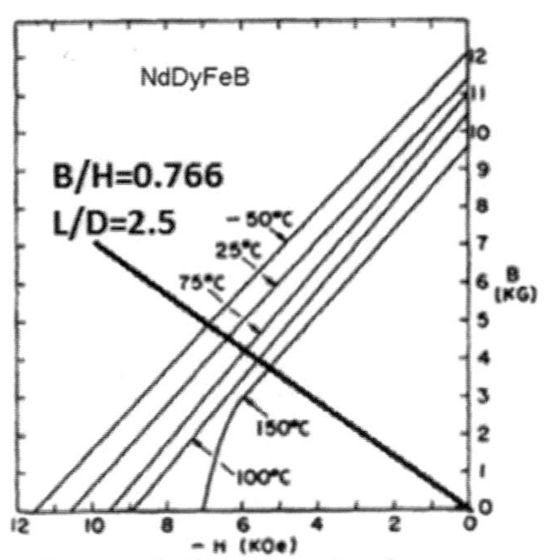

Demagnetization curves at various temperature **Narasimhan 1986**

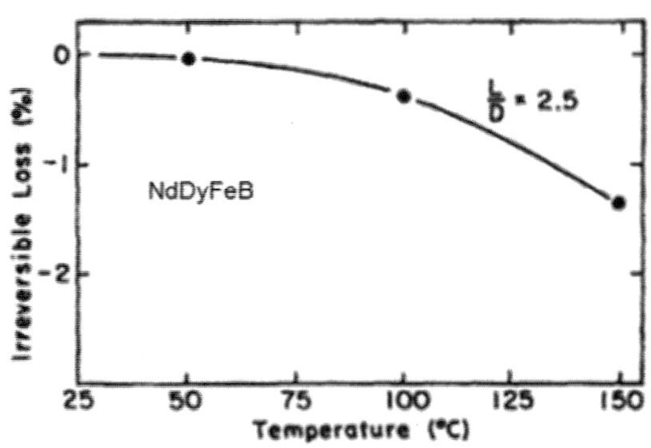

Irreversible losses in a NdDyFeB magnet ,

B/H ,Permeance Coefficient, calculated based on the magnetic circuit

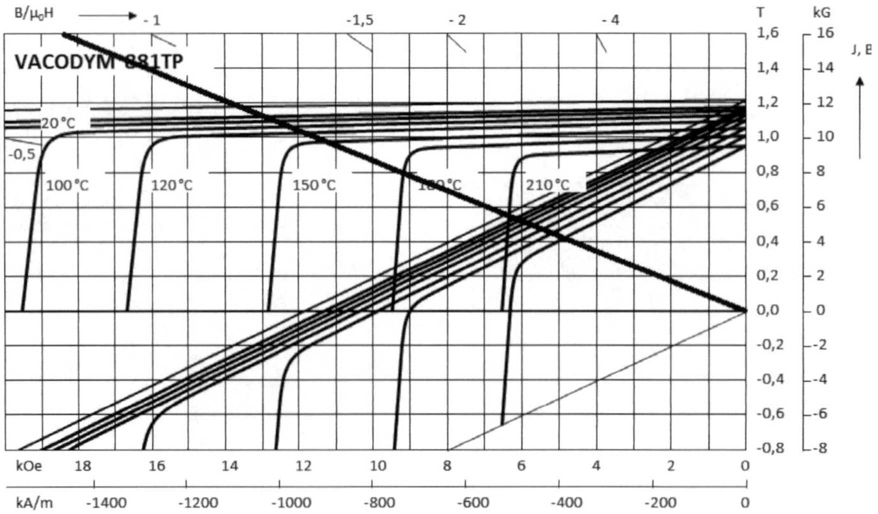

Courtesy Brain Bell Vaccumshmelze

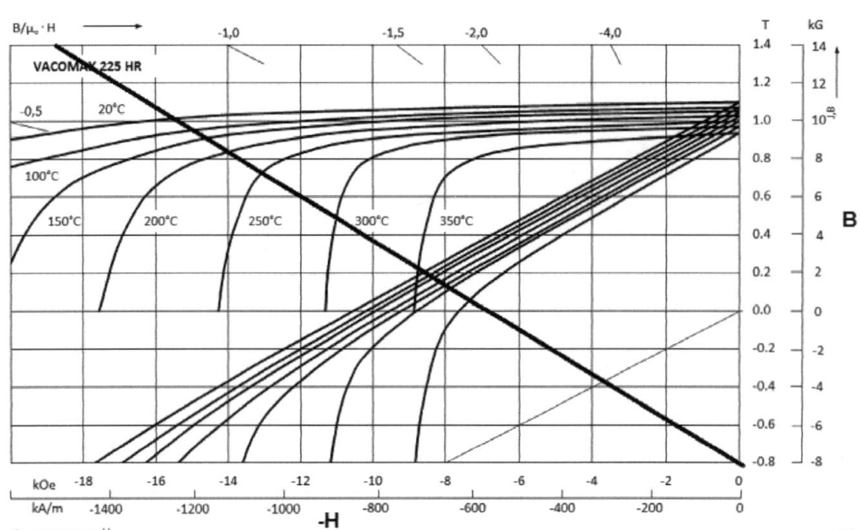

Courtesy Brain Bell Vaccumchmelze

Material	Reversible induction temp.coefficient % per ^{0} C 20 to 150C *	temp.coefficient Hci % per ^{0} C 20 to 150C
$Nd_2Fe_{14}B$	-0.11	-0.6
$Sm_2(FeCoCuZr)_{17}$	-0.035	-0.19
$SmCo_5$	-0.045	-0.15
Ferrites	-0.20	+0.27
Alnico 5-7	-0.02	+0.03

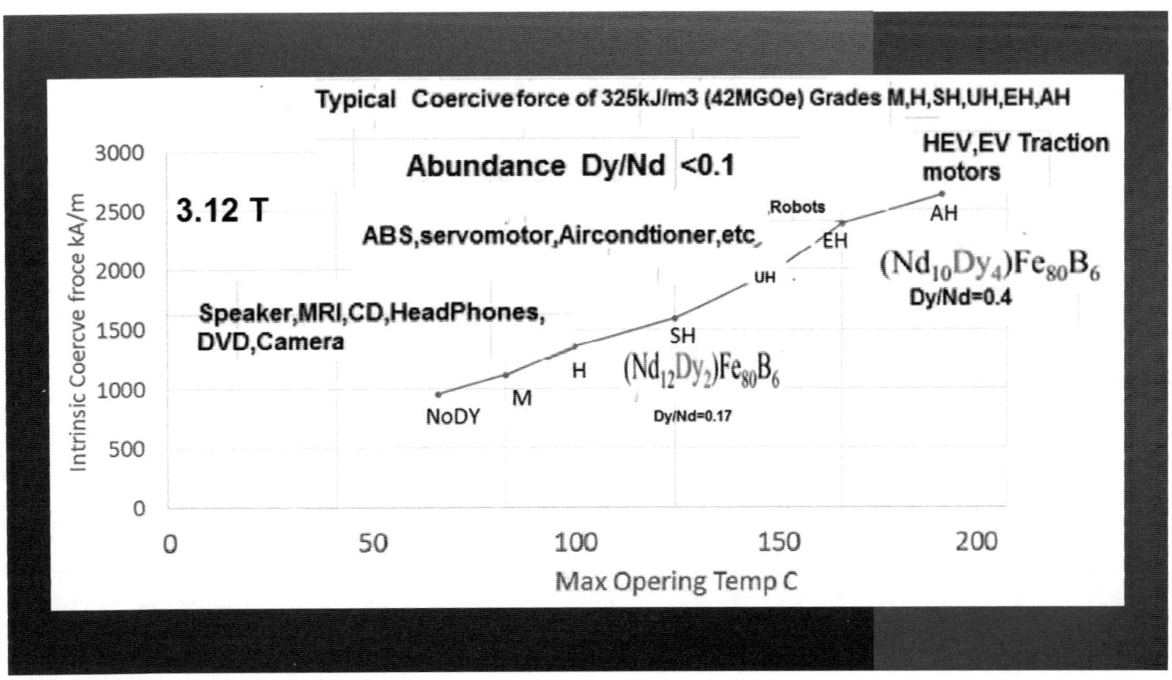

Target Magnetic Properties for EV Motors (existing design)

Hc>3.0T

Remanence >1.35T

At 180C Hc>0.8T

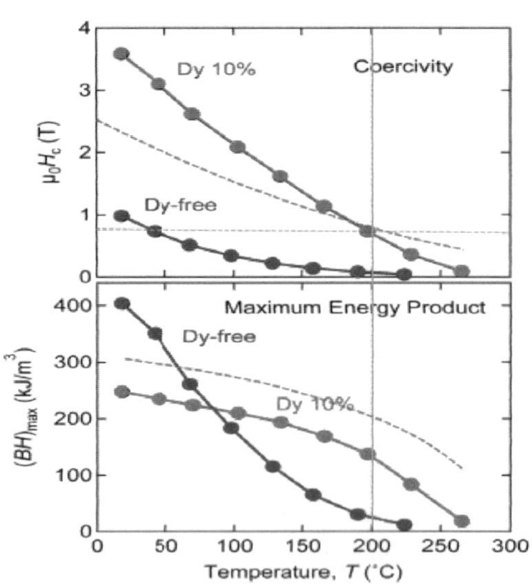

Towards Dy-free high coercivity Nd-Fe-B permanent magnets

K. Hono

Magnetic Materials Unit
&
Elements Strategy Initiative Center for Magnetic Materials
National Institute of Materials Science (NIMS)

Grain boundary phase role in coercivity

- **Grain Boundary Phase 3nanometer thick known for sometime as Neo rich phase .**
- **Recent atom probe analysis revealed the composition to be $Nd_{65}Fe_{35}Cu_{1}$**
- **Thin film of this composition was found by 3DAP to be soft ferromagnetic**

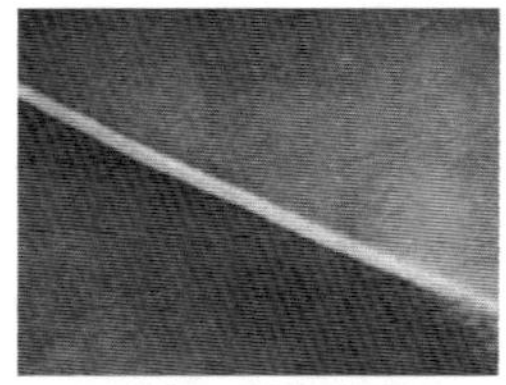

Transmission Micrograph on sintered magnet showing Nd rich grain boundary phase,Courtesy of Late J.D.Livingston ,sample provided by Narasimhan from a production run at Hoeganaes Corporation

Grain Boundary Phase (contd)

Also In situ analysis of the grain boundary by X-ray magnetic dichroism, the Grain boundary phase magnetization to be 0.85T-1T at room temperature with Curie temperature of 260C.Leads to exchange coupling at the grain boundray

Ga Doped material($Fe_{77.6}RE_{14.8}B_{5.1}Cu_{0.1}Ga_{0.5}$) showed 80%higher coercivity compared to standard magnet($Fe_{79.5}RE_{13.9}B_{5}Cu_{0.1}$). Also Ga doped magnets grain boundary is non magnetic which Leads to exchange decoupling with grain boundary phase.

Fine grain size in sintered or hot deformed magnets leads to higher coercive force

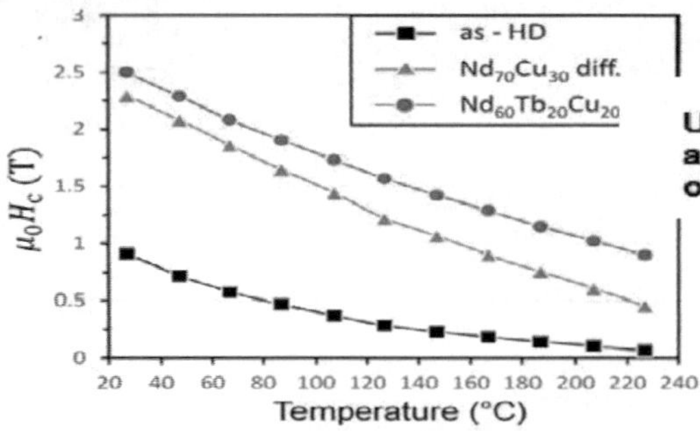

Using melt spun flakes,fine grain, and hot deformed to get grain orientation.

Temperature dependence of coercivity of as-hot-deformed and eutectic diffusion-processed Nd-Fe-B magnets

Jiangnan Li, Hossein Sepehri-Amin, Taisuke Sasaki, Tadakatsu Ohkubo & Kazuhiro Hono (2021) Most frequently asked questions about the coercivity of Nd-Fe-B permanent magnets, Science and Technology of Advanced Materials, 22:1, 386-403, DOI 10.1080/14686996.2021.1916377

Alternate method is Press Less process(Sagawa) or Low oxygen process (Narasimhan 1980)

Low Oxygen Processing of Rare Earth Magnets,(Narasimhan,1980)
Built under Airforce contract ; Stable rare earth magnets

Alternate method to reduce HRE content,

Grain boundary diffusion is not effective as the magnets used in these turbines and other large electrical devices are 100x100x20mm .

FEA analysis indicated coercivity required is large at the edges of magnets .

Compacted Dy free in the center and Dy containing magnet at the outer edges to achieve high coercive force at the edges

- Researchers at ABB, Jacim et.al developed a two component magnet.

(A technique similar to what Bosch did for ferrite magnets in late 1970) ABB was developing these magnets for use in wind turbines.

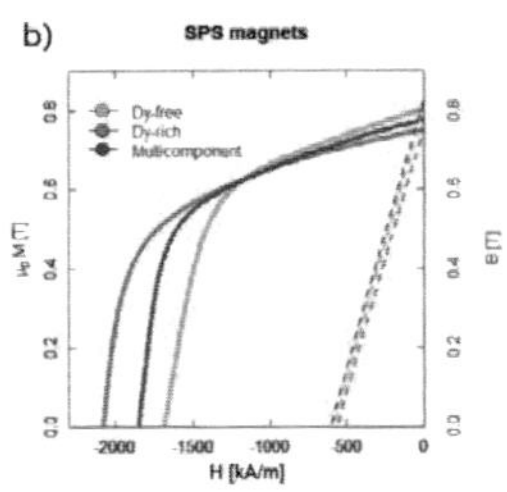

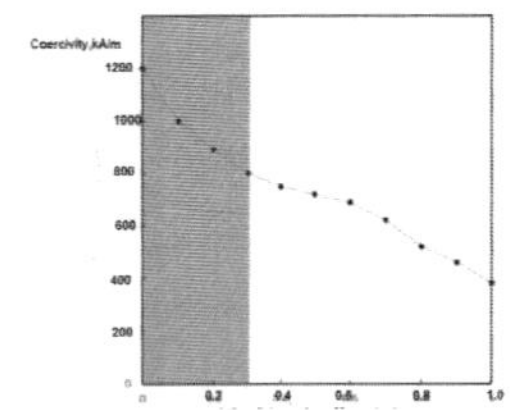

Multicomponent permanent magnets for enhanced electrical device efficiency

Tomaž Tomše[a,b], Darren Tremelling[c], Reto Kessler[d], Thomas Christen[d], Lavinia Scherf[d], Reinhard A. Simon[d], Felix Greuter[d], Lorenz Herrmann[d], Jean-Marie Dubois[a,b], Spomenka Kobe[a,b], Jaćim Jaćimović[d,*]

[a] Jožef Stefan Institute, Department for Nanostructured Materials, Jamova cesta 39, SI-1000 Ljubljana, Slovenia

How to use more abundant rare earths

- **Reduce Nd with more abundant La, Ce .**
- **Refine the grain size to compensate for coercive loss by the replacement ,finer grain higher coercive force.**
- **Replace iron with Cobalt ;compensate loss in coercive force with Al or other addition.**

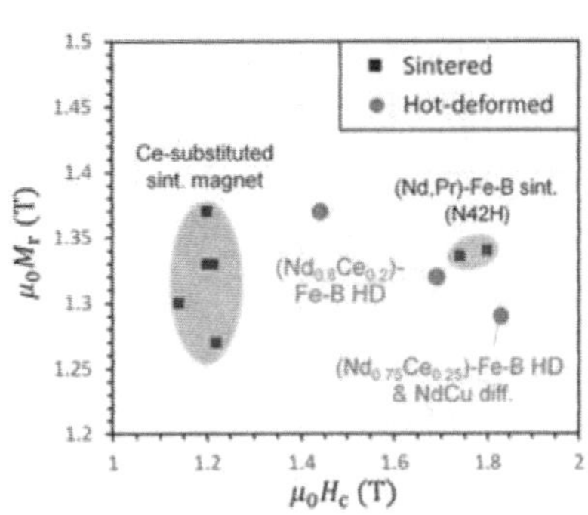

Magnets scenario at 200C

- **Finding a new magnet :**
- **We know from past 50plus years of industrial practice**
- **Hc ≤Ha/3 (Ha= Anisotropy field)**
- **Mr =0.9 Ms (about 10% secondary phases)**
- **BHmax= $Ms^2/4$; Hc >Mr/2**
- **Hc=Ha/3=0.9Ms/2**
- **Ha=1.35 Ms Lower Boundary for hard magnetism**

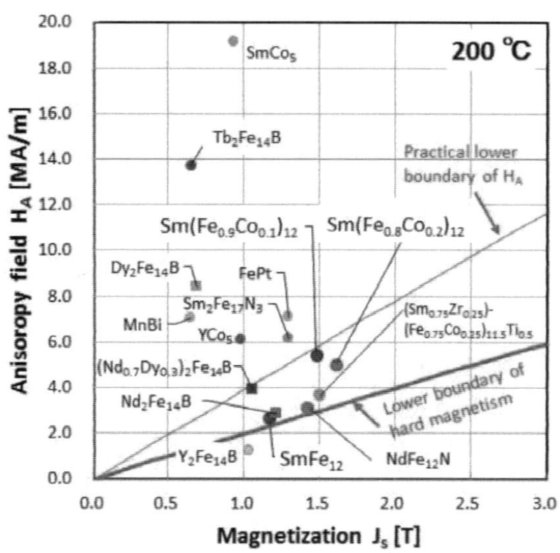

IEEE TRANSACTIONS ON MAGNETICS, VOL. 55, NO. 2, FEBRUARY 2019 2100506

Permanent Magnets Beyond Nd-Dy-Fe-B

Satoshi Hirosawa

Elements Strategy Initiative Center for Magnetic Materials, Research Center for Magnetic Materials,

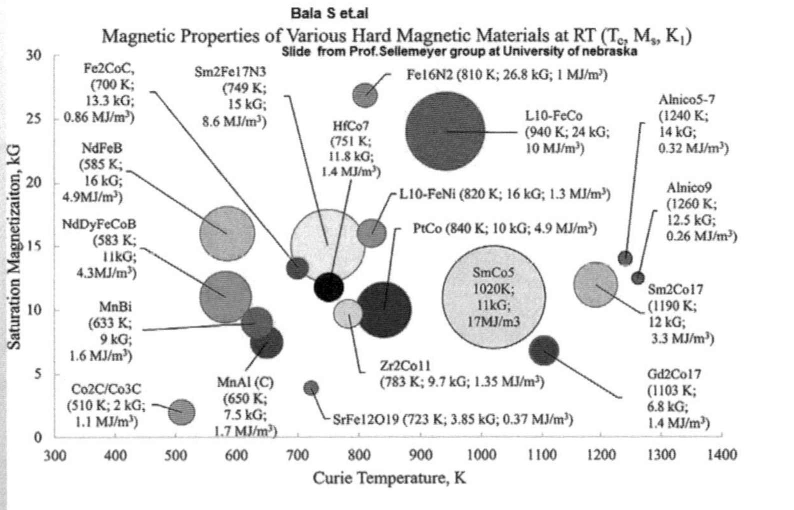

Conclusions

- Neo magnets still continue to be a preferred lower cost option
- HRE Dy,Tb,Gd substitution for Neo increase the coercive force but at a cost.
- Past few years enormous research in Japan and China in understanding the origin of coercive force by grain boundary studies opened new avenues to reduce or eliminate HRE.

Conclusions

- Finer powders and using other eutectic alloys that do not contain HRE have shown dramatic improvement in coercive force.
- Usage of more abundant Ce in the magnets is limited to 22%
- Further understanding of anisotropy and lower curie temperature of iron dominated alloys will help propel the usage of neo magnets .
- Research into newer magnet alloys should and will continue

MAGNETICS 2022

REIA

A Circular System for Assessing Rare Earth Sustainability
CSyARES

9 February 2022

RARE EARTHS FOR A SUSTAINABLE WORLD

WHO WE ARE: the GLOBAL RARE EARTH INDUSTRY ASSOCIATION

REIA

The only global association advocating the Rare Earth Industry

A non-profit organization founded with the support of the EU commission in 2019

A multicultural and experienced Board and Advisory Board

40 members from all over the world

REIA is the only platform to shape the Rare Earth supply chain to deliver on the sustainability demands of both consumers and investors

RARE EARTHS FOR A SUSTAINABLE WORLD

OUR MEMBERS

REIA

Upstream

Appia
AUXICO RESOURCES
CAN
E-TECH RESOURCES
GREENLAND MINERALS LTD
ionic RARE EARTHS
JOGMEC
LEADING EDGE MATERIALS
Medallion RESOURCES
MKANGO
NAMIBIA CRITICAL METALS
NORSK MINERAL
PEAK RESOURCES
PENSANA RARE EARTHS
PHOENIX TAILINGS
REE MINERALS
UCORE
USA Rare Earth
BEC
JL MAG HIGH END MAGNETICS
RockLink
UMAG Ideas Realized

Down-stream

B&C SPEAKERS
GRUNDFOS
MAGNETSYSTEME BRUGGER
mtc rare earths solutions

Research Org.

BGS British Geological Survey
Canada
CARESTER
Fraunhofer IWKS
HS PF
IUE
Jožef Stefan Institute
KU LEUVEN
MINVIRO
Roskill
SRC
UNIVERSITY OF EXETER

RARE EARTHS FOR A SUSTAINABLE WORLD

SUSTAINABILITY IS OUR PRIMARY FOCUS

REIA

Sustainability is the key priority for a healthy REE industry

RARE EARTHS FOR A SUSTAINABLE WORLD

REIA

Today's society simply cannot do without RE. So, the only way forward is to collectively and globally do better, cleaner and stop the negative spiral around these essential metals, referred to as 'The Vitamins of Modern Society'

RARE EARTHS FOR A SUSTAINABLE WORLD

REIA'S MISSION

REIA

Develop a strong and balanced global stakeholder network throughout the whole value chain

Support the development of sustainable and diversified value chains & create transparency and certification of products and processes

Bridge the gap between our members and policy/decision makers

Develop collaboration within the Industry and intelligent strategic partnerships with global influencers and experts

Launch an active communication on REE's potential: Concentrate on the benefits of RE and best ESG practices

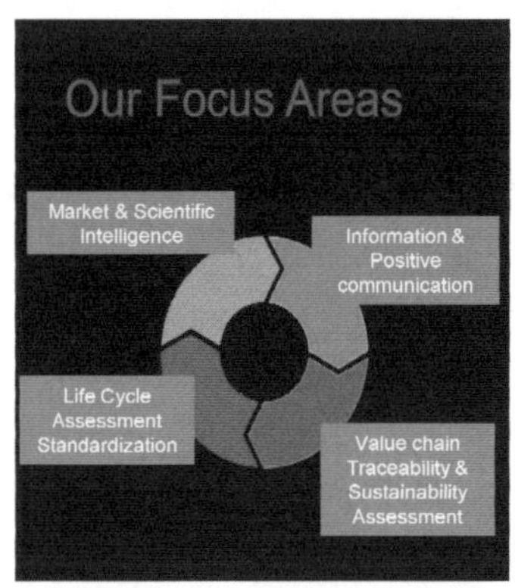

RARE EARTHS FOR A SUSTAINABLE WORLD

Rare earth value chain challenges

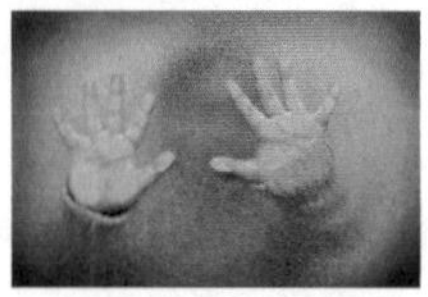

Lack of Transparency

Price Volatility

ISO-TC 298 ☺

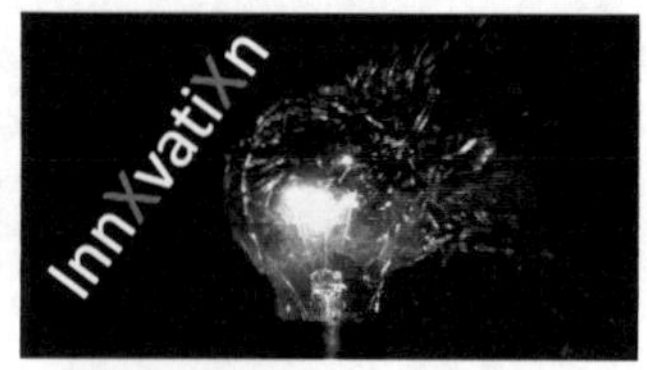

RARE EARTHS FOR A SUSTAINABLE WORLD

Where is the REE industry today?

- Unclear/ambiguous **definitions & quantification methodologies** throughout the value chain
- No framework and no system definition for the **collection of data and modeling**
- No **factual data**
- Risk of **data tampering/manipulation**
- Insufficient **collaboration and consensus** within the industry (esp. between up- and downstream)

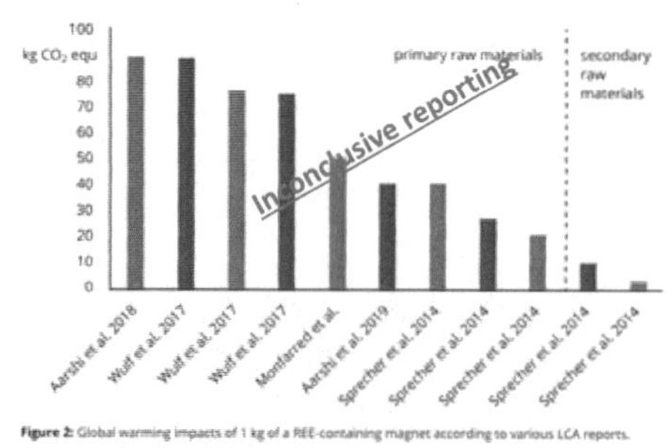

Figure 2: Global warming impacts of 1 kg of a REE-containing magnet according to various LCA reports.
Source: Roland Gauss presentation from Euromat, Stockholm, 2019

RARE EARTHS FOR A SUSTAINABLE WORLD

Focus on **CSyARES:** A CRUCIAL PROJECT FOR THE FUTURE OF THE INDUSTRY

REIA

eit RawMaterials

CSyARES is funded by the European Institute of Innovation and Technology (EIT), a body of the European Union, under Horizon 2020, the EU framework Programme for Research and Innovation

Partners involved alongside REIA :

BEC GESELLSCHAFT FÜR PRODUKTMANAGEMENT MBH — BEC develops customized magnetic solutions for different types of industries, with a focus on sintered NdFeB permanent magnets

CIRCULARISE — Circularise is a supply chain traceability and transparency scale-up enabling actors to trace materials and products on blockchain and share such sensitive data

GRUNDFOS — Grundfos is a global water technology company committed to pioneering solutions to the world's water and climate challenges and improving the quality of life for people

MINVIRO — Minviro is a consultancy and technology company that focuses on a stronger integration of life cycle assessment in the mining, metals and recycling industries

RARE EARTHS FOR A SUSTAINABLE WORLD

CCSyARES

REIA

- ✓ Creates a standardised sustainability certification for rare earth elements (REE), focusing on a Product Environmental Footprint (PEF)
- ✓ Industrial initiative that cooperates closely with upstream and downstream organizations to increase environmental, economic and social standards along the entire supply chain of raw magnets and its downstream applications

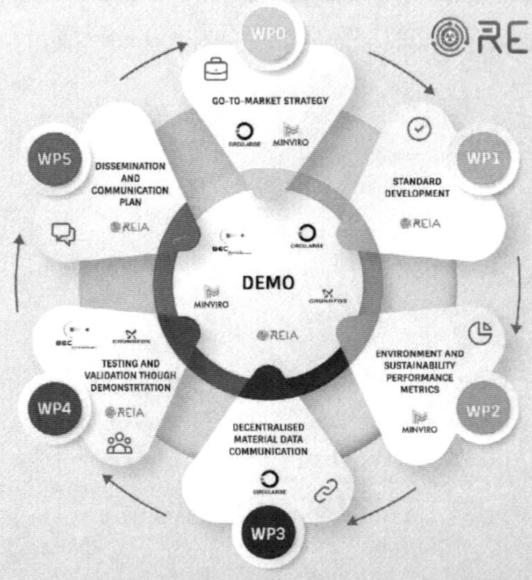

RARE EARTHS FOR A SUSTAINABLE WORLD

Focus on **CSyARES:** A CRUCIAL PROJECT FOR THE FUTURE OF THE INDUSTRY

REIA

Project USP: Bringing **transparency, standard certification and life cycle data** to global RE supply chains and empowering raw material businesses to take steps towards a **circular economy, without sharing or storing any data**

Some of our objectives:

- Provide certified transparency about the origin of materials, production processes, sustainability and material properties through a scaled blockchain application
- Increased environmental impact comprehension of REE sourcing and processing routes along the whole value chain using accessible, robust life cycle assessment (LCA) software
- Demonstrate and validate the business model for certified sustainable material

RARE EARTHS FOR A SUSTAINABLE WORLD

Focus on **CSyARES:** A CRUCIAL PROJECT FOR THE FUTURE OF THE INDUSTRY

REIA

Output

- An open standard platform and procedure for audits and certifications of the end-to-end REE value chain with respective compliance checklists and auditor accreditation
- Education and training material on sustainable mining and the establishment of the global sustainable mining standard
- Assessment system to enable the calculation of REE supply chain data with integrated measuring and improving socio-environmental impact
- A blockchain digital ledger with inbuilt data security via cryptography, featuring the ability to identify supply-chain vulnerabilities and opportunities

RARE EARTHS FOR A SUSTAINABLE WORLD

Quantifying environmental impacts

Internationally recognised approach

REIA

What is a life cycle assessment?

Life Cycle Assessment service is an inventory of environmental impacts tailored for mining, mineral processing and refining projects.

The LCA models a range of environmental impacts, ranging from CO_2 intensity to water use and particulate matter formation and complying with ISO 14040-14044 standards. ISO 14067 follows the same guidelines, only reporting on the climate change impact category.

Our integrated approach makes the environmental impacts of REE material projects clear and transparent through quantification.

Environmental hotspots are identified, providing insights into suitable mitigation strategies ensuring that the raw materials for the low-carbon economy are sourced at minimum environmental impact.

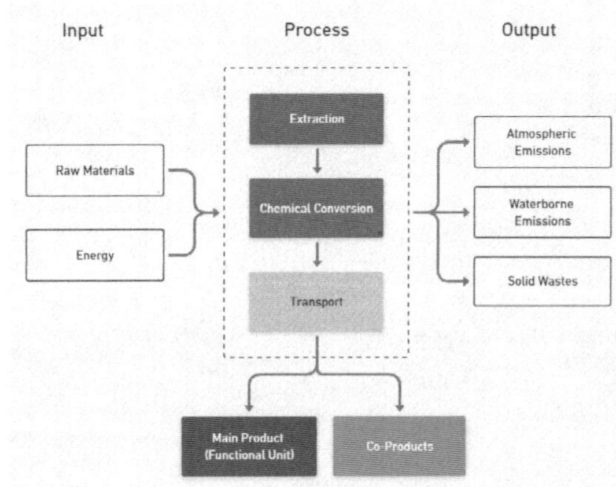

RARE EARTHS FOR A SUSTAINABLE WORLD

Climate Change is one of many impact categories

Global Warming Potential (kg CO_2 eq. per kg product)

Mining industry commonly reports on foreground processes:

- Scope 1 emissions: represents direct combustion of fuel and energy sources on site
- Scope 2 emissions: represent embodied emissions of consumed electricity
- Scope 3 emissions (upstream) represents embodied emissions of other consumables (eg. reagents)

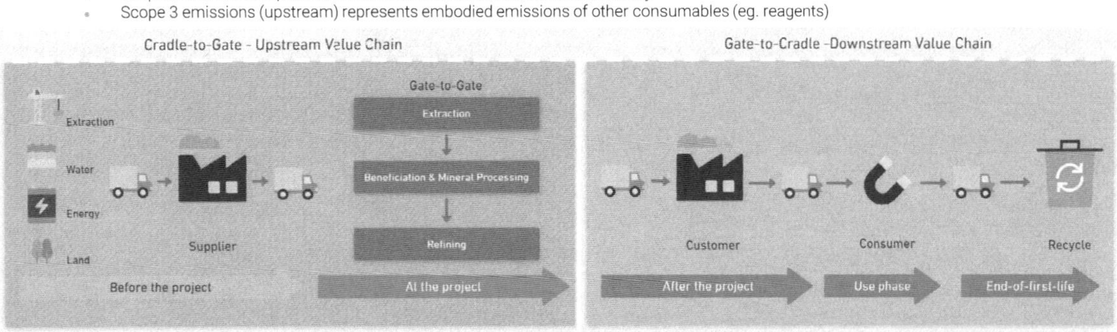

Scope 1, 2 and upstream scope 3 impact is responsibility of miner.

Downstream scope 3.

RARE EARTHS FOR A SUSTAINABLE WORLD

More than carbon accounting

Life Cycle Impact Categories

1 **Global Warming Potential**
(kg CO2 eq)
Radiative forcing as Global Warming Potential (GWP100)

2 **Ozone depletion**
(kg CFC-11 eq)
Steady-state ozone depletion potential

3 **Human Toxicity**
(CTUe)
Comparative toxic unit for humans as provided in the USEtox 2.1.

4 **Particulate Matter**
(Disease incidence)
Human health effects associated with exposure to PM2.5 from the PM method recommended by UNEP

5 **Ionising Radiation**
(kBq U)
Human exposure efficiency relative to U235 using the Human health model as developed by Dreicer et al 1995

6 **Photochemical ozone formation**
(kg NMVOC)
Tropospheric ozone concentration increases from LOTOS-EUROS as applied in ReCiPe 2008

RARE EARTHS FOR A SUSTAINABLE WORLD

Internationally accepted and best practice

Life Cycle Impact Categories

7 **Acidification**
(Mol H+ eq)
Accumulated Exceedance

8 **Eutrophication**
(Mol N eq)
Accumulated Exceedance

9 **Ecotoxicity freshwater**
(CTUe)
Comparative toxic units for ecosystems derived from USEtox 2.1.derived from the HC20 instead of the HC50.

10 **Land Use**
(Dimensionless)
Soil quality index (biotic production, erosion resistance, mechanical filtration and groundwater replenishment) based on LANCA

11 **Water Use**
(kg world eq. deprived)
User deprivation potential (deprivation-weighted water consumption) from the AWARE method

12 **Resource Use**
(MJ)
Abiotic resource depletion from fossil fuels using CML

RARE EARTHS FOR A SUSTAINABLE WORLD

Focus on **CSyARES:** A CRUCIAL PROJECT FOR THE FUTURE OF THE INDUSTRY

MINVIRO

- Within the CSyARES project, Minviro will be using an LCA software base to receive data from the Circularise system to automate a portion of the LCA and easily generate impact results
- Environmental performance complementary to blockchain REE supply information
- Life cycle impacts will be seamlessly validated against REIA environmental standards
- Suitable for raw material extraction, mineral processing facilities and downstream OEMs.

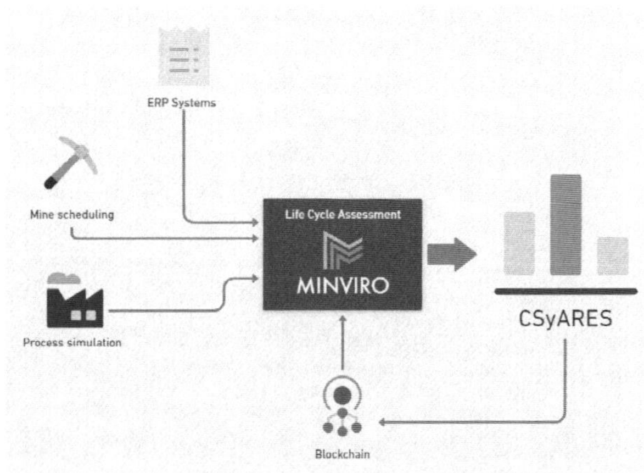

RARE EARTHS FOR A SUSTAINABLE WORLD

THE PROBLEM

Traceability today

CIRCULARISE

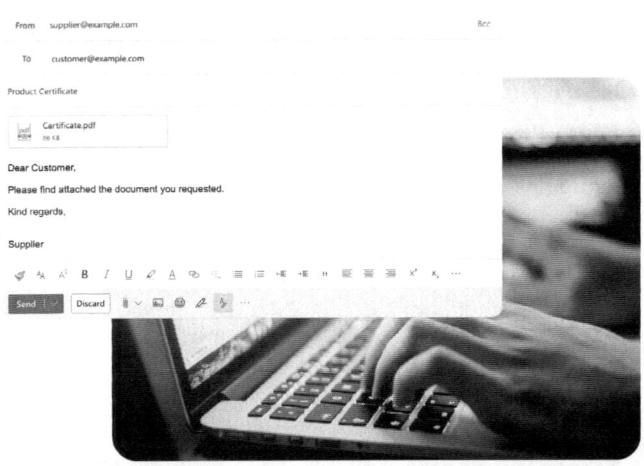

Resource intensive

- Labour intensive
- Prone to error and/or fraud
- Usually reactive
- Not scalable

RARE EARTHS FOR A SUSTAINABLE WORLD

OUR SOLUTION

The Circularise Digital Twin

POLYMER

Covestro

covestro

Token ID: 0xe0...AB94

25 kg

Mass Balance

ACCESS VIA SMART QUESTIONING

- Product Name
- Manufacturing Site
- Recycled Content
- Energy Consumption
- CO_2e Emissions
- Water Usage
- Hazardous Subs..
- Certifications

Token history

12/10/2021, 18:12
Raw Material DA sent

01/10/2021, 15:40
Raw Material DA created, token ID created

RARE EARTHS FOR A SUSTAINABLE WORLD

Focus on CSyARES: A CRUCIAL PROJECT FOR THE FUTURE OF THE INDUSTRY

CIRCULARISE

The Circularise Digital Twin

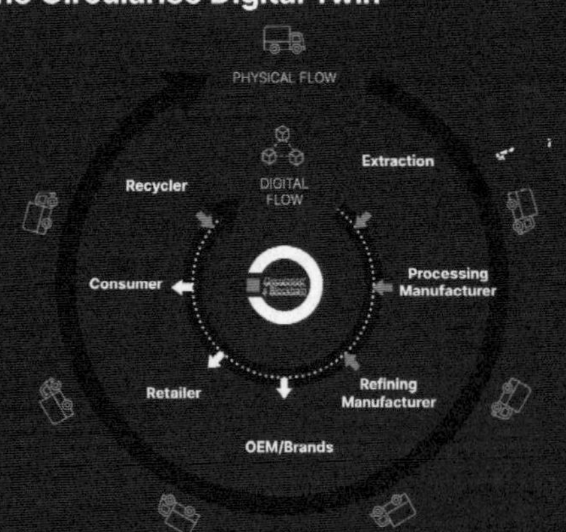

Materials & Products

Token & Data

Upload information to the blockchain

Retrieve information with confidentiality

- Circularise provides a **blockchain software for supply chain traceability and transparency**
- Circularise's patent-pending 'Smart Questioning' solution enables supply chain actors to **share** such **sensitive data** as origins, certificates, CO2 footprint, and impact assessment without risking privacy and confidentiality
- Circularise works with the **most complex supply chains** including automotive, electronics, packaging, construction, chemicals, plastics, metals, rare earths and others

RARE EARTHS FOR A SUSTAINABLE WORLD

CASE STUDY

Porsche 2020 Project Video

RARE EARTHS FOR A SUSTAINABLE WORLD

JJOIN REIA and BE PART OF THE JOURNEY!

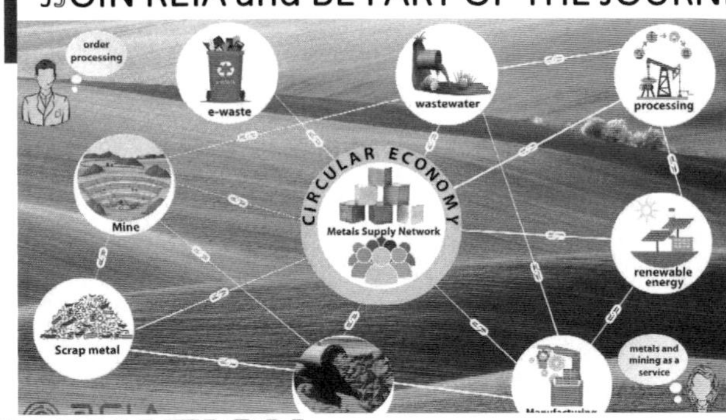

February 8, 2022
6:59 AM GMT+1
Last Updated 13 hours ago

REUTERS

Commodities

Blockchain rare earth scheme to certify sustainable output for EVs

SGNEWS

hain rare earth scheme to certify able output for EVs

08-02-2022

GRUNDFOS

Grundfos partners with four organisations tc develop a blockchain based Circular System for Assessing Rare Earth Sustainability

NOVATION
WS NETWORK

A leads collaboration to assess earth sustainability

U.S.News & WORLD REPORT

Blockchain Rare Earth Scheme to Certify Sustainable Outp

RARE EARTHS FOR A SUSTAINABLE WORLD

REIA

www.global-reia.org

Rare Earth Industry Association
Diestsevest 14
3000 Leuven (Belgium)
Tel:+32466246131

CONTACTS

Nabeel Mancheri
Secretary General
nabeel.mancheri@global-reia.org

Florence Gomez
CCO/Press relations
florence.gomez@global-reia.org
+33699464346

RARE EARTHS FOR A SUSTAINABLE WORLD

MAGNETICS 2022

Your partner for magnetism and twist testing

100% Quality Control of Permanent Magnets for Industrial Applications

Dipl. Phys. Matthias Schmidt,

Matesy GmbH - Magnetic Technologies & Systems

Jena | Germany

matesy

The Matesy GmbH
Quality – Made in Jena

- Is an innovative technology company located in the center of the university town of Jena
- The company was founded in 2008 as a spin-off of the R&D institution "INNOVENT Technology Development"
- Specializes in visualization, characterization and generation of magnetic fields and optical shaft twist testing

The Matesy GmbH
Quality – Made in Jena

Your partner for magnetism and twist testing

The Matesy GmbH
Quality – Made in Jena

- We develop and produce customized systems and technologies of the highest application standards
- We are service providers (consulting and measurements) for all aspects around magnetism
- We work together with INNOVENT and the National Metrology Institute of Germany - the PTB - for calibration, reference magnets and the development of new standard measurement methods

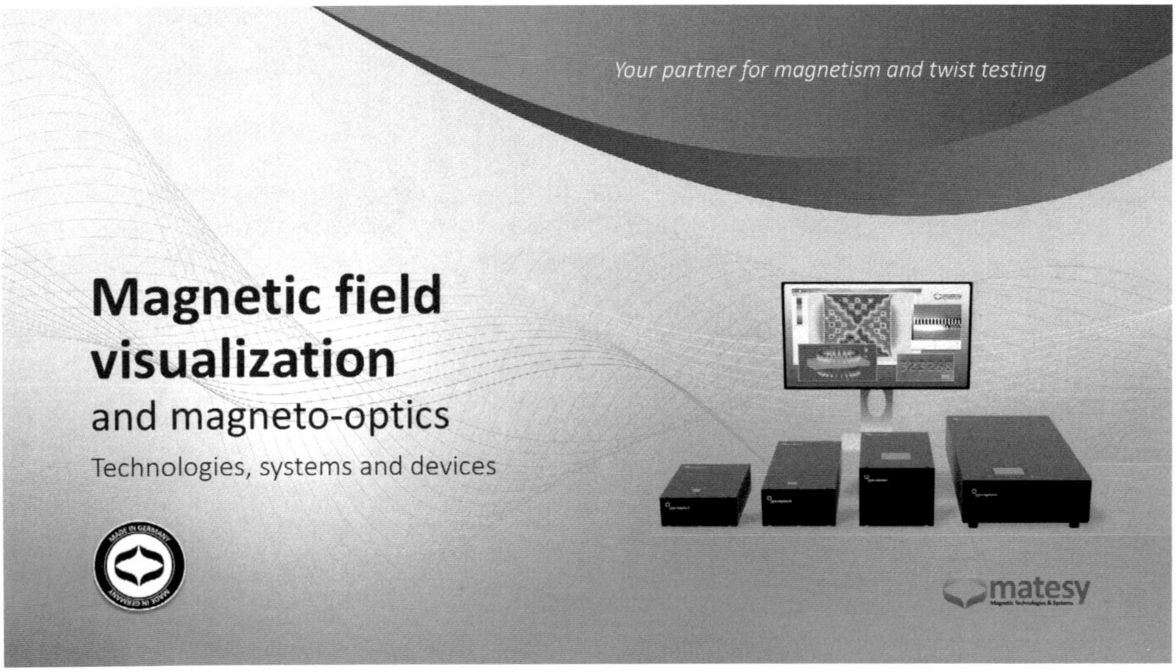
Your partner for magnetism and twist testing
Magnetic field visualization
and magneto-optics
Technologies, systems and devices
MADE IN GERMANY
matesy

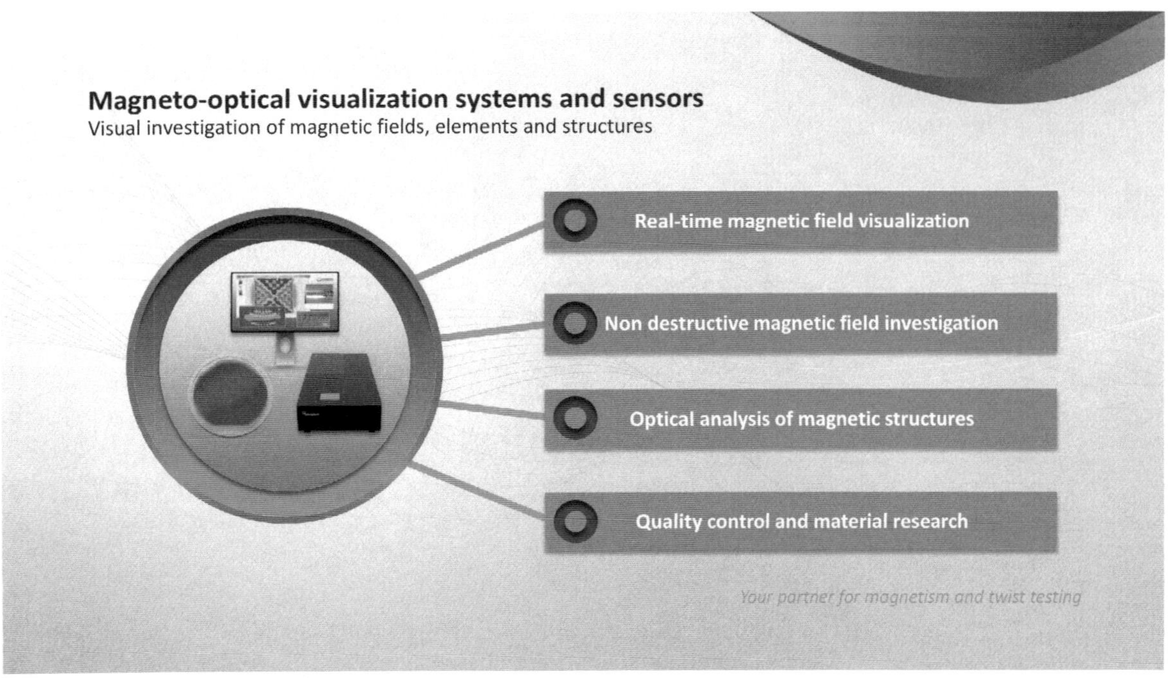
Magneto-optical visualization systems and sensors
Visual investigation of magnetic fields, elements and structures
Real-time magnetic field visualization
Non destructive magnetic field investigation
Optical analysis of magnetic structures
Quality control and material research
Your partner for magnetism and twist testing

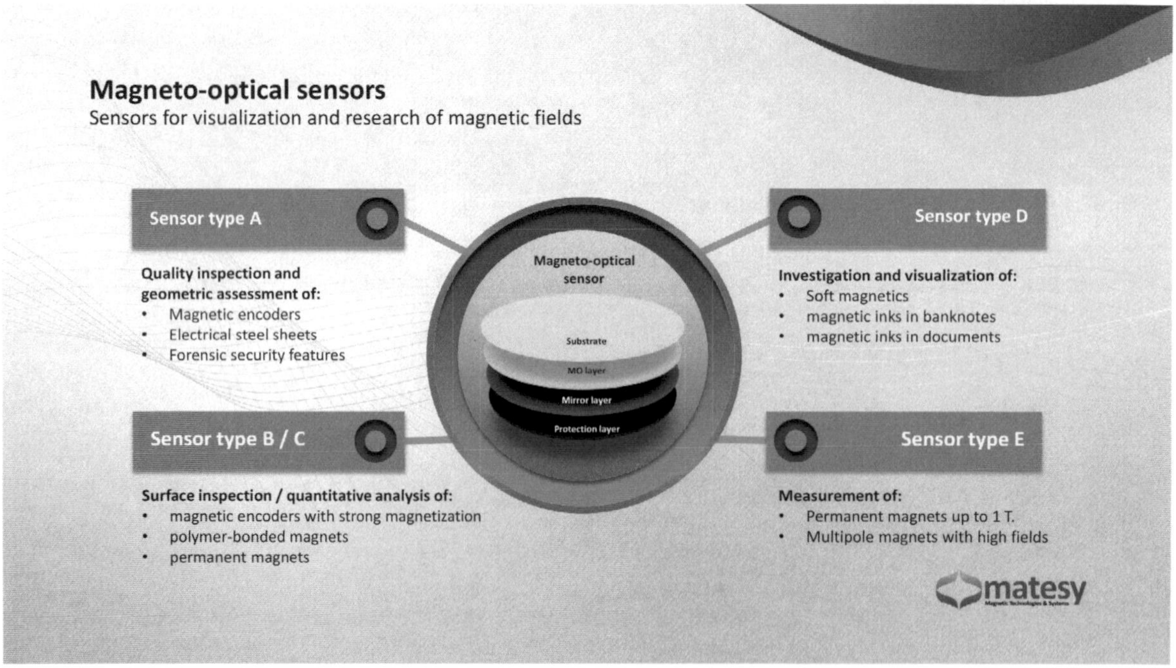
Magneto-optical sensors
Sensors for visualization and research of magnetic fields
Sensor type A
Quality inspection and geometric assessment of:
• Magnetic encoders
• Electrical steel sheets
• Forensic security features
Sensor type B / C
Surface inspection / quantitative analysis of:
• magnetic encoders with strong magnetization
• polymer-bonded magnets
• permanent magnets
Magneto-optical sensor
Substrate
MO layer
Mirror layer
Protection layer
Sensor type D
Investigation and visualization of:
• Soft magnetics
• magnetic inks in banknotes
• magnetic inks in documents
Sensor type E
Measurement of:
• Permanent magnets up to 1 T.
• Multipole magnets with high fields
matesy

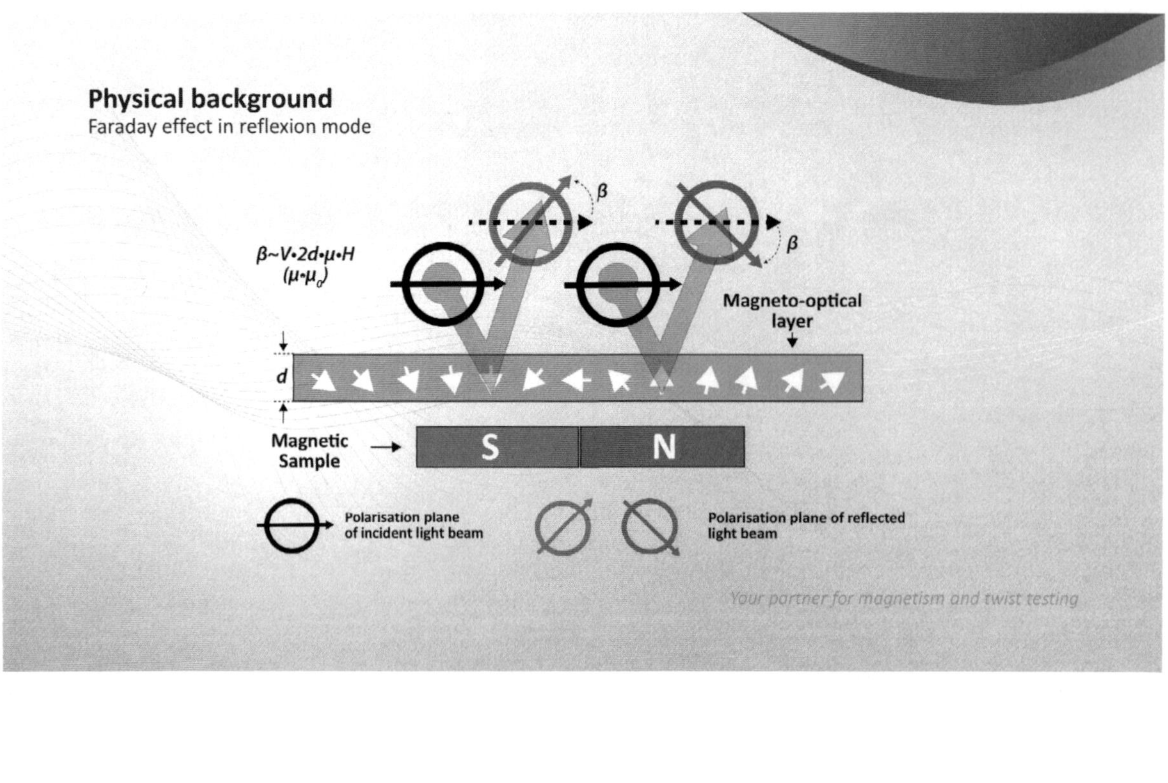
Physical background
Faraday effect in reflexion mode
β~V•2d•μ•H
(μ•μ0)
β
β
Magneto-optical layer
d
Magnetic Sample
S
N
Polarisation plane of incident light beam
Polarisation plane of reflected light beam
Your partner for magnetism and twist testing

Applications

For magneto-optical visualization systems and sensors

Visualize domain structures

Verification of banknotes

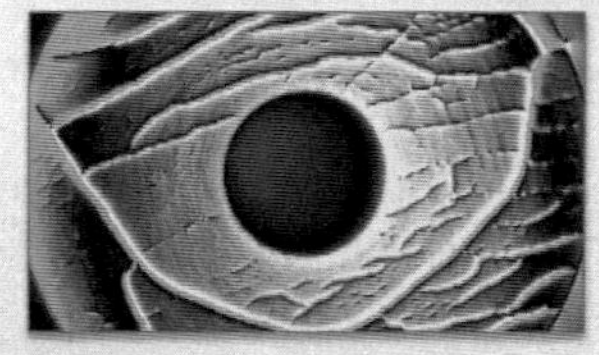

Quality control of permanent magnets

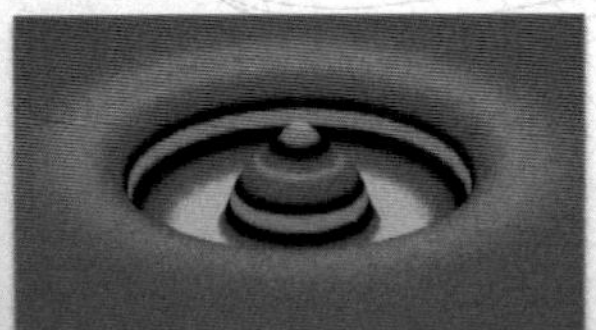

3D visualization of magnetic fields

Quality control of encoders & rotary encoders

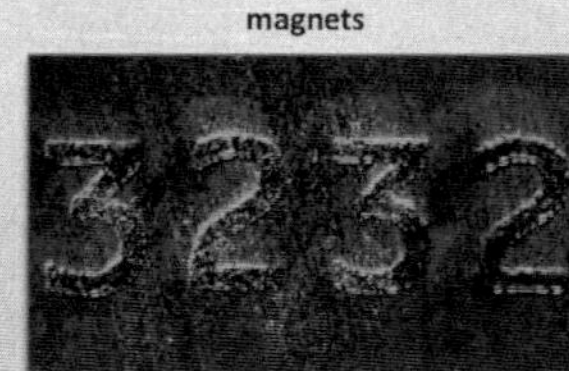

Analysis of serial numbers

cmos-magview

automated image analysis

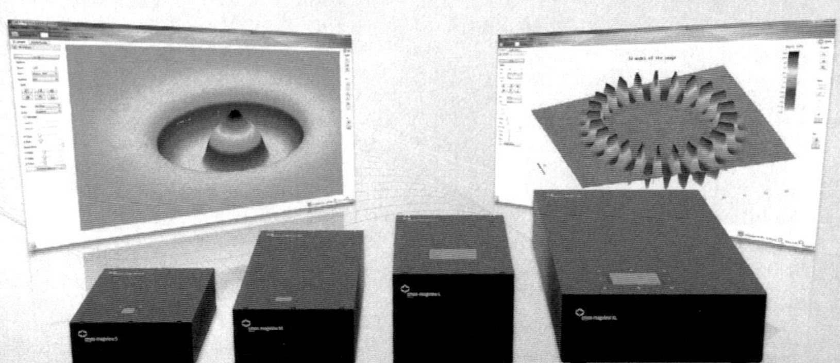

matesy
Magnetic Technologies & Systems

10

cmos-magview
automated image analysis

- Costumer specific software for automated detection of magnetic pole widths,
- Repeatability of angular measurements 0.02°
- Rotation encoders up to 38 mm diameter possible,
- Calibrated measurement range: ± 125 mT,
- Lateral resolution up to 60 µm with 45 mm x 60 mm sensor

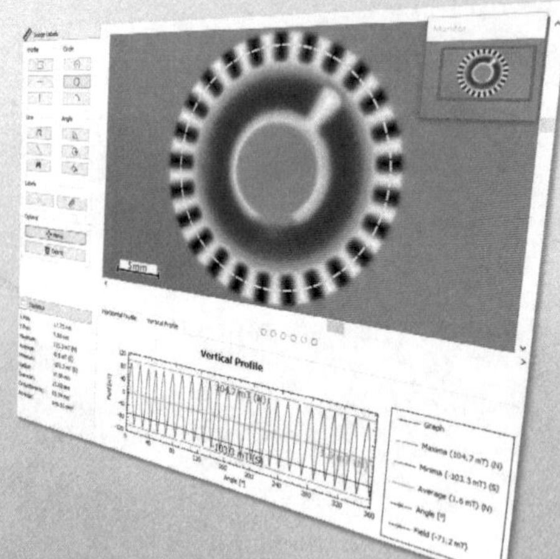

11

Your partner for magnetism and twist testing

Magnet measurement

m-axis system

Permanent magnet measuring and calibration

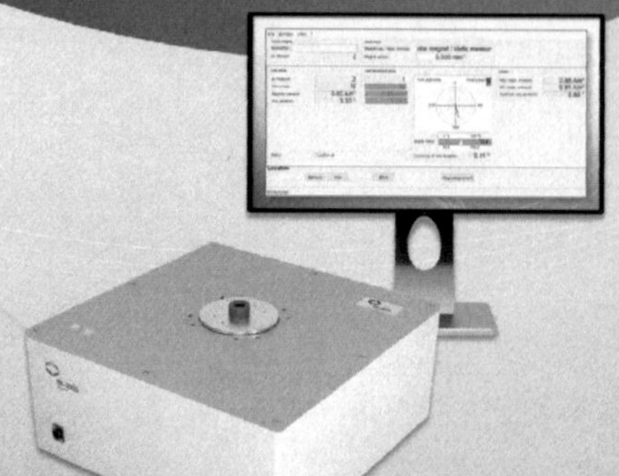

matesy

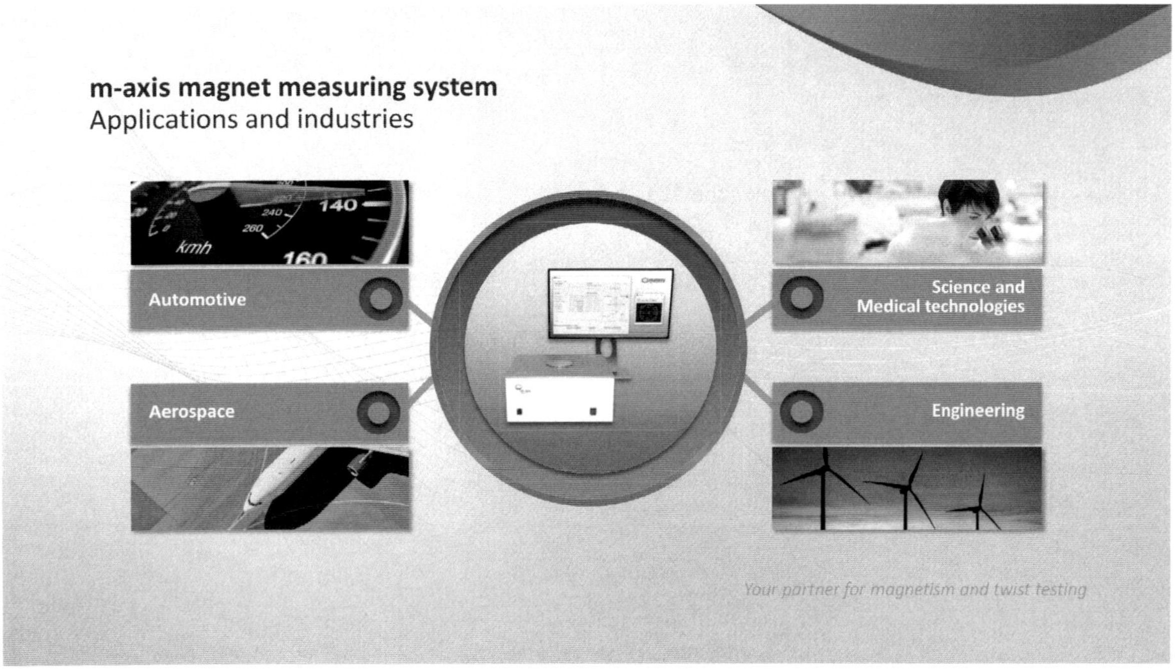
m-axis magnet measuring system
Applications and industries
Automotive
Aerospace
Science and
Medical technologies
Engineering
Your partner for magnetism and twist testing

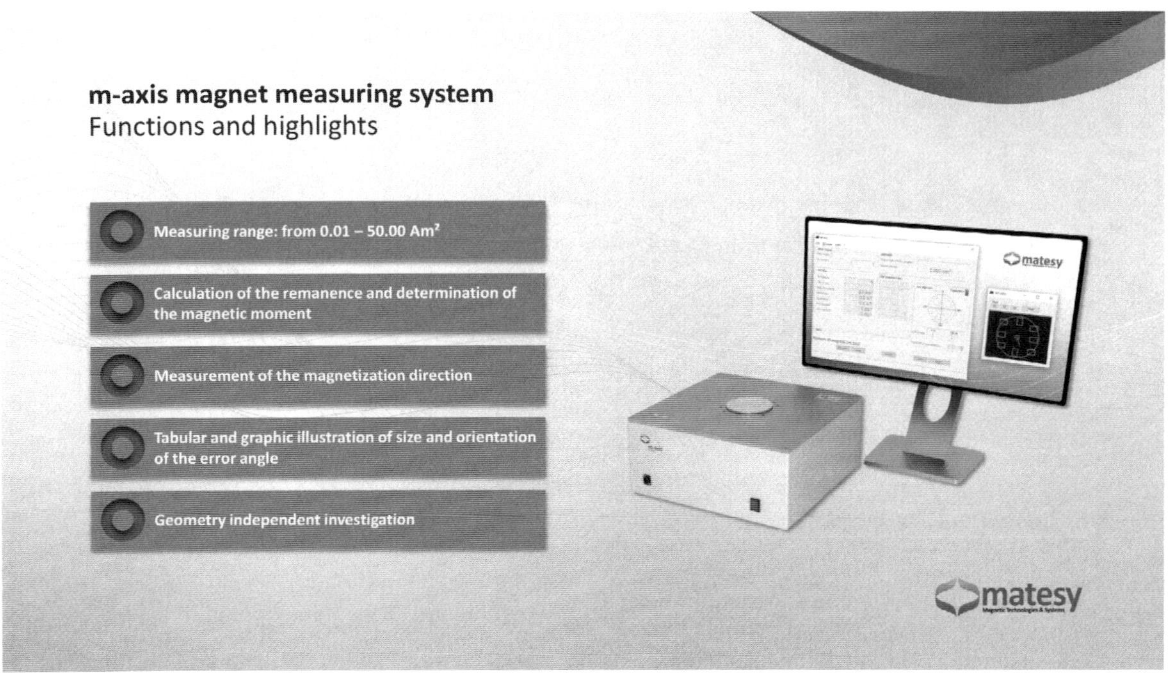
m-axis magnet measuring system
Functions and highlights
Measuring range: from 0.01 – 50.00 Am²
Calculation of the remanence and determination of the magnetic moment
Measurement of the magnetization direction
Tabular and graphic illustration of size and orientation of the error angle
Geometry independent investigation
matesy

Measurement process

- The calculation routine is based on the determination of the dipole parameters of permanently magnetic materials using an integrated AMR sensor set-up
- That way the three-dimensional position (x, y, z) of the magnet as well as its magnetic moment (m) and the angular direction (φ, θ) of the magnetization are determined simultaneously

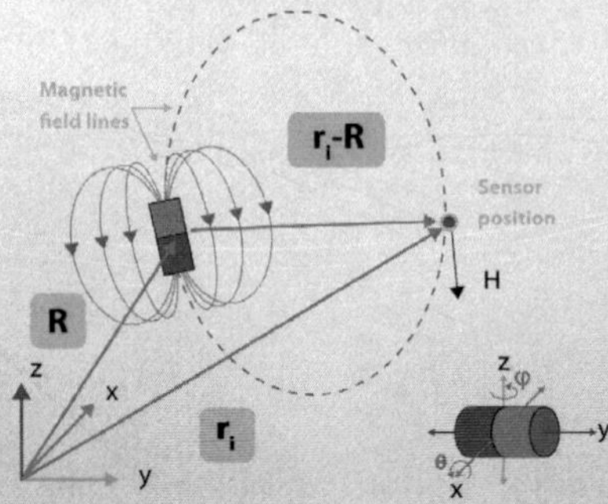

Your partner for magnetism and twist testing

Measurement process

- Because of the universally applicable approach the evaluation of axially as well as diametrically magnetized dipole permanent magnets regarding their quality and strength.
- By implementation of various user defined magnet types and measurement processes in the comprehensive user software the system delivers a real time classification of numerous dipole possibilities.

matesy

Comparison

m-axis – Helmholtz coil

Your partner for magnetism and twist testing

Comparison

m-axis – Helmholtz coil

m-axis:

- Same accuracy within the measuring range
- fast and accurate measurement of magnetic moment and angle
- easy to automate due to free access to the sample
- Disturbed measurements can be recognized directly via the quality function!

Helmholtz coil:

- maximum accuracy only if the magnet geometry fits into the homogeneous area of the coil
- Exact measurement of angle and magnetic moment is only possible with a three-axis coil
- not easily automatable due to limited access to the sample
- Disturbances during the measurement process are not recognized!

Automated magnet measuring line in automotive industry

Measurement and alignment of the magnets

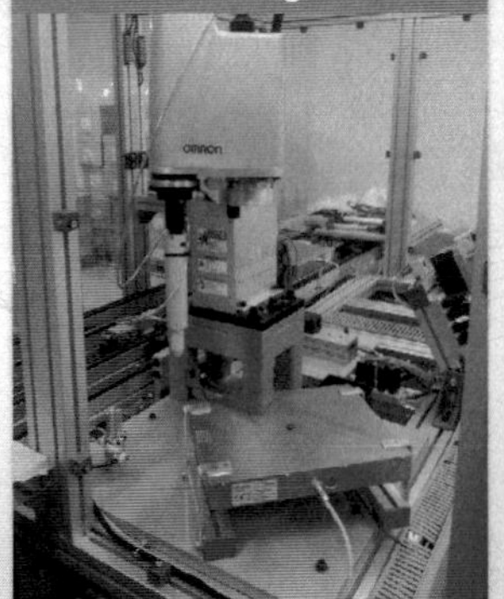

100% end-of-line test of the product

Your partner for magnetism and twist testing

19

Automated magnet measuring line

magnet producer

20

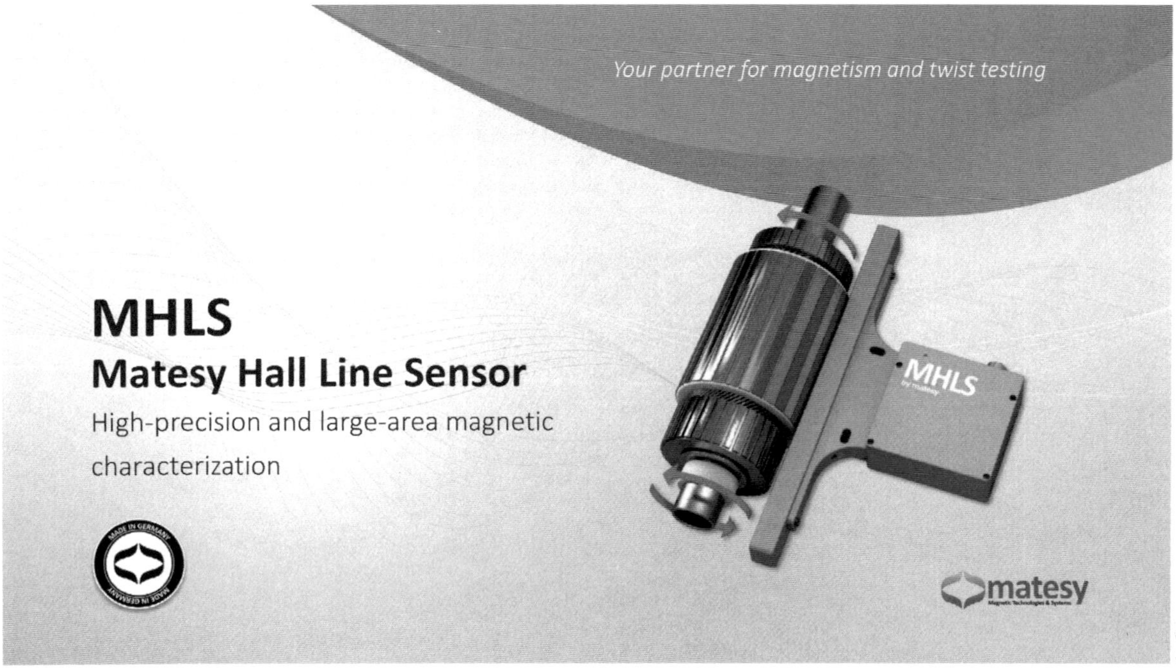
Your partner for magnetism and twist testing
MHLS
Matesy Hall Line Sensor
High-precision and large-area magnetic characterization
MADE IN GERMANY
MHLS
matesy

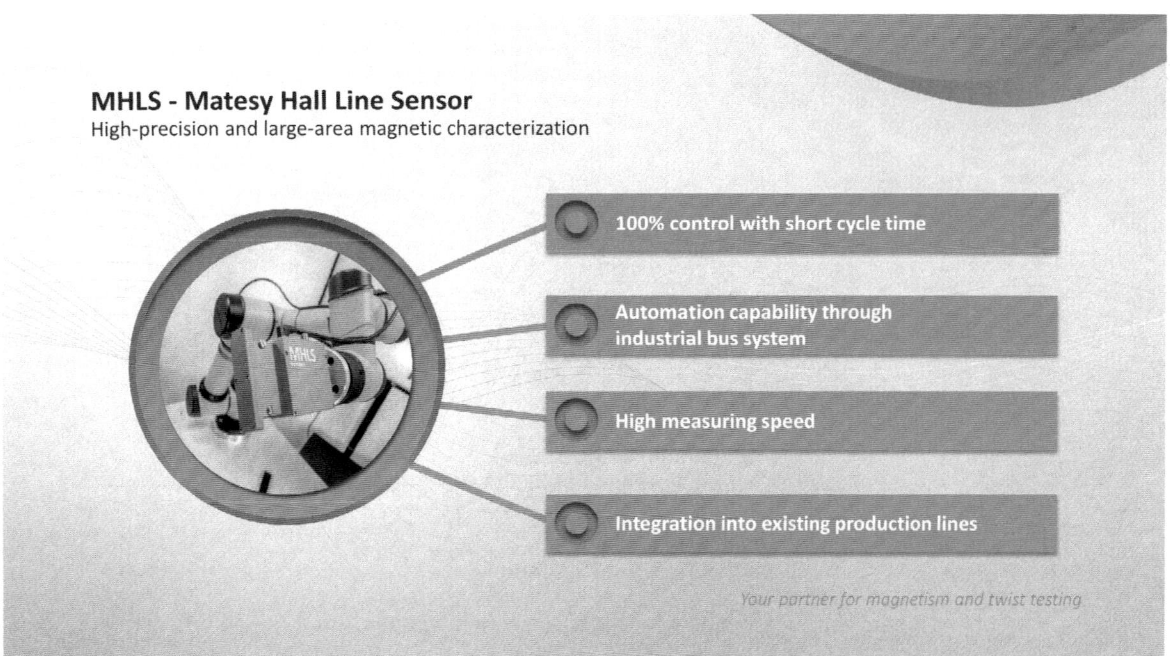
MHLS - Matesy Hall Line Sensor
High-precision and large-area magnetic characterization
100% control with short cycle time
Automation capability through industrial bus system
High measuring speed
Integration into existing production lines
Your partner for magnetism and twist testing

MHLS - Matesy Hall Line Sensor

High-precision and large-area magnetic characterization

- MHLS is extremely flexible in use due to its compact and robust design
- Application / quality control in the development of efficient electric motors in areas such as automotive engineering or wind energy
- Ultra-flexible, compact and high-precision measuring device with extremely high measuring speed
- Available in 4 different sizes with configurable measuring ranges

matesy

MHLS - Matesy Hall Line Sensor

Application areas

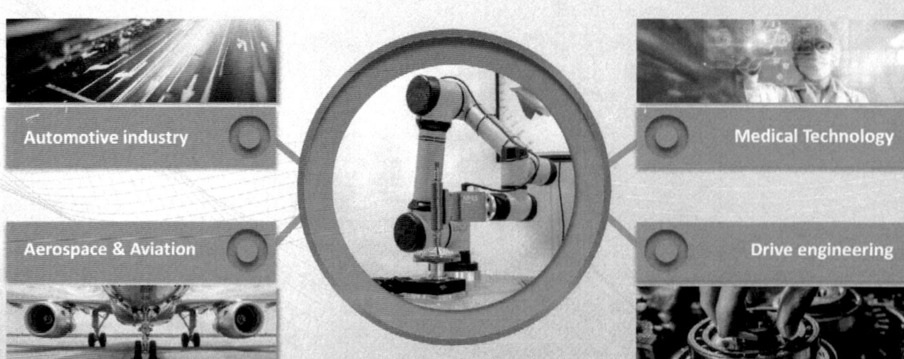

Your partner for magnetism and twist testing

MHLS - Matesy Hall Line Sensor

Measurement and visualization

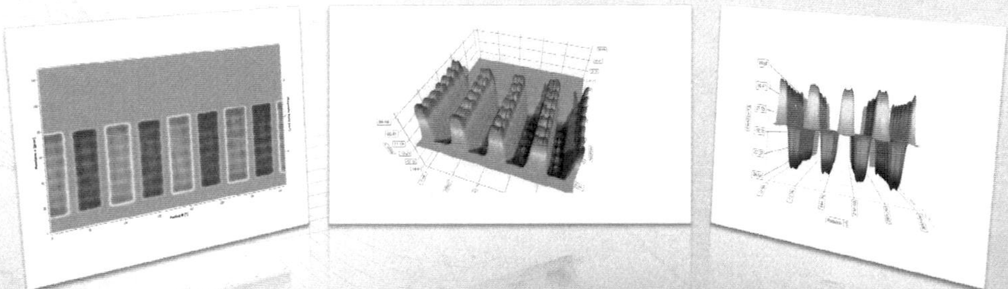

2D and 3D visualization of rotors and magnet assemblies

matesy

MHLS - Matesy Hall Line Sensor

Structure and functionality

- Ultra precise and complex arrangement of highly integrated 3 axis hall sensors
- All sensor triplets have an extremely small sensor volume
- Pinpoint field and vector determination of the magnetic stray fields
- Linear arrangement and interconnection of the sensor triplets with a distance of 2.5mm for high accuracy and a high measuring frequency (sampling rate)

Your partner for magnetism and twist testing

MHLS - Matesy Hall Line Sensor

Structure and functionality

Sensor arrangement :

0.6mm below the housing cover, 16 to 64 high-precision Hall sensor ICs are located at a distance of 2.5mm. Each sensor has its own temperature sensor and is therefore temperature compensated in addition to the magnetic field calibration. Up to 317.5 mm measuring length.

matesy

MHLS - Matesy Hall Line Sensor

Variants

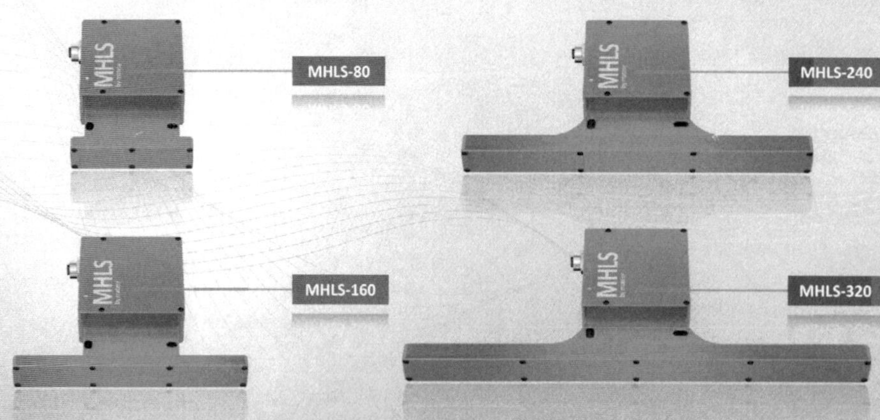

Your partner for magnetism and twist testing

MHLS - Matesy Hall Line Sensor

Magnetic measurement mounted on a robot

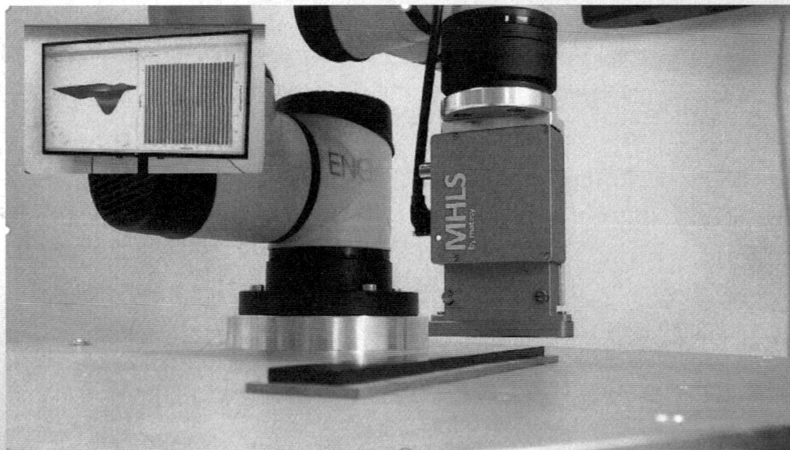

MHLS - Matesy Hall Line Sensor

Measurement

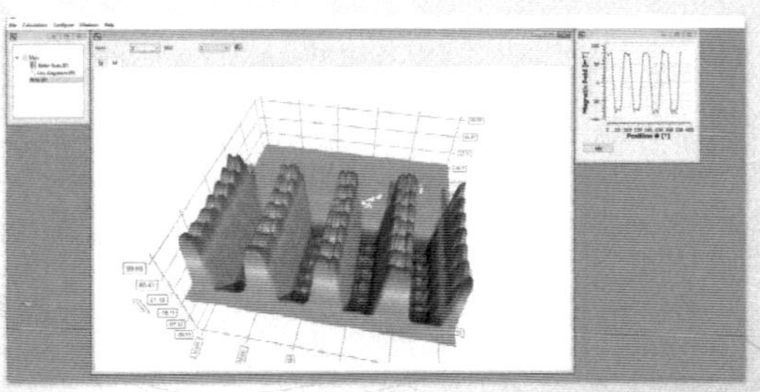

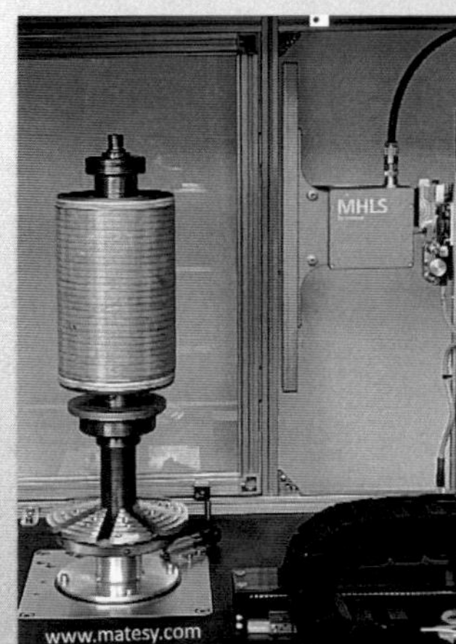

- Easy integration to our rotor mapping system and industrial production lines
- Fast and precise measurements for 100% control
- Triggered measurements via hardware or software

MHLS - Matesy Hall Line Sensor

Technical data

- 3-axis Hall sensor system
- Cascaded version in steps 80, 160, 240, 320
- Sensor pitch: 2.5mm
- Measurement accuracy 3D: 0.5% to ±800 mT
- Minimum measurement distance*: 0.6 mm
- Measuring frequency (3D): 200 S/s
- Interface: USB, UART (RS422)
- Digital data output
- Trigger - input / output
- Integrated sensor monitoring

*Z-sensor to housing surface

matesy

Your partner for magnetism and twist testing

Matesy GmbH

Magnetic Technologies & Systems

Address and location :

- Loebstedter Str. 101-103
- 07749 Jena
- Germany

Contact:

- Tel: +49 (0) 3641 79799 00
- Fax: +49 (0) 3641 79799 01
- E-mail: info@matesy.de
- Web: www.matesy.de

matesy

Newly Developed Rare-Earth Lean High-Performance Permanent Magnets

Durga Paudyal

CMI Critical Materials Institute

AMES LABORATORY Creating Materials & Energy Solutions U.S. DEPARTMENT OF ENERGY

This research is supported by the Critical Materials Institute, an Energy Innovation Hub funded by the U.S. Department of Energy, Office of Energy Efficiency and Renewable Energy, Advanced Manufacturing Office. The Ames Laboratory is operated for the U. S. Department of Energy by Iowa State University of Science and Technology under Contract No. DE-AC02-07CH11358.

Science challenges and opportunities to reduce the use of critical elements

- Start to end ratio
  - What percentage of starting material ends up in the finished magnet
- Functionally graded materials
  - Can we put critical elements only where they are needed
- Replace
  - Can we completely remove or replace Dy with something else to enhance high temperature coercivity
- Replace
  - Can we use something other than Co to enhance Curie temperature

Permanent magnet technology, challenges, and solutions

Technology

- ✓ Motors
- ✓ Generators
- ✓ Heat engines
- ✓ Electronics

Challenges

Maintain magnet performance

Reduce use of critical elements

Solutions

Playground: structures, sites, interstitials, defects, interfaces, and strain

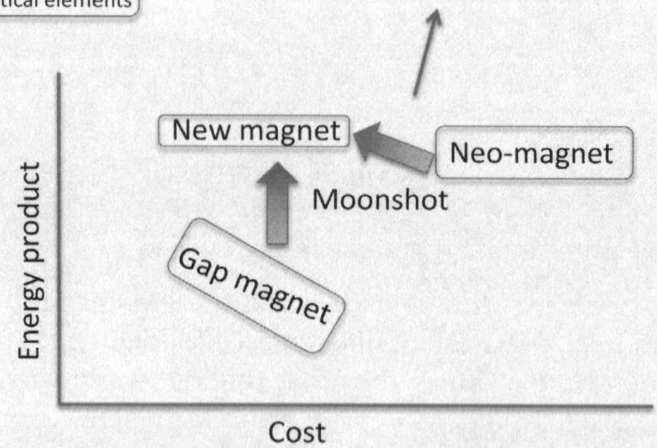

Rare earth magnets

✓ Plus

- ✓ 4f electrons produce high magneto-crystalline anisotropy
  - ✓ high coercivity
  - ✓ high energy product compared to other magnets

❑ Minus

- ❑ rare earth elements
  - ❑ not rare
  - ❑ expensive to process
  - ❑ reactive
    - ❑ prone to corrosion
  - ❑ low volume magnetization

CMI Critical Materials Institute
AN ENERGY INNOVATION HUB

Outline

- ✓ Rare-earth (RE) and transition metals (TMs): building blocks for magnets
- ✓ Origin of magnetic anisotropy, magnetic moment, and Curie temperature: anisotropic charge densities and structure, exchange interactions from TMs
- ✓ Challenge of uplifting the magnetic performance of hexaferrite
- ✓ Rare earth free permanent magnets
- ✓ Itinerant versus localized nature of Ce 4f and Co 3d in $CeCo_5$
- ✓ Substitution of Nd by Ce/La to reduce the usage of critical elements
- ✓ Are there alternatives to $Nd_2Fe_{14}B$?
- ✓ Summary

AMES LABORATORY IOWA STATE UNIVERSITY OF SCIENCE AND TECHNOLOGY U.S. DEPARTMENT OF ENERGY 5

CMI Critical Materials Institute
AN ENERGY INNOVATION HUB

Rare-earth (lanthanide) and transition metals: building blocks for permanent magnets

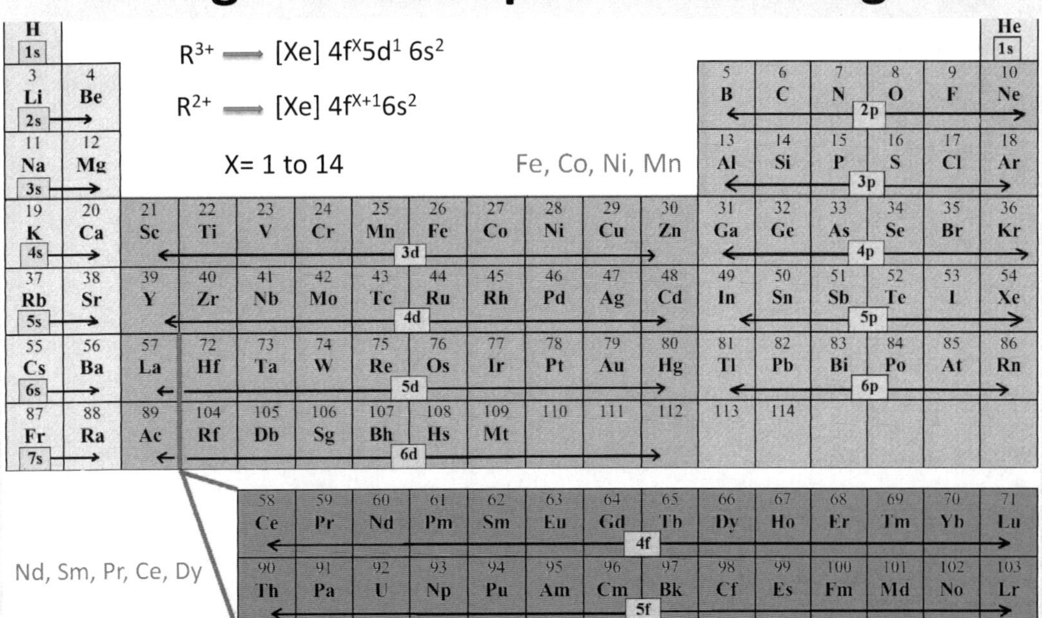

AMES LABORATORY IOWA STATE UNIVERSITY OF SCIENCE AND TECHNOLOGY U.S. DEPARTMENT OF ENERGY 6

Origin of magnetic anisotropy: anisotropic atomic orbitals

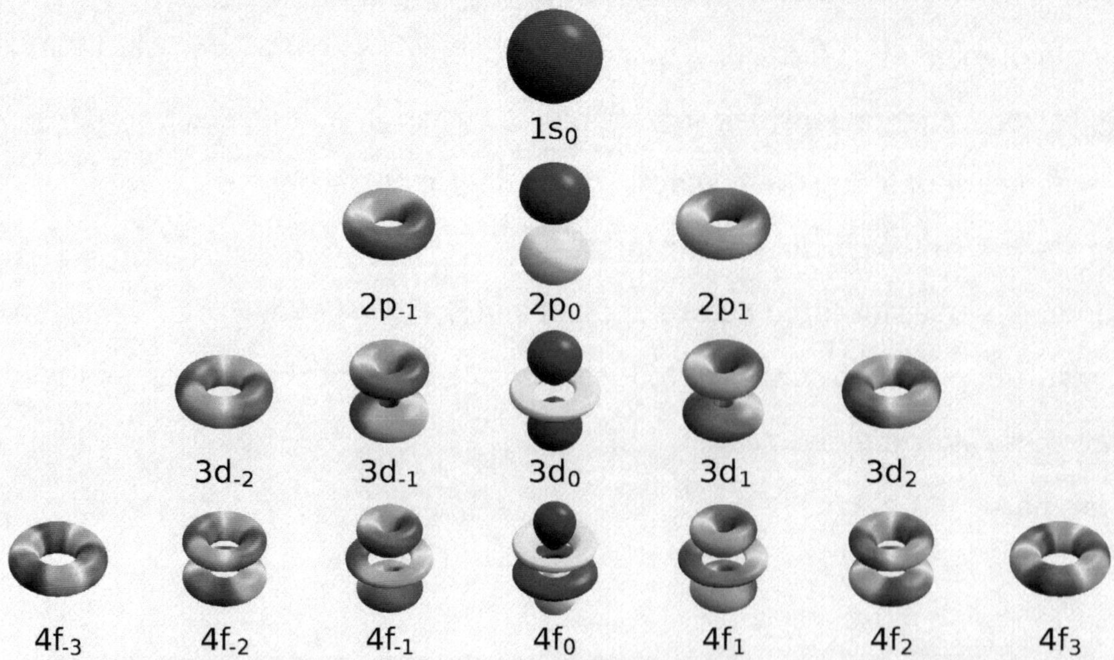

Anisotropy and quenched orbital moment in Sm-Co magnets

Crystal Structure

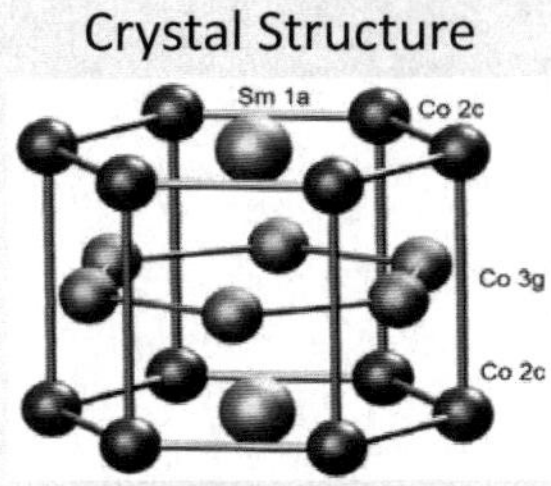

Fe substitution

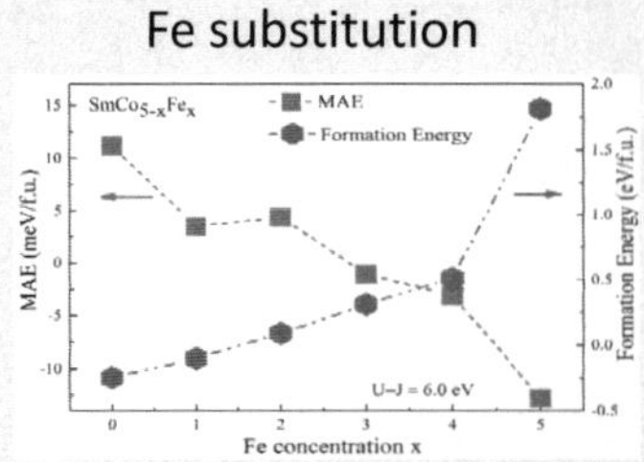

Charge distribution

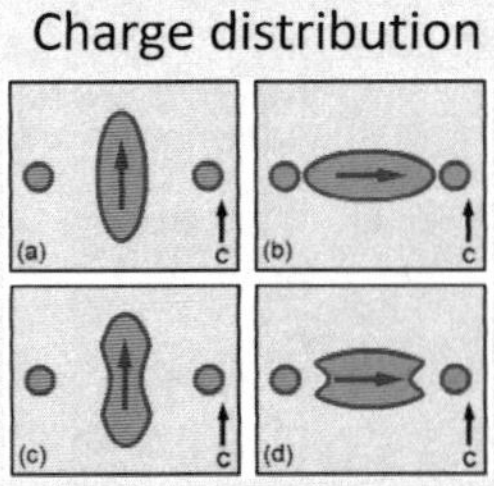

Valence charge density

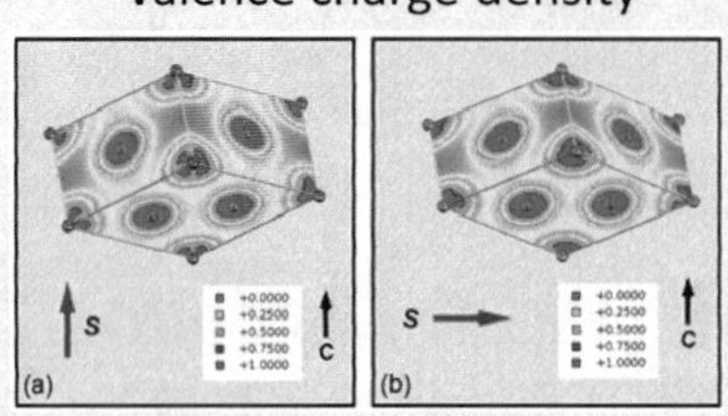

- ✓ Peculiar crystal structure
- ✓ One Co out of five can be substituted by Fe
- ✓ Sm 4*f* charges distort differently in the c- and the planar directions
- ✓ Valence charges also differ in the c- and the planar directions

Ames Lab Press Release: Scientists discover potential path to improving samarium-cobalt magnets

B. Das, R. Choudhary et al., Phys. Rev. B ***100****, 024419 (2019)*

Challenge of uplifting the magnetic performance of hexaferrite: What is known so far

$LaFe_{12}O_{19}$

Fe (2a) changes from 3+ state to 2+ state with extra electron coming from La

Magnetic anisotropy gets doubled as compared to that of $SrFe_{12}O_{19}$

Looking for possibilities to increase magnetic moment

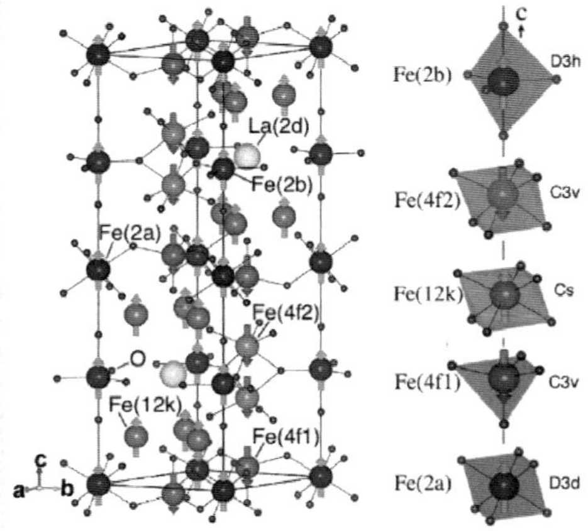

Unit cell of $LaFe_{12}O_{19}$ hexaferrite. The five nonequivalent Fe sites are octahedral (2a), bipyramidal (2b), tetrahedral (4f1), octahedral (4f2), and 12k. The three- and six-fold local axis are parallel to the hexagonal axis c of the crystal, which is also the easy axis of magnetization.

Ames Lab News Release (2021): A well-known iron-based magnet is also a potential quantum information material

*C. B. Bhandari, M. E. Flatté, and D. Paudyal, Phys. Rev. Materials **5**, 094415 (2021)*

AMES LABORATORY IOWA STATE UNIVERSITY OF SCIENCE AND TECHNOLOGY U.S. DEPARTMENT OF ENERGY 9

CMI | Critical Materials Institute AN ENERGY INNOVATION HUB

Rare earth free permanent magnet: MnBi

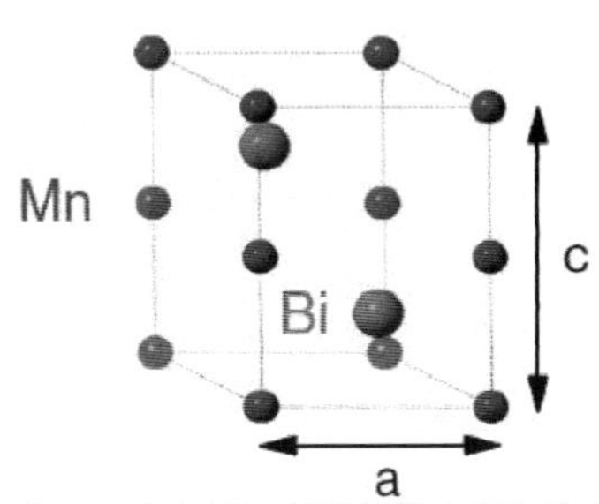

NiAs-type hexagonal crystal structure of MnBi.

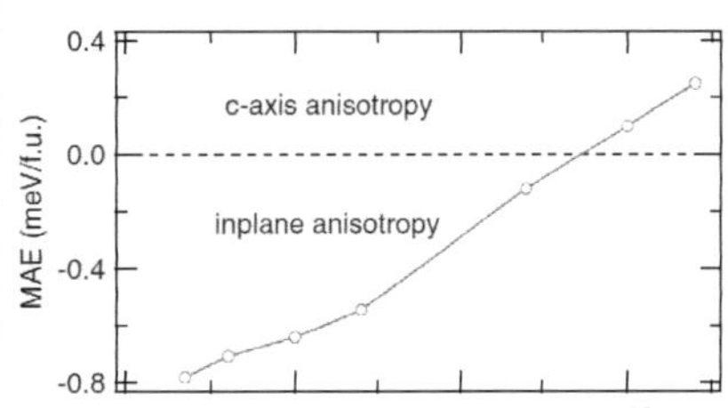

Anisotropy could be tuned from planar (not useful) to uniaxial (useful) utilizing the variation of lattice constants in MnBi

How about MnAl and FeNi ?

*Choi et al., Phys. Rev. B **94**, 184433 (2016)*

AMES LABORATORY IOWA STATE UNIVERSITY OF SCIENCE AND TECHNOLOGY U.S. DEPARTMENT OF ENERGY 10

Itinerant versus localized nature of Ce 4*f* and Co 3*d* in $CeCo_5$

$CeCo_5$

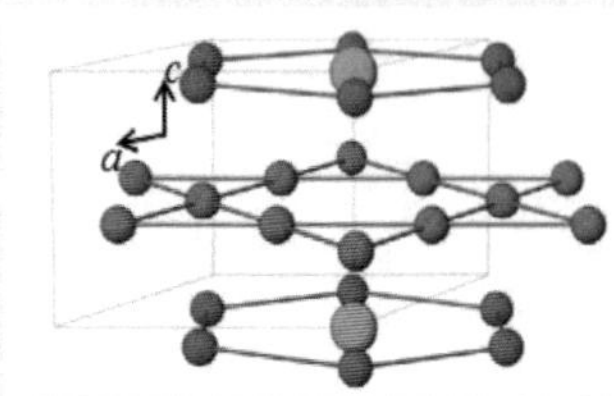

Co atoms in non-equivalent sites behave differently

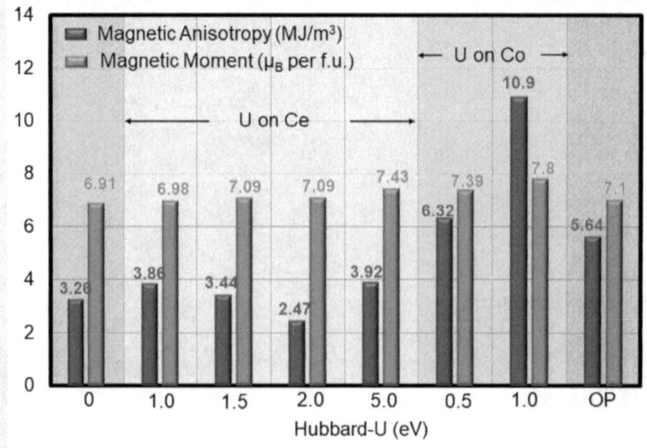

Weakly localized nature of Co 3*d* but not Ce 4*f* in intermetallic compounds is unusual but only helps to explain high magnetic anisotropy in $CeCo_5$

R. Choudhary et al., J. Alloys and Compounds 839, 155549 (2020)

Substitution of Nd by Ce/La to reduce the usage of critical elements

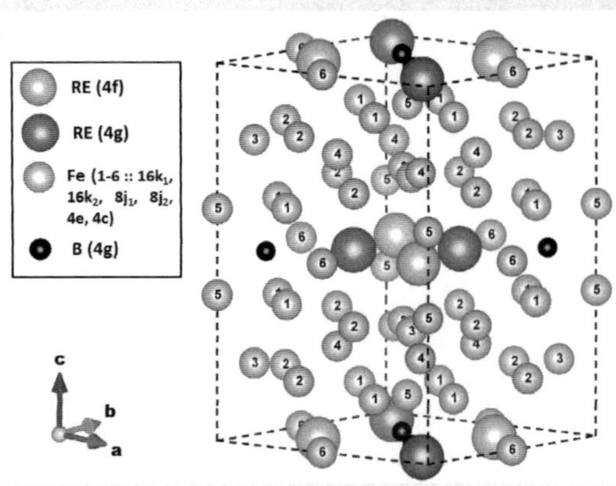

Tetragonal $Nd_2Fe_{14}B$

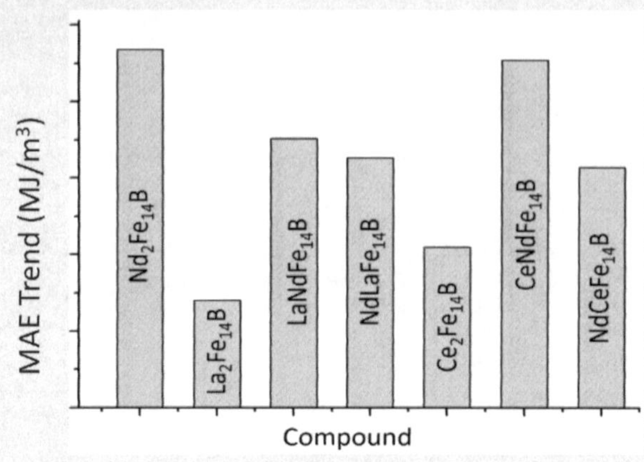

$CeNdFe_{14}B$ is competitive to $Nd_2Fe_{14}B$

Chouhan et al., arXiv:1806.01990

(La,Ce,Nd) $Fe_{14}B$ Based Electric Motors

Critical Materials Institute
AN ENERGY INNOVATION HUB

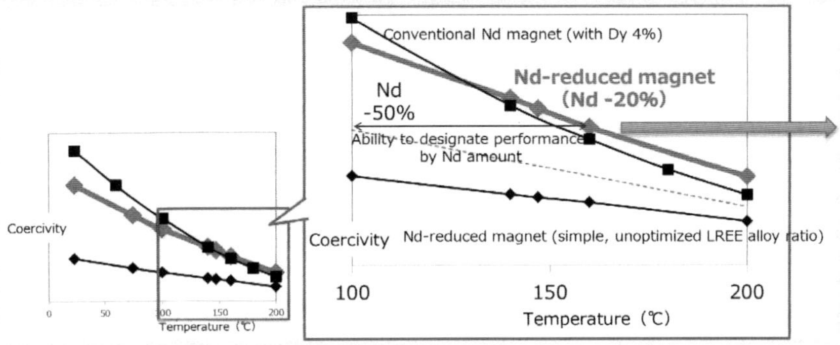

High temp. Coercivity is higher in Nd reduced compositions

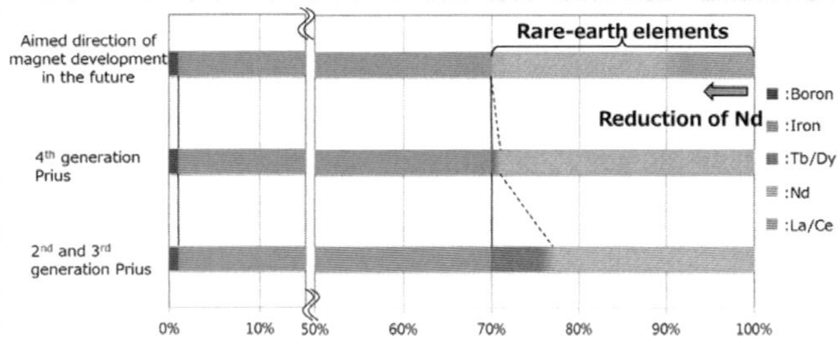

Use of motors in various areas such as automobiles and robotics, as well as maintaining a balance between the supply and demand of valuable rare earth resources

https://newsroom.toyota.co.jp/en/corporate/21139684.html

Are there alternatives to $Nd_2Fe_{14}B$?

Critical Materials Institute
AN ENERGY INNOVATION HUB

$ThMn_{12}$ – type tetragonal $NdFe_{12}N$

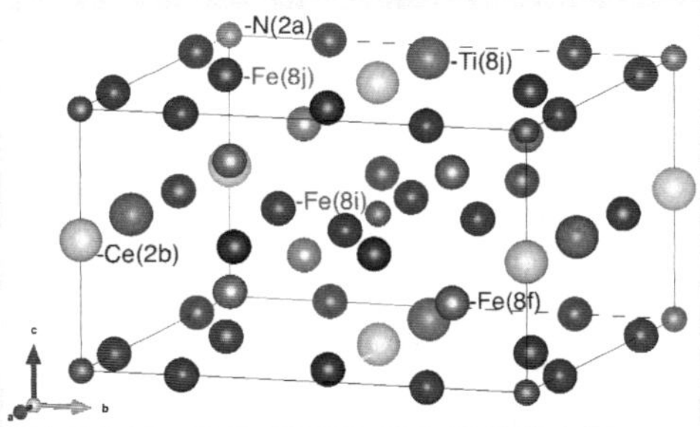

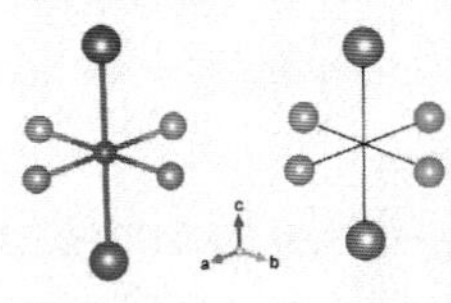

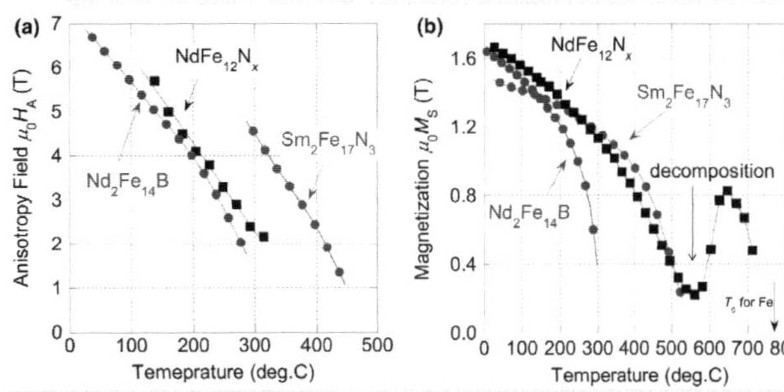

$NdFe_{12}N$ has magnetic moment, magnetic moment, and Curie temperature superior to those of $Nd_2Fe_{14}B$ but the synthesis in the bulk form and decomposition at high temperature are challenges and obstacles

*Hirayama et al., JOM **67**, 1344 (2015)*

Critical Materials Institute
AN ENERGY INNOVATION HUB

Summary

Challenge - First, understand model permanent magnetic materials and then discover new permanent magnetic materials that have high uniaxial magneto-crystalline anisotropy and magnetic moment with reduced critical elements

Opportunity - Identify and substitute the non-relevant REE sites in terms of magnetic anisotropy by abundant REEs to discover new permanent magnetic materials

AMES LABORATORY IOWA STATE UNIVERSITY OF SCIENCE AND TECHNOLOGY U.S. DEPARTMENT OF ENERGY 15

Acknowledgment –

Churna Bhandari (Current post-doc)
Huseyin Ucar (Visiting Faculty Program)
Renu Choudhary (Post-doc 2018-2020)
Rajiv Chouhan (Post-doc 2015-2017)

AMES LABORATORY IOWA STATE UNIVERSITY OF SCIENCE AND TECHNOLOGY U.S. DEPARTMENT OF ENERGY 16

INTERACT ANALYSIS | Inspiring intelligent insight

Predictive Maintenance in the Motor & Drive Markets

PRESENTED BY:

BLAKE GRIFFIN
Senior Analyst, US
+1 512 596 3092
Blake.Griffin@interactanalysis.com

FEBRUARY 2022

INTERACT ANALYSIS | Inspiring intelligent insight

Outline of Presentation

- Current State of Motor & Drives Markets
- What's Going On With Prices?
- Predictive Maintenance: What? When? How?

Biggest Takeaways From This Presentation

- Gain a sense for the challenges of 2022
- Understand the value behind predictive maintenance
- Recognize where we are on the predictive maintenance timeline

Methodology Overview

40+ hours of interviews per edition

Deep splits modeled from national manufacturing survey data

Estimates continuously iterated upon through ongoing conversations with stakeholders

LOW VOLTAGE AC MOTORS – 2022 REPORT

INTERACT ANALYSIS Inspiring intelligent insight

State of the Industries

Both markets rebounded heavily from 2020 COVID lows

- Motors market grew 21.5% in revenue terms, 6.6% in units shipped
- Drives market grew 7.7% in in revenue terms, 5.2% in units shipped

Supply chains and energy markets are still disrupted

Resultingly, prices & lead times were up for both motors and drives

- Lead times for motors & drives up 4x compared to normal times

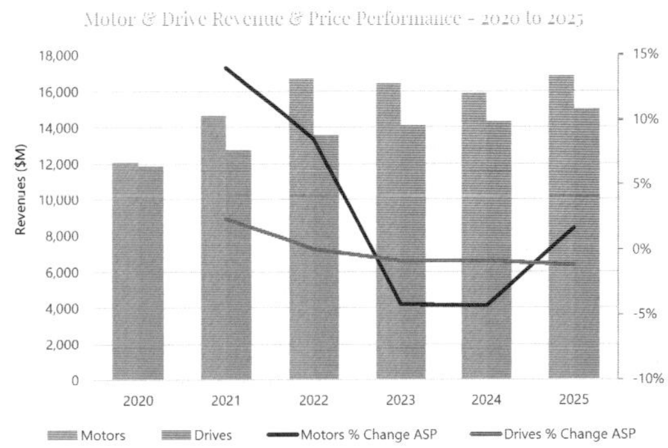

LOW VOLTAGE AC MOTORS – 2022 REPORT

INTERACT ANALYSIS Inspiring intelligent insight

2021 Was All About Price Increases

Motors:

- Magnetic Steel Prices Up 140% in July of 2021
- Aluminum Prices Up ~50% in 2021
- Copper Prices Up ~50% in 2021

Drives:

- Silicon up >7%

Both:

- Average Price for 40ft shipping container up 740%!

Changes in Key Costs

Cost	% Change from 2020
Aluminum	49.6%
Copper	50.6%
Magnetic Steel	140.0%
Silicon	7.0%
40 ft Shipping Container	740.0%
Drive Price	2.4%
Motor Price	14.0%

© 2021 Interact Analysis

What's Going on With Shipping and What's Next?

March–July 2020

Global COVID-19 economic shutdown
Ships and containers decommissioned
Mass dislocation of containers

January 2021 to Present

China's trade balance becomes heavily out of skew
Ports are bottlenecked globally
COVID-19 variants continue to challenge labor supply
Truck drivers are exiting the industry all over US

Coiled demand becomes released
A supernova in e-commerce
Demand begins outstripping supply

Aug.–Dec. 2020

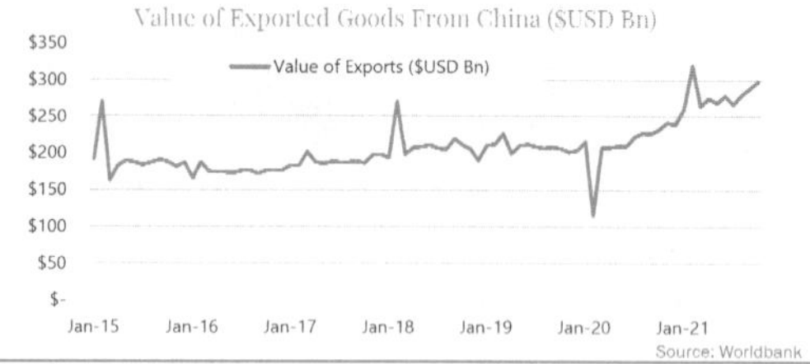

What's Going on With Shipping and What's Next?

3 factors could represent a peak of the short-term crisis

- Beijing Olympics
- Chinese New Year
- Omicron

Long-term, this is a systemic issue

- The labor shortage will drive a long-term trend towards more congested shipping
- We may not see rates return to levels seen before this crisis for a long time

INTERACT ANALYSIS Inspiring intelligent insight

How Does This Impact Motor & Drives?

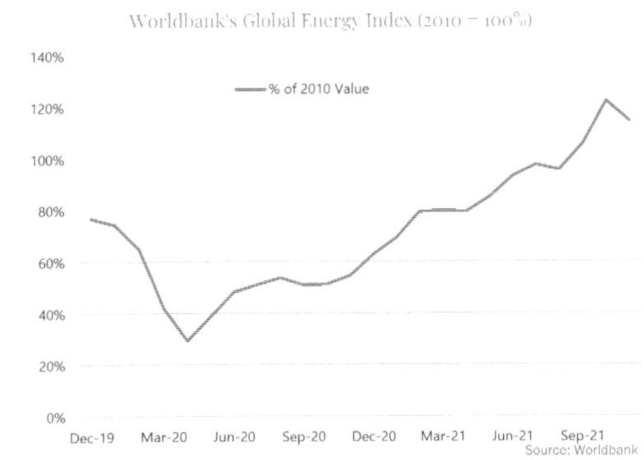

Higher Costs of Good

More Time Needed for Sourcing Components

Higher Energy Costs

INTERACT ANALYSIS Inspiring intelligent insight

Why Are Energy Markets Paralleling Motor Pricing?

- LNG and hydropower production were disrupted heavily in 2021 by weather related events.
- The world started heavily substituting towards coal power
- The largest coal producer, China, saw dramatically increased demand for its coal
- Coal supplies became constrained and China was forced to limit production from energy intensive industries, namely steel
- Steel prices surged
- The price of steel in 2022 will largely be dictated by the severity of Europes winter
- If Europe demands high levels of imported LNG, it could again cause heavy substitution towards coal and force China to again limit production from the steel industry

The result, higher steel prices and subsequently higher motor prices

Our Expectations for Future

- Demand from EVs on magnetic steel could lead to shortage
- Semiconductor shortage persists and threatens supply lines and price levels of drives (through late 2022 early 2023)
- Prices for motors see increased pressures in early 2022 but stabilize in back half of year
- Prices for drives return to 2020 levels by 2024 time-frame
- Increased predictive maintenance offerings and adoption by end-users

First Things First: What is Predictive Maintenance?

- **Predictive Maintenance** – The use of technology to gather data on an asset, such as its temperature or vibration levels, and to perform analysis on the data to predict when the asset needs repair to eliminate risk of failure.

Which of the following digitalization initiatives have you evaluated, piloted, or implemented? (CPG)

	Have Not Evaluated	Evaluating	Piloting	Implemented	Evaluated and Rejected	# of Responses
Big Data (on premise)	56.9%	23.5%	3.9%	13.7%	2.0%	51
Big Data (cloud-based)	50.0%	26.0%	12.0%	12.0%	-	50
Digital twin (simulation)	80.4%	7.8%	5.9%	3.9%	2.0%	51
Predictive maintenance	25.5%	29.4%	21.6%	23.5%	-	51
Augmented and/or virtual reality	70.6%	13.7%	9.8%	3.9%	2.0%	51
Collaborative robots	64.0%	14.0%	4.0%	14.0%	4.0%	50
Mobile robots	68.0%	14.0%	2.0%	12.0%	4.0%	50
Additive manufacturing	70.6%	19.6%	3.9%	5.9%	-	51
						405

Source: PMMI © 2020 Interact Analysis

- **74.5%** of respondents indicated that they were evaluating, piloting, or had implemented predictive maintenance.
- **44.2%** were either extremely familiar or very familiar with our definition.
- Education is needed!

  Predictive maintenance often gets conflated with terms like preventative maintenance, and condition monitoring.

Familiarity with Predictive Maintenance Definition (CPG)

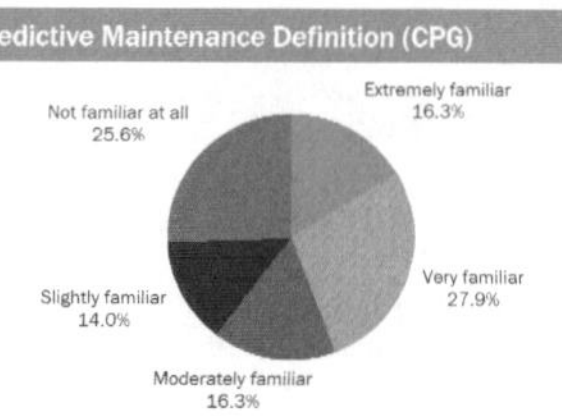

Source: PMMI © 2020 Interact Analysis

INTERACT ANALYSIS Inspiring intelligent insight

Why Is This important?

Predictive maintenance technology bridges the labor gap

- Unplanned downtime is a huge problem... and without technology, it will get worse

Motors are some of the most process critical equipment. Almost all are offline!

Predictive maintenance represents a flurry of business opportunities

- Enhanced service level agreements
- Opportunity to differentiate
- New business models

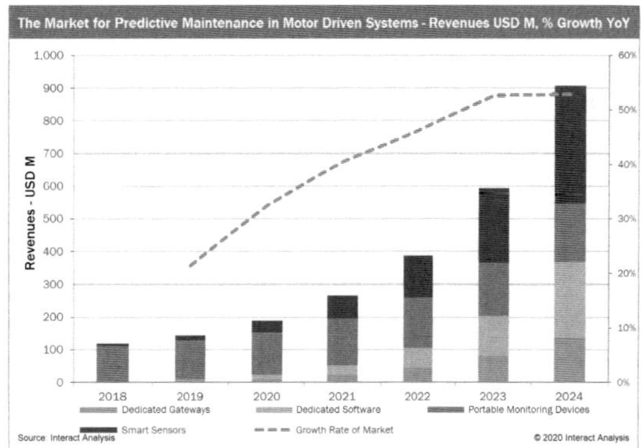

INTERACT ANALYSIS Inspiring intelligent insight

Predictive Maintenance Is Not New.... Why Now?

Smart sensors: Wireless sensors which can communicate asset health related data to an edge device, or a smart device.

↓

The advent of smart sensors has drastically reduced the cost of implementing predictive maintenance!

↓

Suppliers include

ABB	Siemens	WEG	Nidec	SKF	Augury	Petasense	Many more...

Smart Sensors Are Not The Only Solution

Software approaches
- Tapping into historian
- Reading data off PLC

Drive as a Sensor
- Current draw analysis
- Aggregating sensor data

Vendors currently offering a drive with predictive maintenance capability included:
- Danfoss
- NORD
- Mitsubishi Electric

Why Smart Sensors And Drives Are Such A Powerful Combination

- Most smart sensors are overly reliant on 'physics of failure'
- Utilizing a drive w/ smart sensors is much better for non-standard applications... and they are both in close proximity to the motor
- More data resolution = higher accuracy in predicting failure

Where Are We Now?

.... and some consideration for the future

- Smart sensors begin being offered by major motor suppliers. Physics of failure and 'traffic light' monitoring are king. Adoption is slow.
- Turnkey PdM providers gain funding and produce competitive offering to industry. Solution still largely relies on 'physics of failure'
- Application specific PdM solutions emerge. Solutions still rely heavily on Smart Sensors to collect majority of the data. Adoption ramping up although still considered a 'nice to have' by most customers.
- Prediction accuracy improves as tech becomes refined. Increasing utilization of data streams beyond smart sensors. Simple PdM solutions begin being offered as standard for some applications.
- Predictive maintenance becomes commonplace. Integration of sensors into motors offers baseline PdM functionality for a large portion of new motors. Most drives come standard with PdM features.

Contact us

REPORT ANALYST TEAM

BLAKE GRIFFIN
Senior Analyst
Blake.griffin@interactanalysis.com
+1 512 596 3092

ADRIAN LLOYD
CEO, US
Adrian.Lloyd@interactanalysis.com
+1 512 598 0087

With offices spanning the UK, US and Asia, we've grown to become the go-to partner for international market research.

in www.interactanalysis.com

NORTHAMPTON
East Northamptonshire Enterprise Centre
Michael Way, Raunds
NN9 6GR
United Kingdom

Phone: +44 (0) 1933 654 245
Email: info@interactanalysis.com

AUSTIN
4111 Medical Pky, Suite 200
Austin
TX 78756
United States

Phone: +1 512 598 0087
Email: info@interactanalysis.com

SHANGHAI
Room 2976, 29/F, Shanghai Tower
501 Middle Yincheng Rd,
Pudong,
China, 200120

Phone: +86 (0) 21 3893 2558
Email: info@interactanalysis.com

METROlab
Magnetic precision has a name

Overview of Magnetic Field Mapping Systems

Antoine Daridon

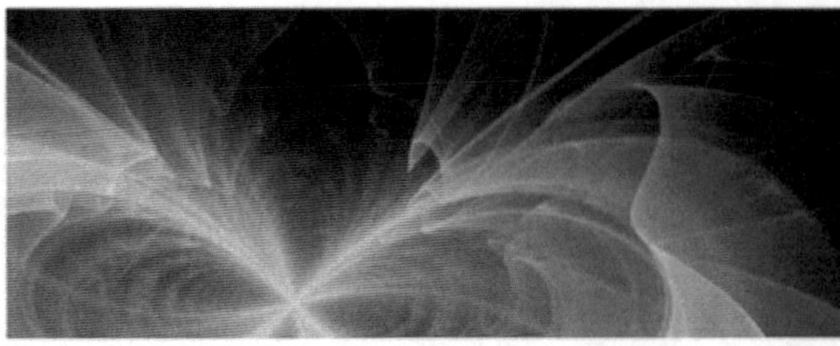

MAGNETICS 2022

February 8-9
Orlando, Fla.

METROlab
Magnetic precision has a name

Magnetic field mapping

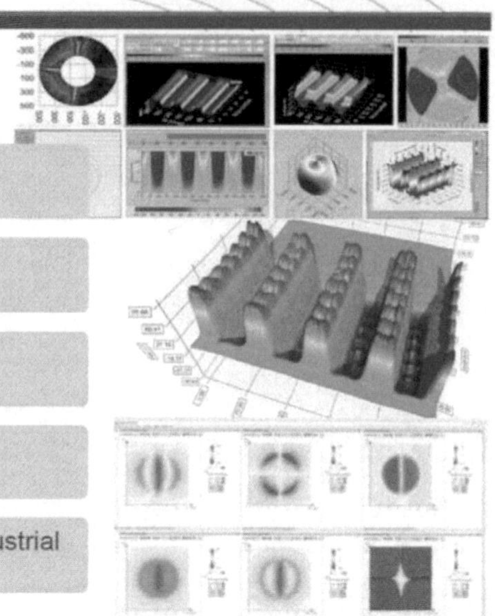

- Measure magnetic flux density (B_x, B_y, B_z) at many positions (X, Y, Z)
- Many different solutions – recent development!
- Different technical approaches
- Different advantages / limitations
- Goal: high-level overview of solutions relevant to industrial users

Some solutions we will NOT talk about

- Iron filings, magneto-optical: qualitative, no 3D vector info
- Ultra-high precision coils & fluxmeters: accelerator magnet production
- Pulsed- & vibrating-wire: small-gap accelerator magnets
- NMR based solutions: MRI magnet production
- Other specialized solutions, e.g. QC of magnet bars for glass sputtering
- Geo-surveying: oil exploration, archeology, geophysics
- VR- or drone-assisted surveys: large & odd-shaped magnet systems

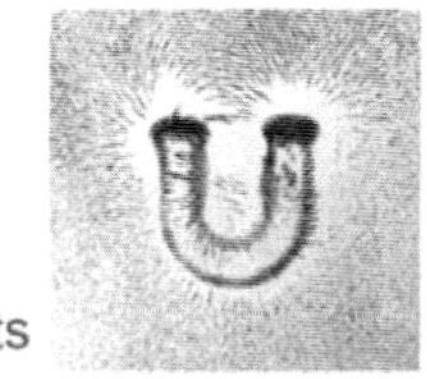

Ways to categorize mapping systems

- Magnetic field range & precision
- Positioning range, precision, resolution & flexibility
- Time to map => AC – DC mapping
- Degree of automation, manufacturing-line integration
- Sophistication of analysis software
- Capital & labor costs

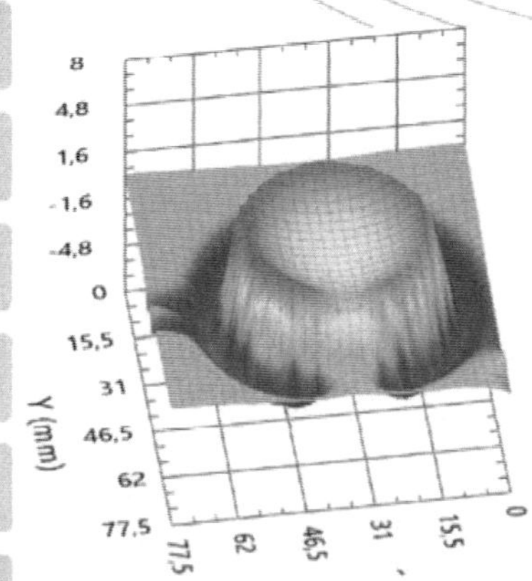

iPhone12 magnetic positioning element mapped by HallinSight® 32x32

METROlab
Magnetic precision has a name

Fully Integrated Hall sensors

Planar Hall sensors measure the field normal to the sensor plane.

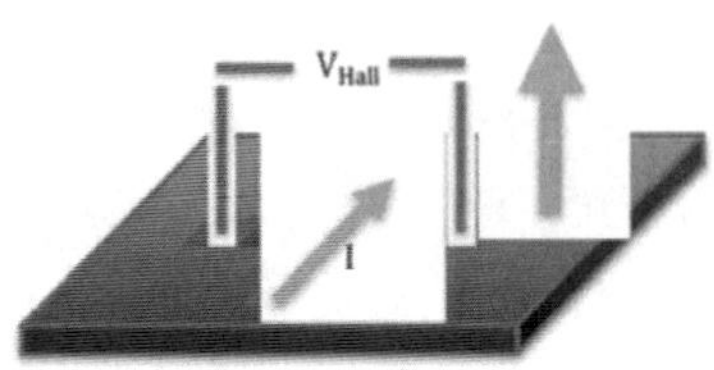

Vertical Hall sensors measure the field in the sensor plane

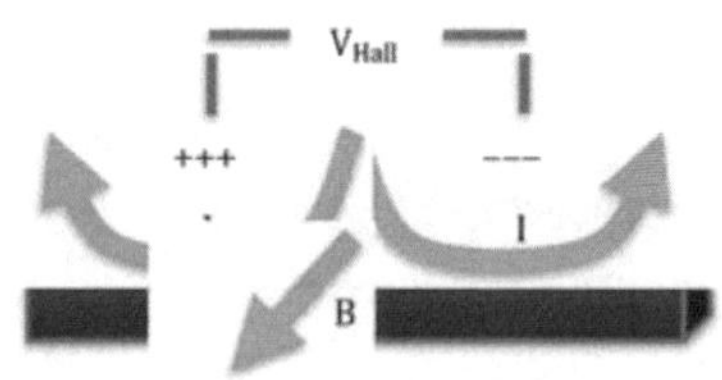

https://youtu.be/r3WGe6R-3RE

METROlab
Magnetic precision has a name

Fully Integrated Hall sensors

One planar Hall sensor

Four vertical Hall sensors

=> **Fully Integrated 3-axis sensors** with tiny sensing volume

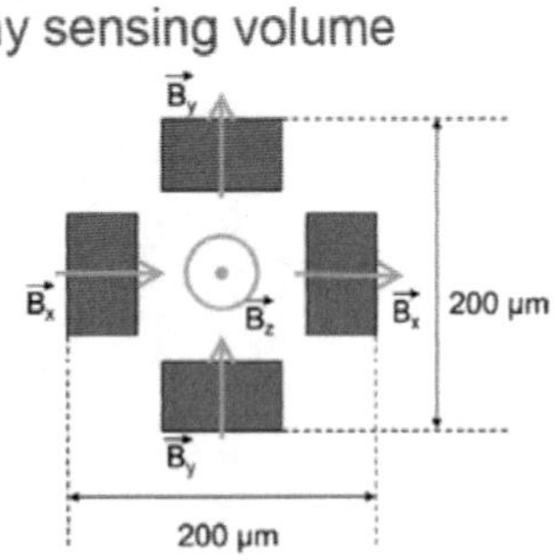

An array of Semiconductor Hall effect sensors

=> **Local field imaging with high spatial, time and field resolution**

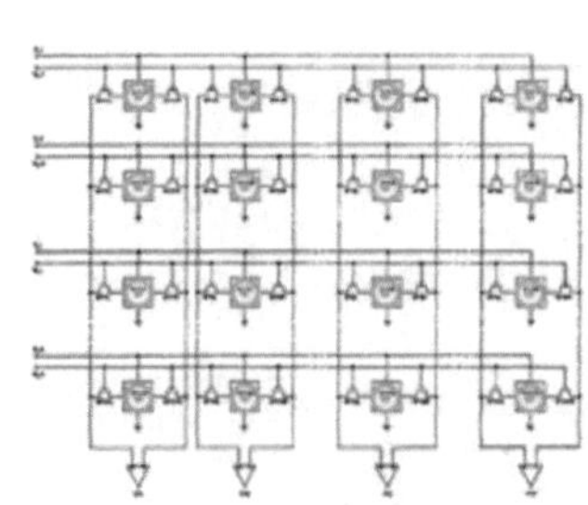

https://youtu.be/r3WGe6R-3RE

https://patents.google.com/patent/US7902820B2

Do-it-yourself 3D mapper

3DFM Automated 3D magnetic flux density mapping system

- Developer: Aaron Purchase, U. of Alberta, Canada

- Open source
- Probe: Metrolab 3-axis compact USB probe
- Robot: "Any 3D CNC/3D printer arm"
- Controller: Arduino with commercial shield for CNC interface
- < 10 k$; flexible; OK precision; slow; incomplete solution; no support

https://github.com/Aaron-Purchase/3DFM

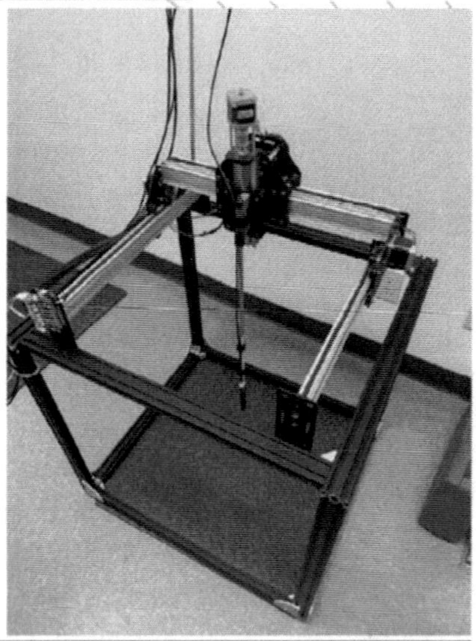

Industrial 3D mapper

SENIS® Magnetic Field Mappers

- Probes: Senis 3-axis Hall; optionally 3-axis AMR, eddy-current (crack detection) & surface probes
- Robots: various costs & sizes, 100x100x45 mm to 570x570x290 mm (bigger custom solutions available)
- Controller: Windows-based PC
- Sophisticated visualization and analysis software
- Options: rotary stage, in-situ calibration, safety cabinet, touch sensor, magnetic moment measurement...
- 10 k$ – 100 k$
- Very complete solution; production use; flexible; precise; relatively slow

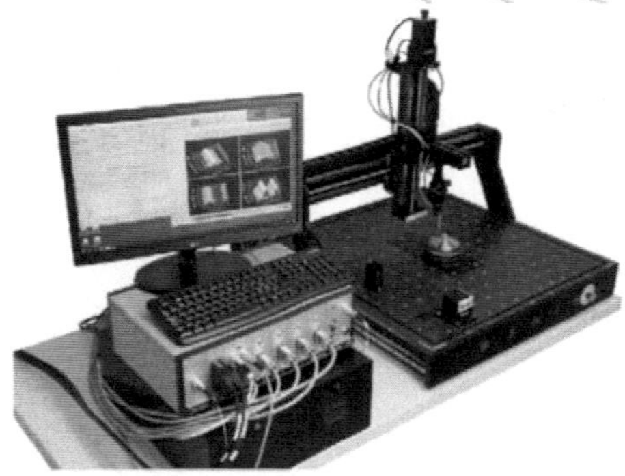

https://www.senis.swiss/mappers

METROlab
Magnetic precision has a name

MAGCAM
advanced
magnet
inspection

Industrial 2D high-res Hall sensor array

Magcam Portal Scanner – Magcam MiniTable

- Probes: compact package: 24 x 24 x 24 mm
  - MiniCube1D: IC array of 128x128 1-axis Hall sensors, 0.1 mm pitch
  - MiniCube3D: reconstruction of all 3 vector components,
- Ranges ±1T, resolution 0.1mT
- Robot: XYZ flat-scan 300x300x300 mm^3 – MiniCube 12.7x12.7 mm^2
- Time for complete scan: < 1 s MiniCube
- Sophisticated visualization and analysis software
- Price ??
- Very complete solution; production use; fast; OK precision (1-axis)

https://www.magcam.com/product/magcam_magnetic_field_scanner

METROlab
Magnetic precision has a name

Industrial 2D medium-res Hall sensor array

HallinSight® by Fraunhofer Institute for Integrated Circuits IIS

- HallinSight®: 2D arrays of 3-axis Hall sensors, 2.5 mm pitch, USB interface, AC or DC mapping
  - 32x32: Al case 310x110x22.5 mm, 40 ms/scan
  - 16x16: Al case 200x60x22.5 mm, 10 ms / scan
  - 32x2: PCB 106x15x2 mm, 4 ms/scan
- Sophisticated visualization software
- Ranges ±100 mT – ±2 T
- 3 k$ – 17 k$
- Precise; fast; nearly complete solution; lab & production use

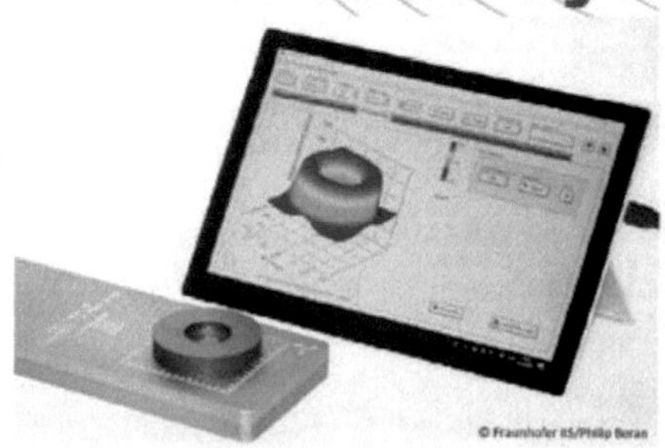

Distributed by Metrolab https://www.metrolab.com/products/hallinsight-hall-magnetic-cameras/

METROLAB
Magnetic precision has a name

matesy
Magnetic Technologies & Systems

Industrial 1D medium-res Hall sensor array

Matesy Hall Line Sensor - MHLS

- Probes : linear array of 32 to 128 3-axis Hall sensors, 2.5 mm pitch
- Compact sensor package: 77.5 – 317.5 mm, USB/RS422 interface
- 2D & 3D visualization software
- Time for complete scan: 200 S/s => 5 ms for 128 3-axis Hall sensors
- Ranges ±100 mT – ±2 T
- 6.9 k€ – 14.9 k€
- Precise; fast; production use; partial solution

https://matesy.de

METROLAB
Magnetic precision has a name

Rotor mappers

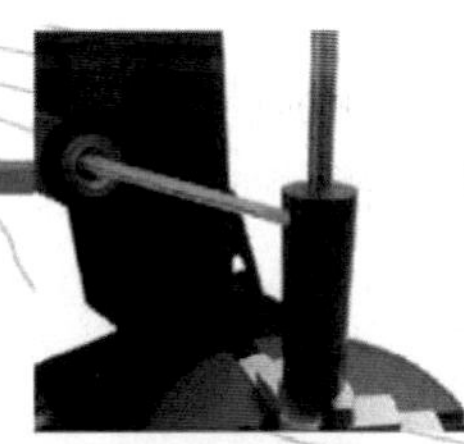

Rotate rotor; probe at fixed radial distance; trigger measurements with angle encoder; scan along rotor length

- Senis 3-axis probe, 55 mm radial x 155 mm Z
- Magcam Portal/Combi Scanner 500 mm radial x 300/450 mm Z
- Matesy MHLS 3-axis Hall probe, 200 mm radial x 350 mm Z
- Do-it-yourself: with Metrolab compact USB probe, HallinSight® 32x2 linear array or other

Specialized solution; compact mechanics; relatively fast

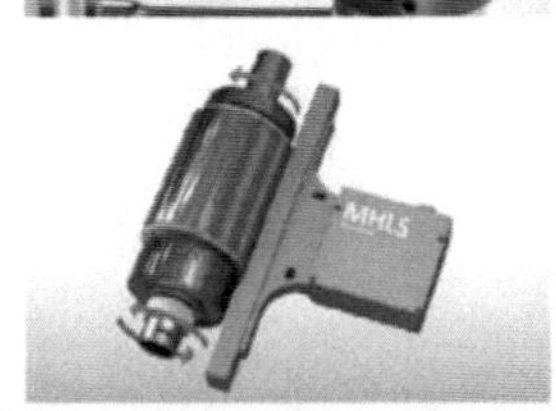

METROLAB
Magnetic precision has a name

Custom medium- to low-res Hall sensor array

Metrolab Hall Magnetic Camera HMC9076

- Standard components: 3-axis Hall sensors, micro-controller, temperature sensor, voltage regulator, firmware/software
- Custom array layout
- Optional temperature regulation for increased precision
- USB power & communication
- ~30 k$
- Precise; fast; customized solution for specialty applications

https://www.metrolab.com/products/hmc9076-hall-magnetic-cameras/

METROLAB
Magnetic precision has a name

Flexible and reconfigurable low-res Hall sensor array

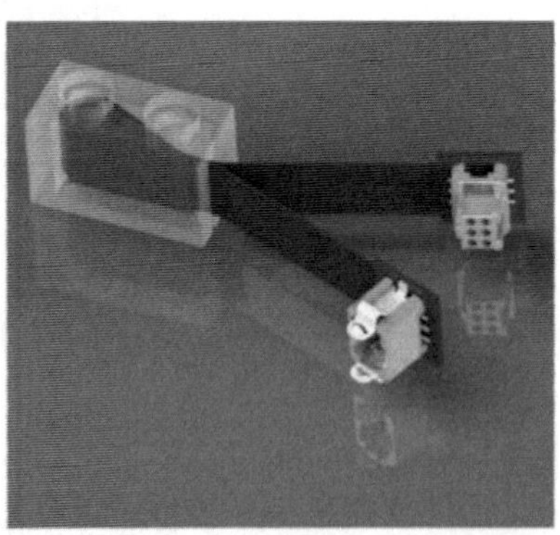

Metrolab MV2Lego (prototype)

- Daisy-chain of standard sensor modules; USB master interface
- Module: 1x2 LEGO brick (8x16x9.6 mm) with 3-axis Hall sensor & microcontroller
- Time for complete scan: as little as 350 μs, regardless of number of modules
- ~4 k$/module
- Precise; very fast; flexible; user-friendly mechanics; relatively low resolution; not yet available

METROlab
Magnetic precision has a name

Summary

	Magnetic Range & Precision	Positioning Range, Precision, ...	Time to Map – AC/DC	Automation, Mfg-Line Integration	Analysis Software	Capital & Labor Costs
DIY U. of Alberta	3	3	1	1	1	5
Senis® XYZ	5	4	1	3	5	1
Magcam MiniCube	3	5	3	3	5	1
Matesy MHLS	5	3	3	3	5	3
Fraunhofer HallinSight®	5	3	4	1 (3)*	4	4
Rotor Mappers	3	3	3	5	5	1**
Metrolab HMC9076	5	3	5	1	1	1
Metrolab MV2Lego	5	1	5	1	3	3

* HallinSight® 32x2 ** Cost of automation

METROlab
Magnetic precision has a name

Thank you!

Luc Van de Perre from Magcam,
Dragana Popovic Renella from Senis, and
Benjamin Wenzel from Matesy for their inputs.

GMW Associates for hosting me on booth #103

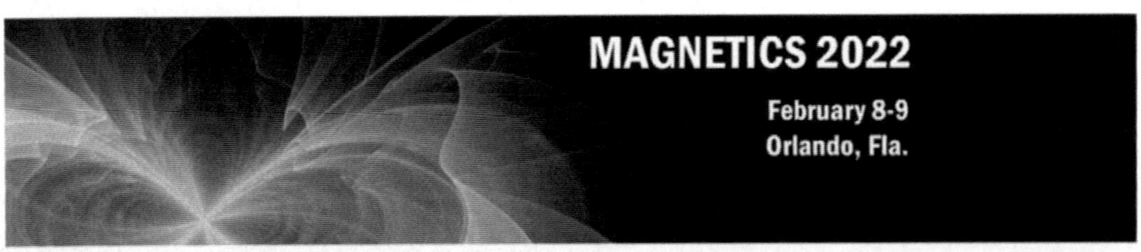

PERFORMANCE COMPARISON OF SURFACE AND FLUX CONCENTRATING PERMANENT MAGNET TRANSVERSE FLUX MOTOR

ALTAIR

Lavanya Vadamodala, Ph.D
Senior Application Engineer

Introduction

- High torque density direct-drive electric machines are gaining popularity especially in in-wheel motors, wind turbines
- Direct drive machines produce high torque at low speed
- Transverse Flux Machine (TFM) is suitable for direct drive applications due to their high torque density
- Claw pole TFM is chosen for this study
- The performance of TFM with Surface Permanent Magnets (SPMs) and Flux concentrating type Permanent Magnets (FCPMs) is being presented in this study
- FCPMs helps in using reluctance torque in addition to magnetic torque

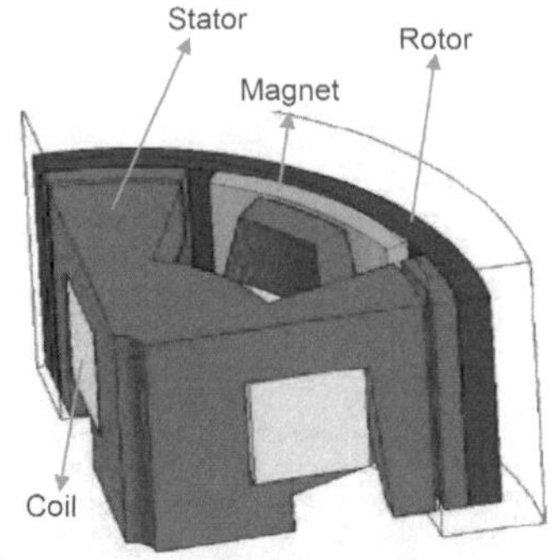

Claw pole TFM

2

ALTAIR

Transverse Flux Motor (TFM)

Flux lines axially across the tooth bottom and radially up the tooth side

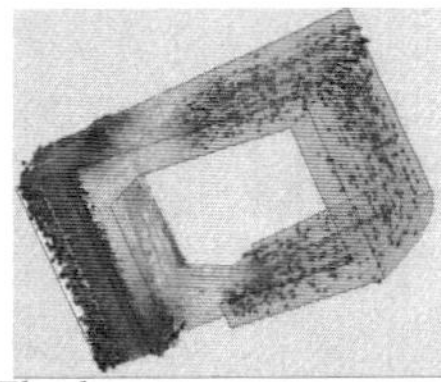

Flux lines transverse across the stator top surface

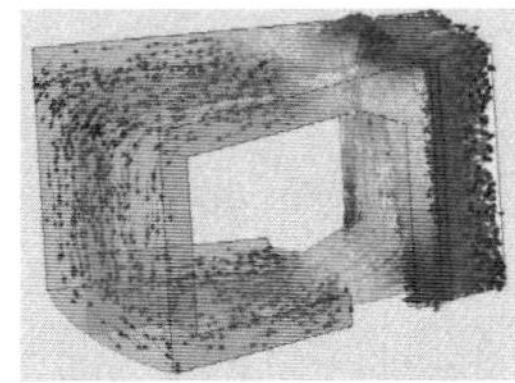

Flux lines radially down tooth side and axially across the tooth bottom

FEATURES

- Each phase is identical and stacked for multiple phases
- Can optimize the design by solving one phase first
- Multi-Phase model can be made by stacking optimized design
- Simple bobbin style winding with high fill and no corners

Advantages

- Low resistance
- High Power Density
- Fewer parts and simple design
- High quality and Reliability

Disadvantages

- Same number of poles and slots
- Winding has high harmonics
- High pole count limits top speed
- Power factor is low

3

ALTAIR

Rotor configurations

- Two rotor configurations are being considered :
  - Surface PMs
  - Embedded PMs: FCPM, IPM
- PMs of alternating polarities are used in the rotor

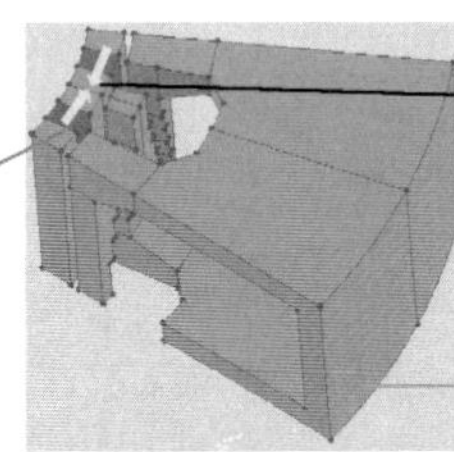

TFM with Flux concentrating PMs (FCPM)

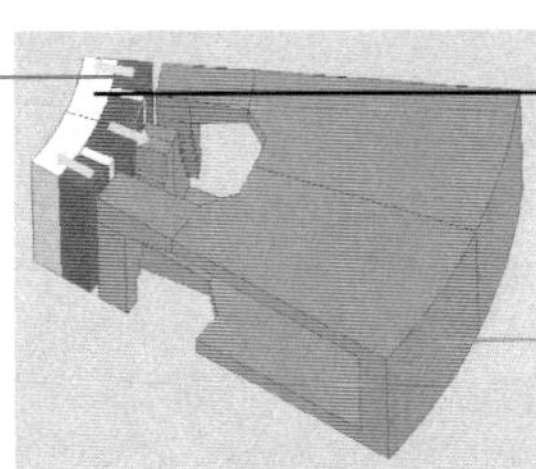

TFM with Surface PMs (SPM)

Magnet orientation

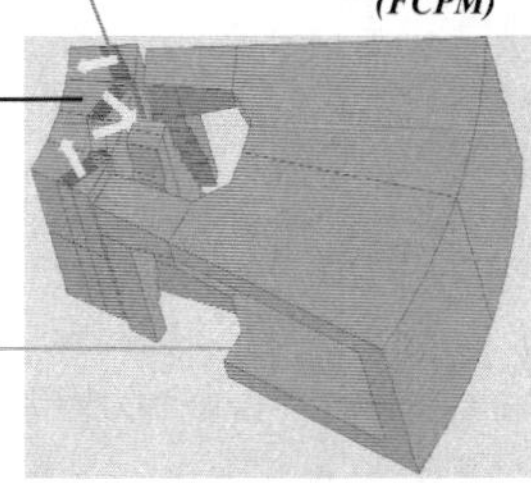

TFM with Interior PMs (IPM)

4

ALTAIR

Machine parameters

Quantity	Value
Stator outer diameter	104 mm
Air gap length	0.8 mm
Air gap diameter	51.2 mm
Stack length for one phase	19 mm
Number of phases	3
Number of turns	50

Part	Material
Stator	ARMCO M22
Rotor	ARMCO M22
Magnet	Bonded NDFEB

ALTAIR

COMPARISON AT NO LOAD CONDITION (1000 RPM)

ALTAIR

Effect of pole count on BEMF

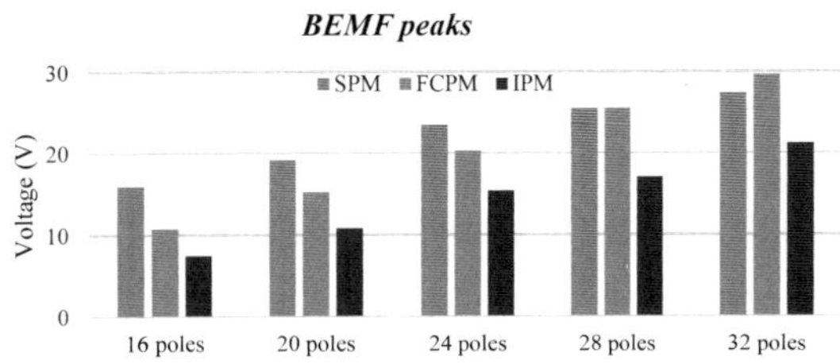

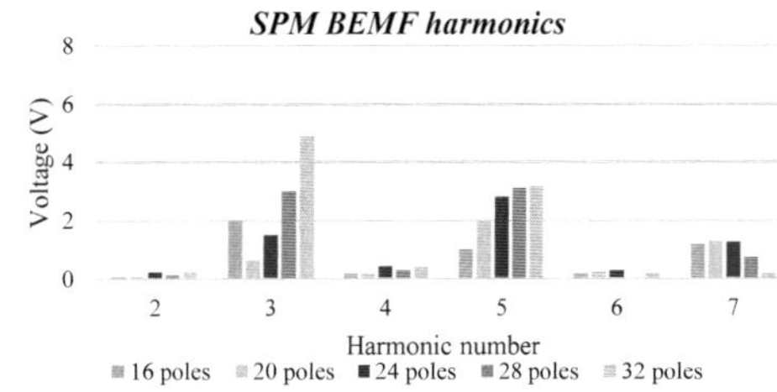

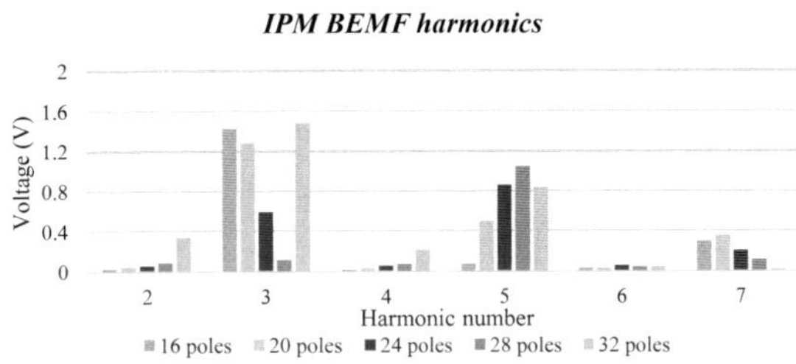

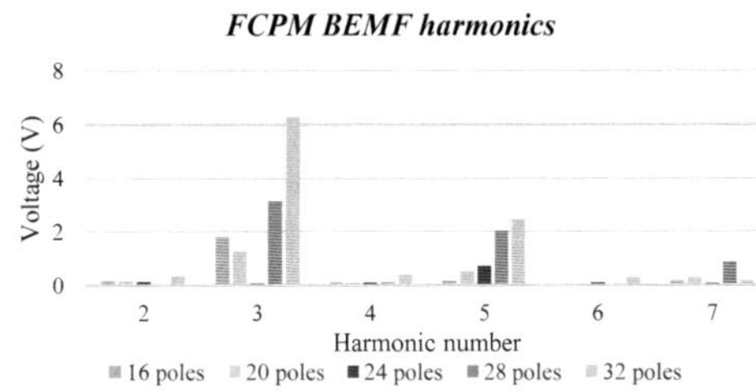

7

ALTAIR

Effect of pole count on Cogging torque

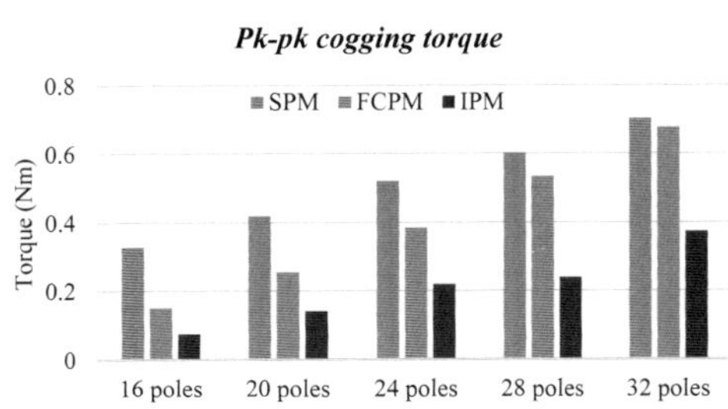

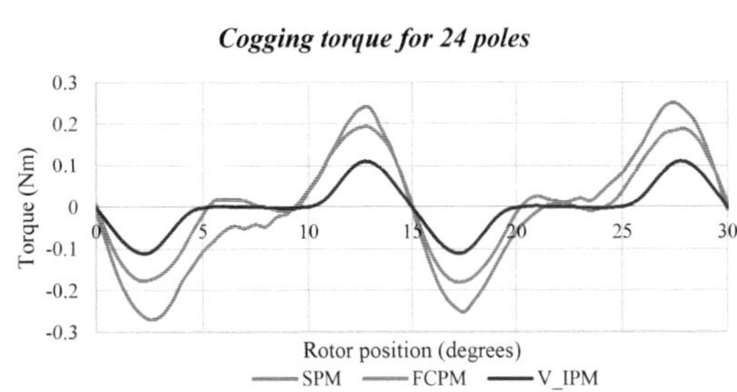

- 24 poles configuration is chosen to compare cogging torque

Quantity	SPM	FCPM	IPM
Pk – pk torque	0.52 Nm	0.38 Nm	0.219 Nm

8

ALTAIR

Comparison of Airgap flux density and BEMF

- 24 poles configuration is chosen to compare airgap flux density and BEMF

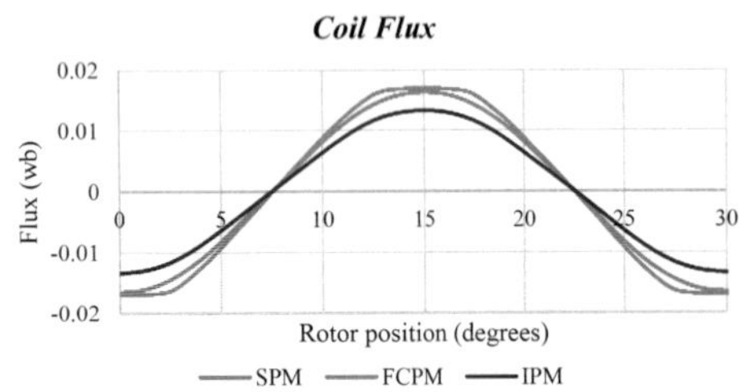

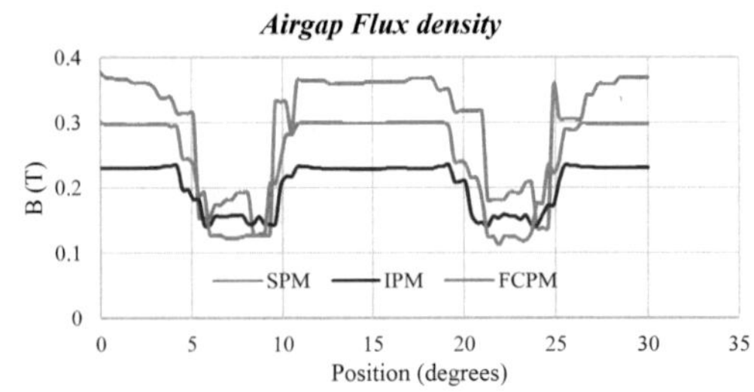

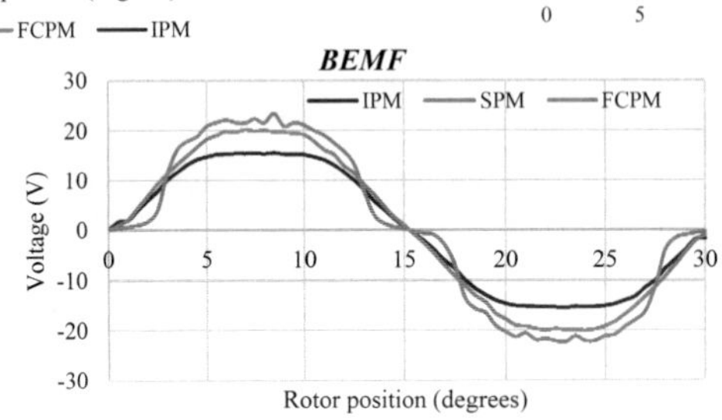

9

ALTAIR

Effect of stator pole skew

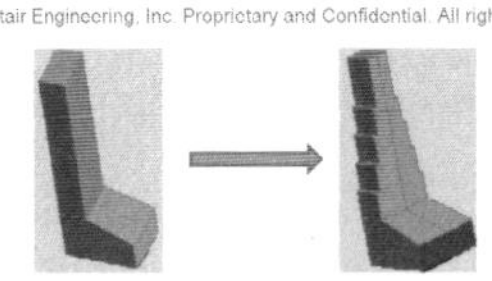

- 24 poles configuration is chosen to compare effect of pole skew
- Stator pole is skewed to an angle of 2 degrees

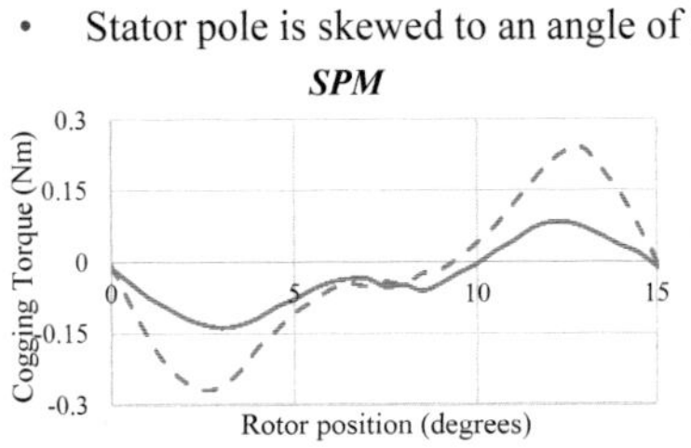

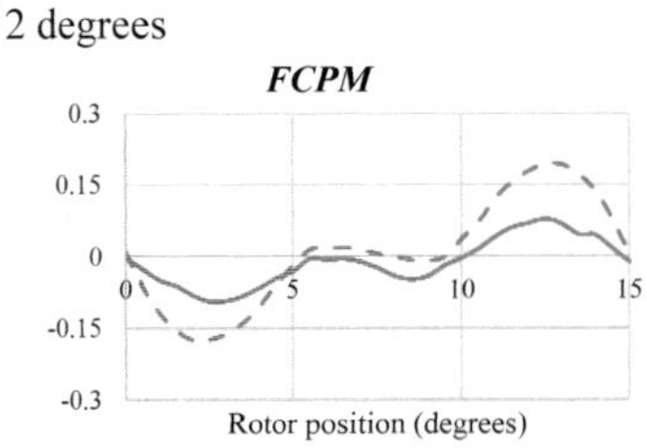

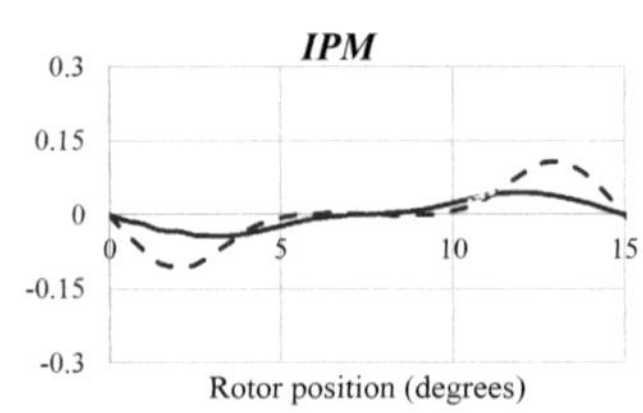

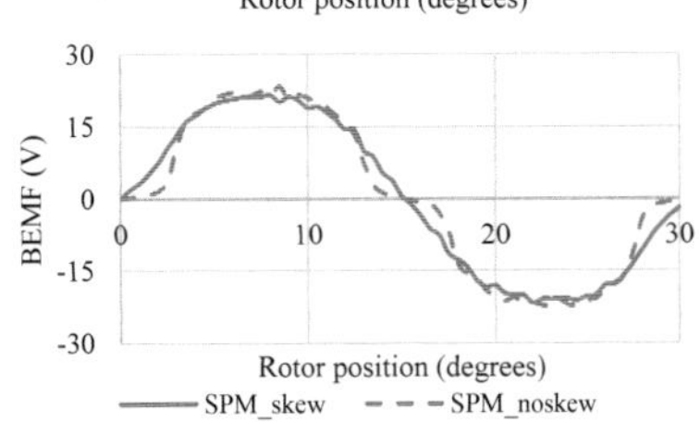

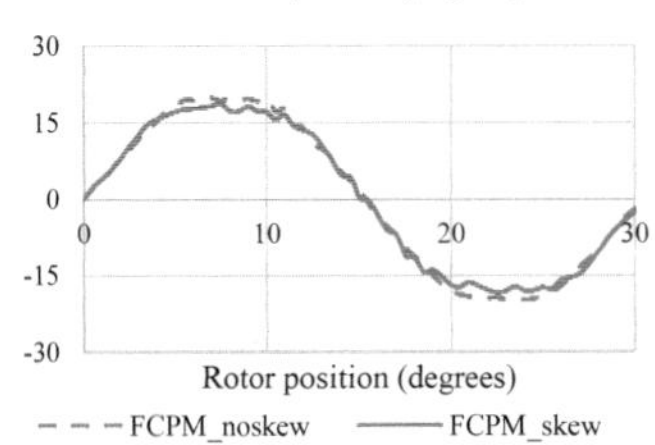

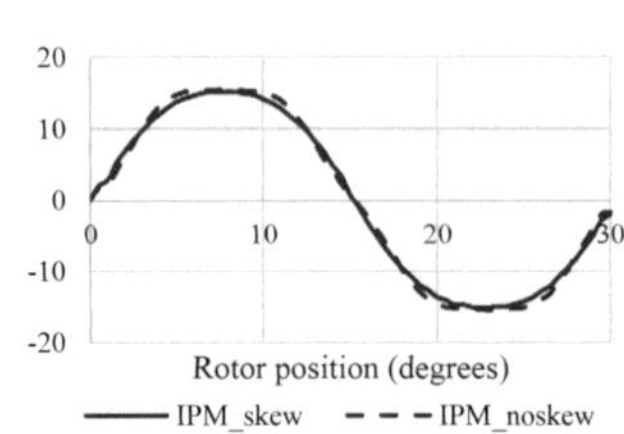

10

ALTAIR

COMPARISON AT LOADED CONDITION

ALTAIR

Performance under loaded condition for Single phase

- Loaded condition: 1000 rpm, 20 A peak input current

Quantity	SPM	FCPM	IPM
Weight of stator (Kg)	0.337	0.337	0.337
Weight of rotor (Kg)	0.0817	0.043	0.0794
Weight of magnets (Kg)	0.023	0.023	0.024
Weight of copper (Kg)	0.0138	0.0138	0.0138
Peak torque (Nm)	1.49	1.254	1.052

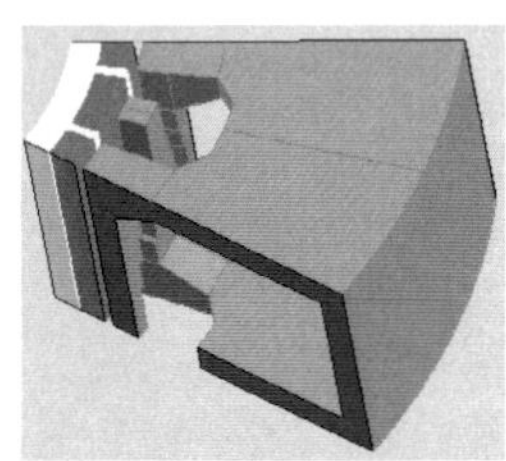

Single phase section of TFM

Single Phase Torque

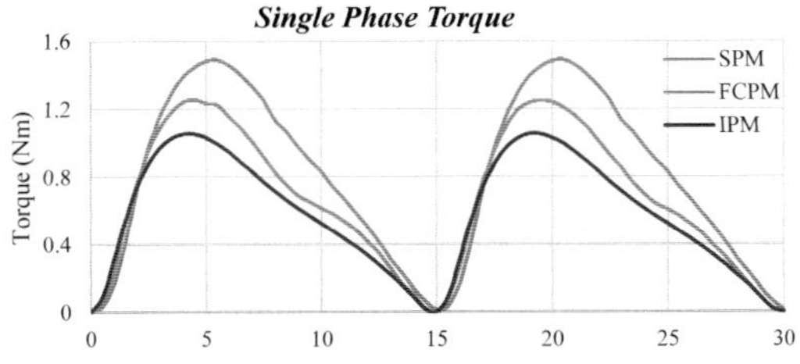

Phase voltage

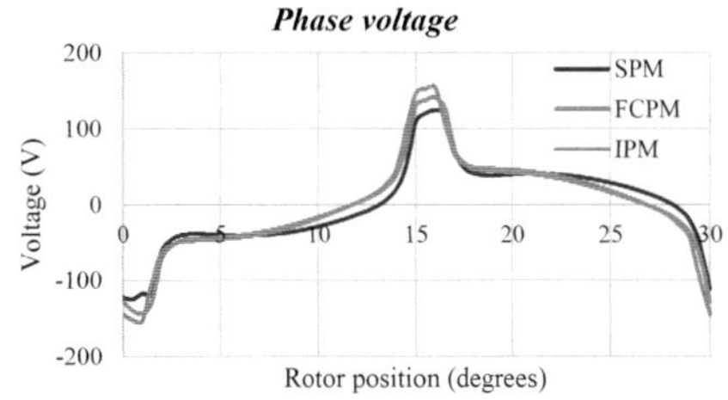

12

ALTAIR

Performance of TFM with Three phases

- Loaded condition: 1000 rpm, 20 A peak input current

Quantity	SPM	FCPM	IPM
Avg. Torque (Nm)	2.41	1.997	1.726
Torque ripple %	18.4	22	24
Iron losses (W)	11.18	11.33	10.55
Copper losses (W)	982.5	982.5	982.5
Efficiency (%)	19.35	16.44	14.49
Torque density (Nm/Kg)	1.82	1.51	1.43

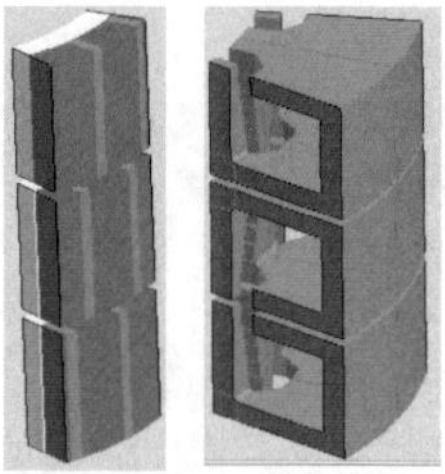

Three phase section of TFM

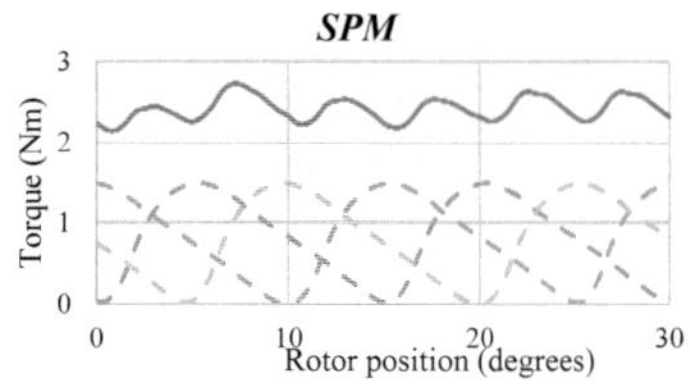

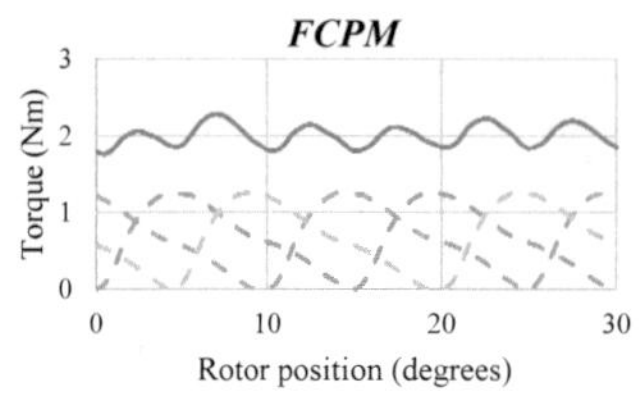

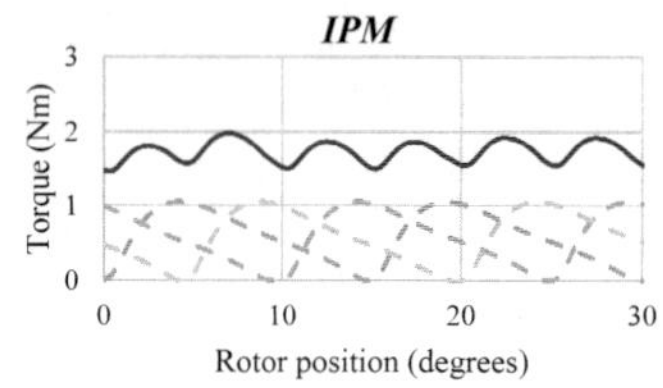

13

ALTAIR

CONCLUSION

ALTAIR

Conclusion

- The complete analysis is performed on a 24 pole TFM with surface and interior PMs
- Claw pole TFM with SPM, FCPM, and IPM rotor configurations are studied
- SPM have high BEMF peaks and prominent odd harmonics compared to FCPM and IPM configurations
- IPM configuration has less peak to peak cogging torque compared to FCPM, SPM configurations
- Stator pole skew reduces the peak-to-peak cogging torque in Claw pole TFM
- In claw pole TFM, FCPM is a better configuration compared to IPM
- By keeping the volume of the machine constant, and optimizing magnet mass, airgap diameter helps in increasing the torque density of FCPM and IPM configurations

Shape optimization

15

ALTAIR

THANK YOU

altair.com

#ONLYFORWARD

ALTAIR

Selecting PM Motor Topologies for Frameless Motor Applications

Presented by: David Coulson
Date: February 8~9, 2022

PM Motor Topologies and Frameless Motors

There are many benefits to integrating a motor parts set into a higher-level assembly. Be sure to understand the different motor topologies available to further improve the system.

Permanent Magnet Motors Family Tree

Family Tree | Frameless Motors | PM Motor Comparison | Motor Technology Selection | Application Examples

Typical / Traditional Motor Family Tree

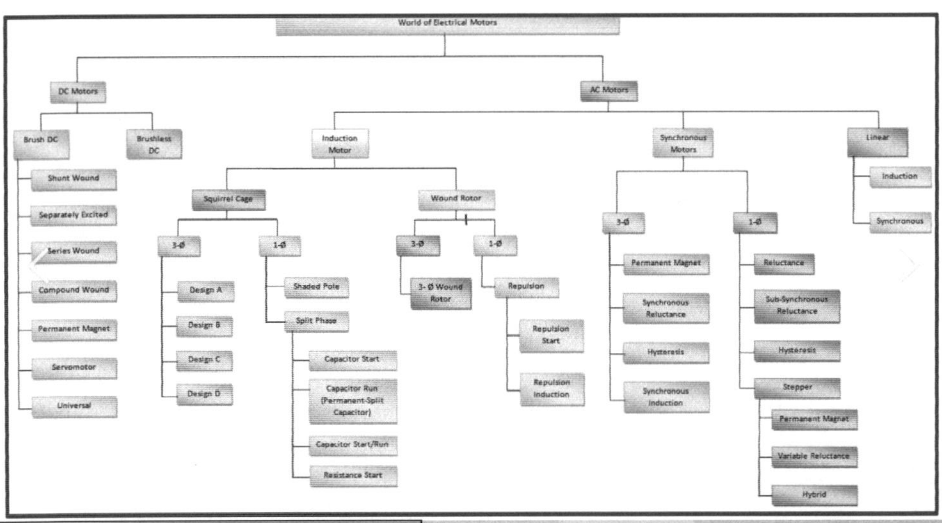

Family Tree | Frameless Motors | PM Motor Comparison | Motor Technology Selection | Application Examples

Typical / Traditional Motor Family Tree

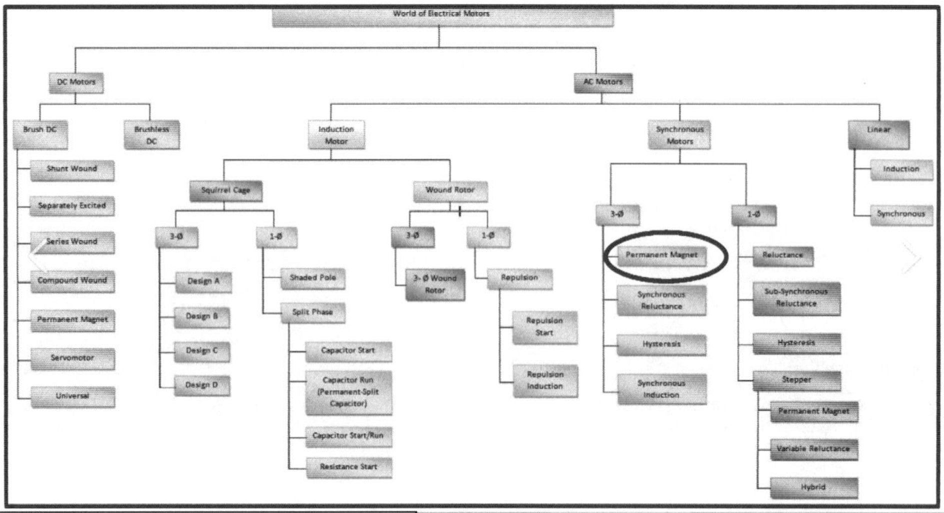

Family Tree | Frameless Motors | PM Motor Comparison | Motor Technology Selection | Application Examples

Permanent Magnet Motors – Direction of Flux

Permanent Magnet Motors

Radial Flux | Axial Flux | Transverse Flux

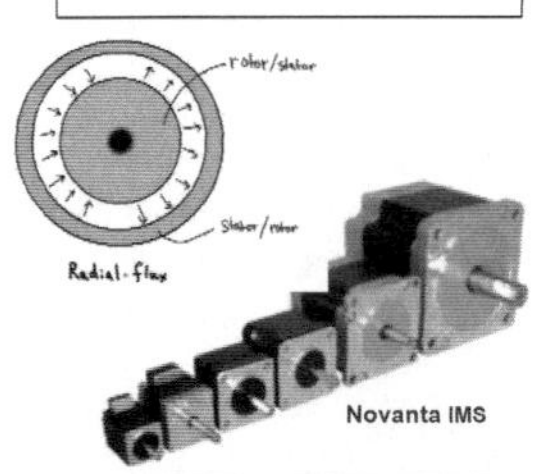

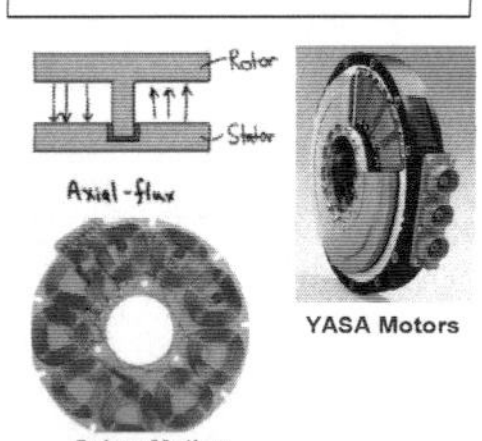

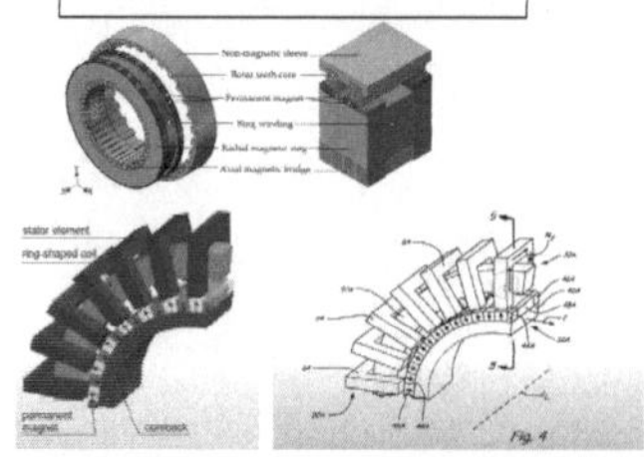

Family Tree | Frameless Motors | PM Motor Comparison | Motor Technology Selection | Application Examples

Permanent Magnet Motors

Permanent Magnet Motors

Radial Flux

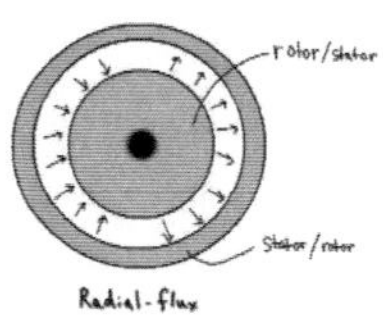

- Radial Flux Motors – the workhorse for frameless applications.
- Axial Flux and Transverse Flux Motors - gaining popularity, torque dense. Each have their own subset of motor topologies.
- Celera Motion has a focused product line for Axial Flux motors (ARC).
- Focus for this presentation – Topologies under the Radial Flux Motor Umbrella.

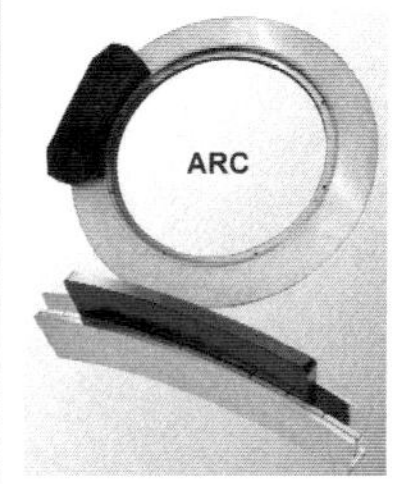

Family Tree | Frameless Motors | PM Motor Comparison | Motor Technology Selection | Application Examples

Focus on AC for Comparison – all sine wave commutated

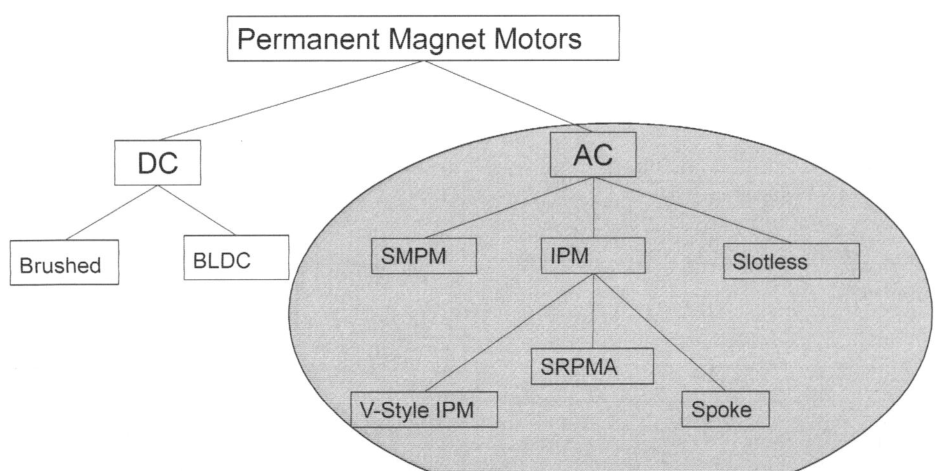

Family Tree | Frameless Motors | PM Motor Comparison | Motor Technology Selection | Application Examples

Permanent Magnet AC motors – cross sections, different rotors and stators

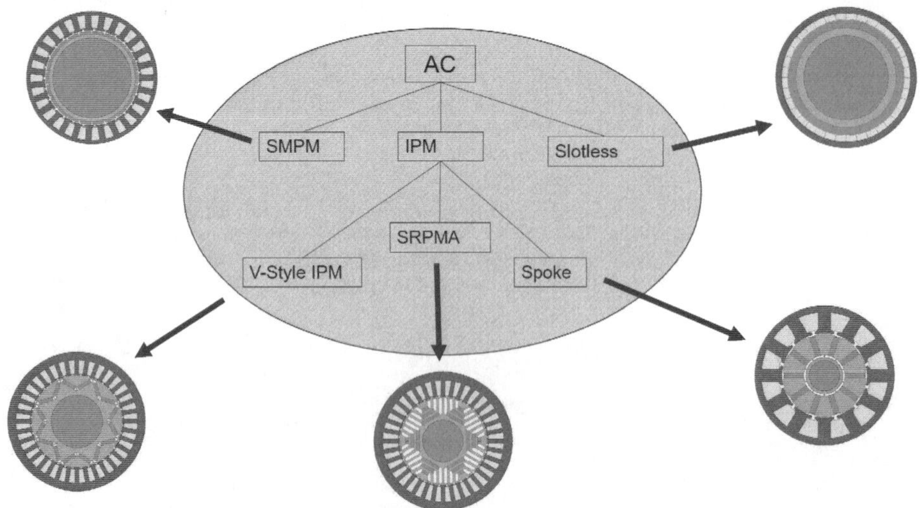

Permanent Magnet AC motors

SMPM – Surface mount PM rotor

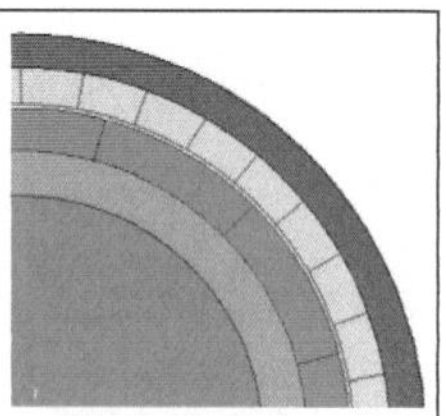

Slotless – Stator has no teeth to differentiate slots

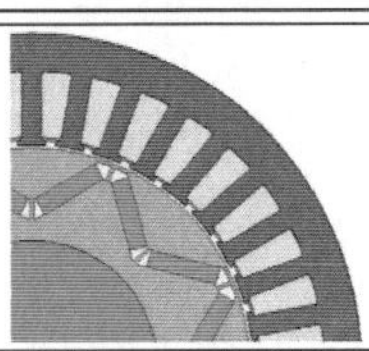

IPM-V – Interior permanent magnet motor

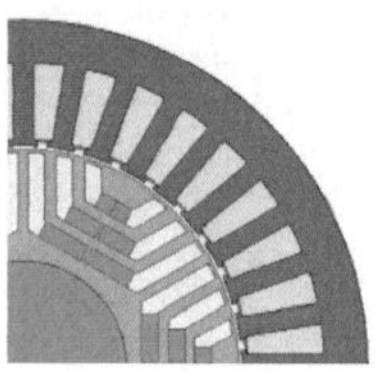

SRPMA – Synchronous Reluctance PM Assist, layers of magnets

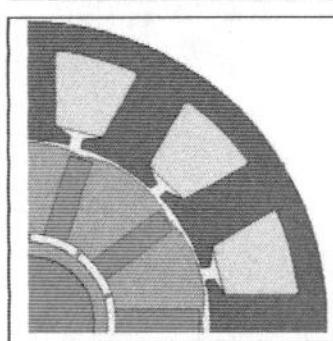

Spoke IPM – IPM with steel pole pieces

Frameless Motors

Family Tree | **Frameless Motors** | PM Motor Comparison | Motor Technology Selection | Application Examples

What is a Frameless Motor?

- Parts set - 2 discrete components - rotor and stator.
- Stator – laminations, insulation, and copper
- Rotor – Backiron/rotor laminations and permanent magnets

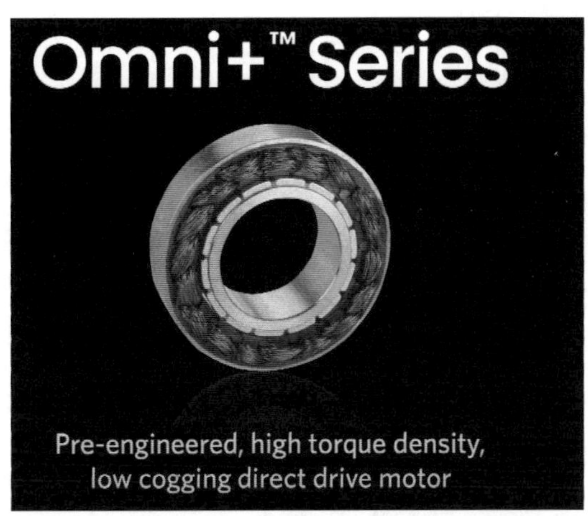

Family Tree | **Frameless Motors** | PM Motor Comparison | Motor Technology Selection | Application Examples

Benefits of Frameless Motor Strategy

- Higher level integration of the motor into the system results in:
  - **Reduced envelope** – torque density and volume constraints may be critical
  - **Reduced components** – leads to lower profile and lower weight – reduced set of bearings and end bells, reduced coupling(s). Weight reduction. Audible noise reduction.
  - **Decreased losses** due to reduced mechanical components (↑ Efficiency)
  - **Dynamic response** – Motor may be directly driving load. Tighter machine performance with reduced mechanical transmissions (Couplings, Gearbox, Pulley, Belts, etc). Stiffer system.

Examples of Frameless Motor Implementation

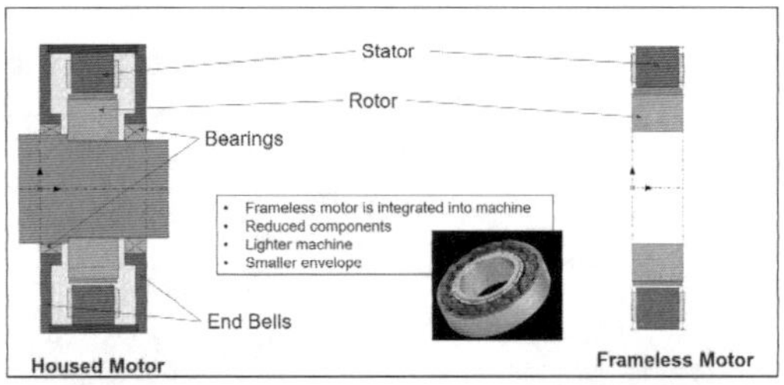

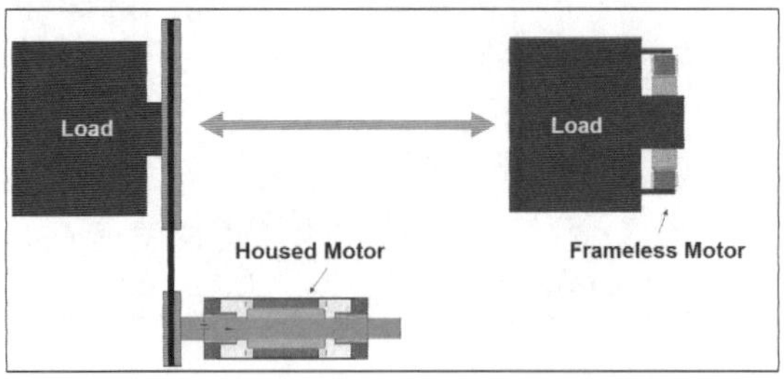

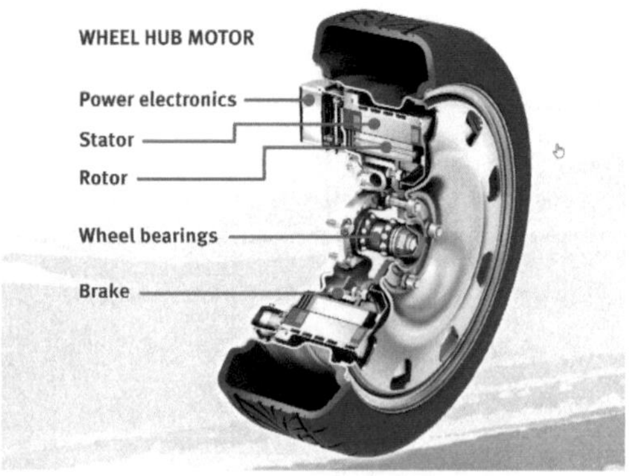

Schaeffler Wheel Hub Assembly

Robot Joint Frameless Motor Integration

Dual encoder robot joint design example

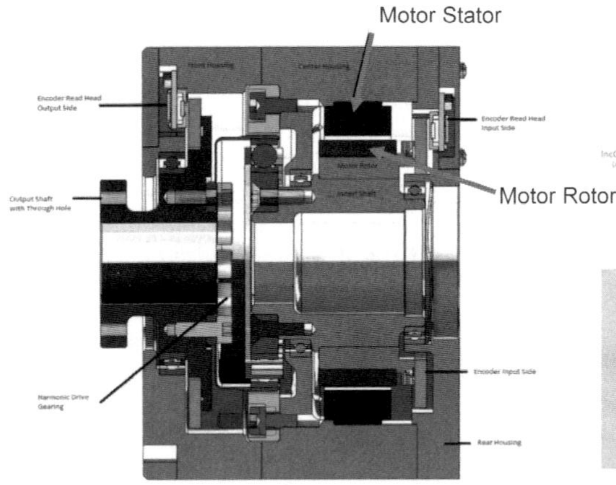

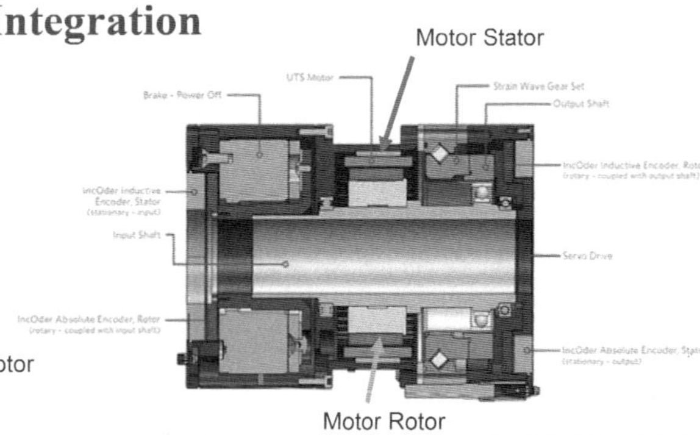

Family Tree | **Frameless Motors** | PM Motor Comparison | Motor Technology Selection | Application Examples

Permanent Magnet Motor Comparison

Family Tree | Frameless Motors | **PM Motor Comparison** | Motor Technology Selection | Application Examples

Permanent Magnet Motor Comparison

- What makes these motors different?
- What are the strengths & weakness of each motor topology?
- What criteria are important relative to frameless motor integration?
  - Torque Density, Peak Torque
  - Motor Constant (Km) – parameter used to compare different motors – ratio of torque to square root watts.
  - Smoothness (cogging and torque ripple)
  - Maximum speed
  - Geometry – Axial Length, Through Bore

Comparison Constraints

- OD = 100 mm
- Stack length = 50 mm
- Bus Voltage = 48 Vdc
- Drive Max Current = 49 Arms
- Max current density = 45 CirMil/A (winding limited)

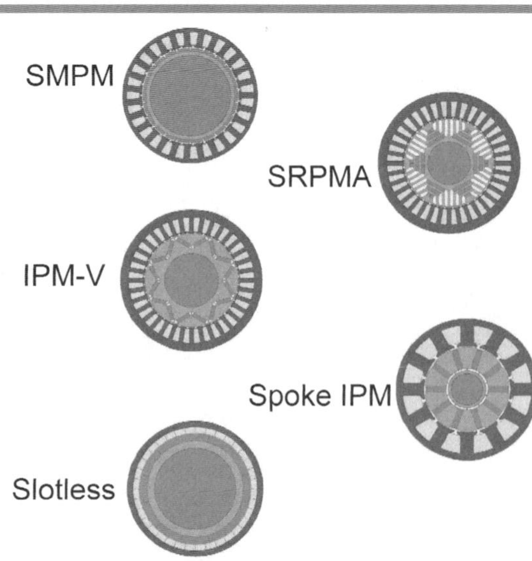

Speed Torque Curve

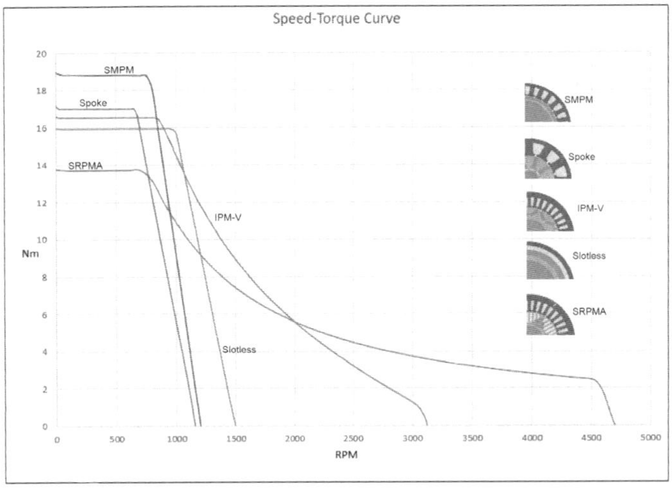

Vbus = 48 Vdc
Drive Current Max = 49 Arms

Family Tree | Frameless Motors | **PM Motor Comparison** | Motor Technology Selection | Application Examples

SMPM Strengths and Weaknesses

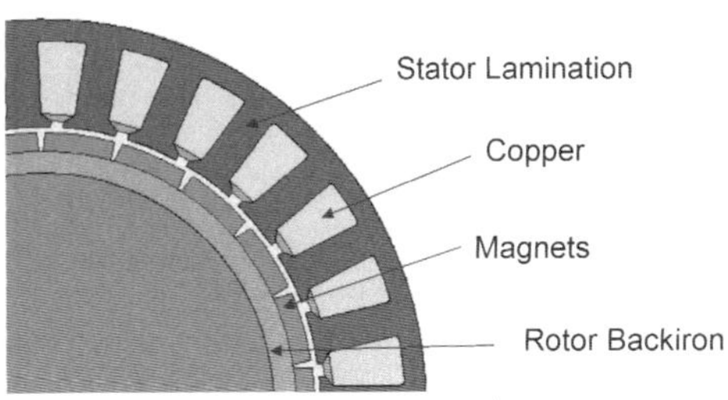

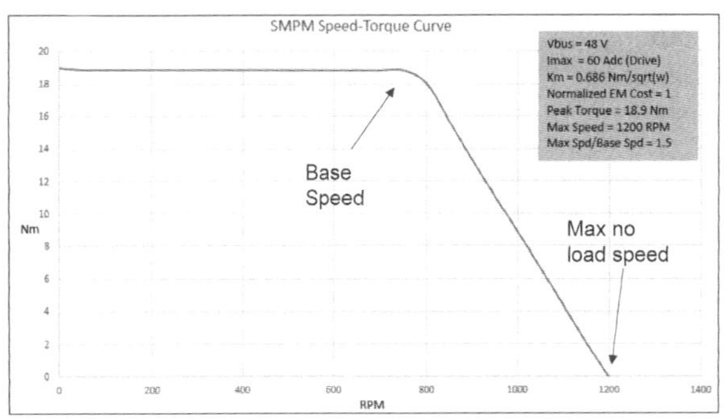

- Peak Torque, 18.9 Nm / Torque Density
- EM Cost – normalized comparison – copper, magnets, steel
- Low Cogging - by design optimization

- Max Speed / Base Speed ratio
- Shock and Vibe – Additional magnet retention may be required

Family Tree | Frameless Motors | **PM Motor Comparison** | Motor Technology Selection | Application Examples

Spoke IPM Strengths and Weaknesses

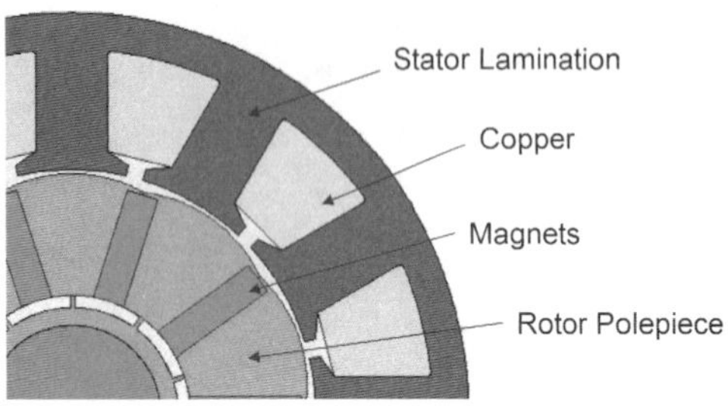

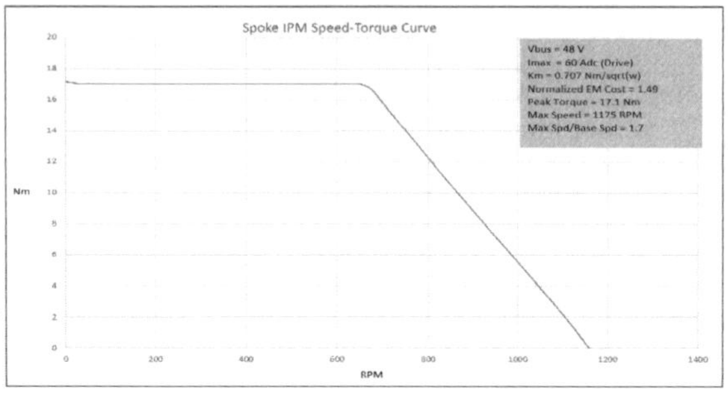

- Shock and Vibe (IPM)
- Good candidate for Ferrite Magnet

- Radial cross section
- Manufacturing - magnet insertion and magnetization
- Rotor Leakage and mechanical structure

IPM-V Strengths and Weaknesses

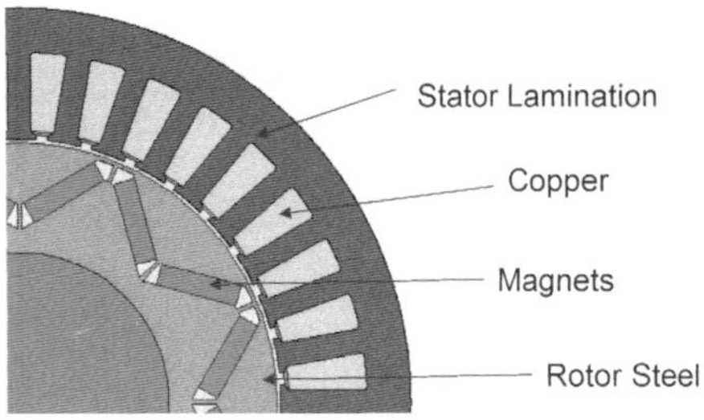

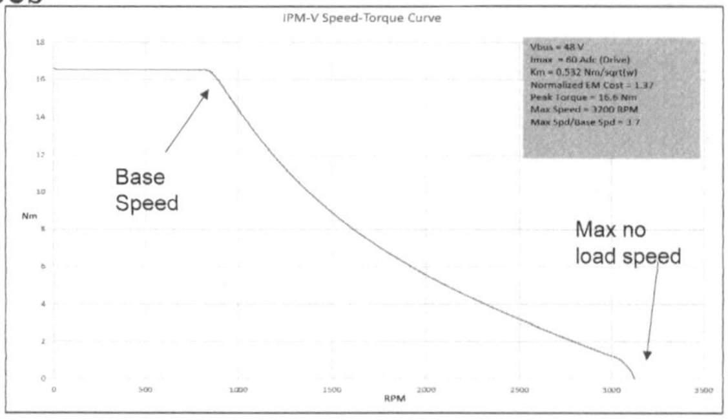

- Good Max Speed/Base Speed
- Good compromise for many items – Peak torque/Tq Dense/EM Cost
- Shock and Vibe (IPM)

- Axial Length – winding type (distributed)
- Smoothness – mitigate with skewing and fine turning of EM design.

Slotless Strengths and Weaknesses

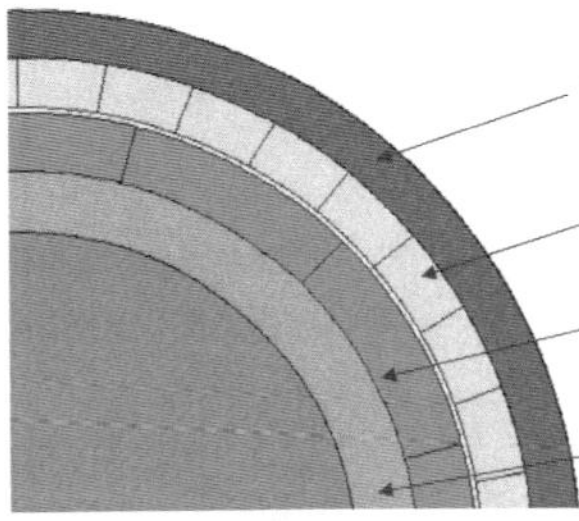

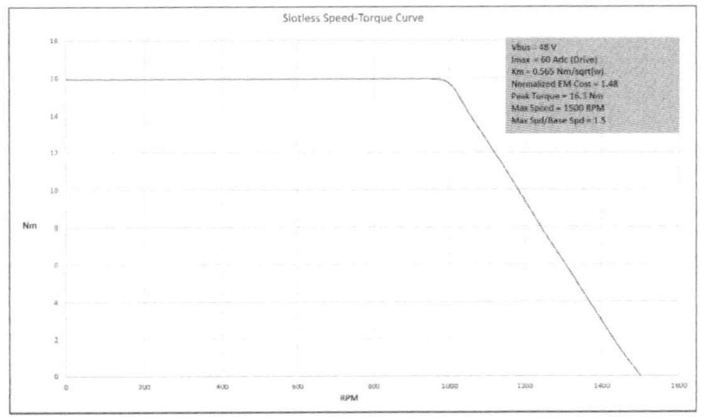

- Smoothness – zero cogging – smoothest operator
- Torque Density, radial cross section

- EM cost – driven by magnet material
- Thermal

Family Tree | Frameless Motors | **PM Motor Comparison** | Motor Technology Selection | Application Examples

SRPMA Strengths and Weaknesses

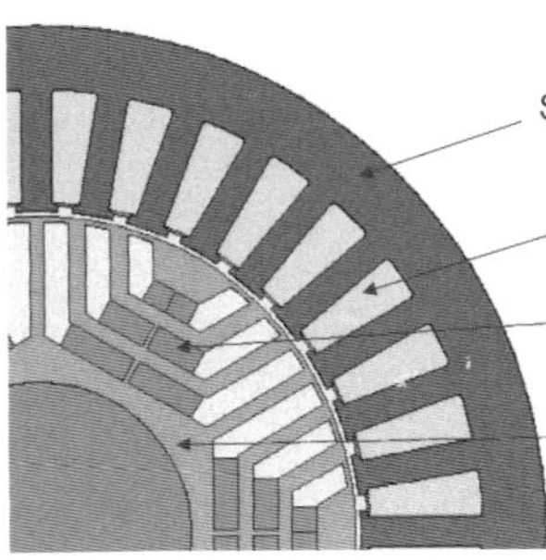

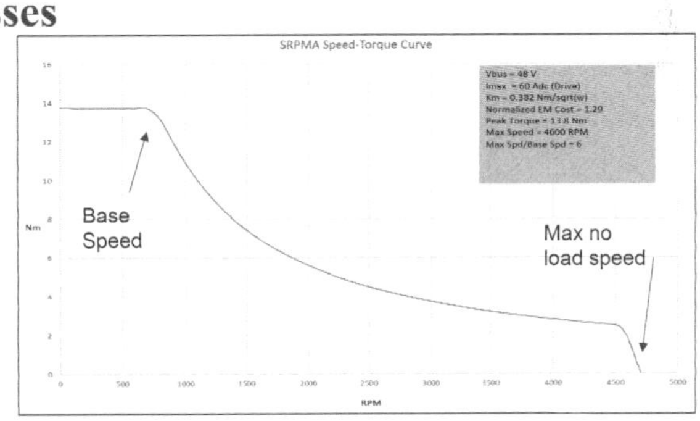

- Best Max speed – Base speed rating
- Good Candidate for Ferrite Magnet Material substitution

- Smoothness – Torque Ripple
- Low end torque / torque density

Family Tree | Frameless Motors | **PM Motor Comparison** | Motor Technology Selection | Application Examples

PM Motor Technology Comparative Summary

		SMPM	Slotless	Spoke	IPM-V	SRPMA
1	Peak Torque	1	2			5
2	Torque Density	1	2			5
3	Rad Cross Section	1	1	5		
5	Axial Length	1		1		
6	Max Speed				2	1
7	Smoothness	2	1			
8	EM Material Cost	1			2	
9	Km	2		1		
10	Best Ferrite Alternative			1		1
11	Shock and Vibe			2	1	1
12	Control Technology					

Speed Torque Curve – Max Torque

Vbus = 48 Vdc
Drive Current Max = 49Arms

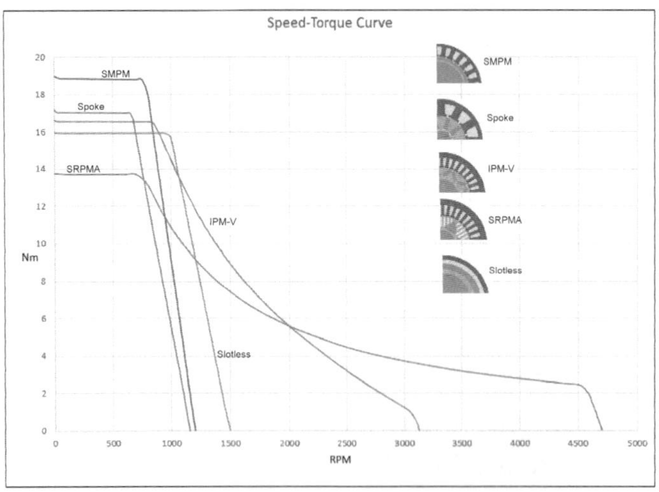

Max torque – SMPM

Smoothness – Slotless

IPM V – best compromise

Ferrite Replacement – Spoke and SRPMA

Max Speed - SRPMA

Motor Technology Selection

Considerations for Frameless Motor Strategy

- How does this impact my machine value to me or my customer? Identify the benefit.
  - Space/envelope, lower maintenance, performance, energy efficiency, speed/productivity?

- Engineering resources – Do I have the technical resources to design the frameless motor into my system?

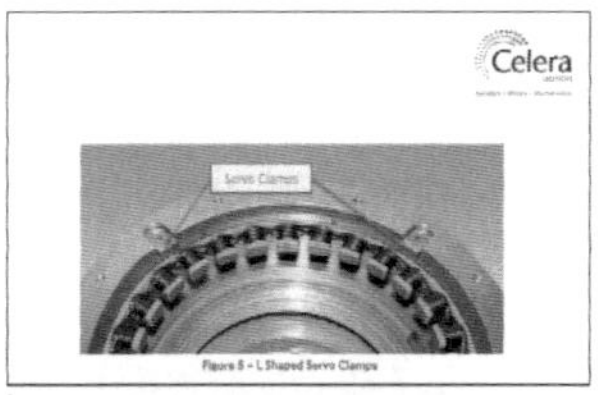

- Mounting and assembly – integration of a parts set during build is critical. Find a supply partner that will help guide you through these steps.

Considerations for PM Motor Technology

1. Performance
   Torque, Speed, max speed, duty cycle, max sp/base speed
2. Dynamics
   Acc time, Dec time, settling time, torque ripple, smoothness/cogging
3. System/Drive
   Bus Voltage, available drive current, control capability of drive.
4. Environmental
   Max temp, ambient temp, ingress protection, shock and vibe, vacuum
5. Physical
   Geometry, OD, Axial Length, weight, Radial cross section, Through bore

Understand your operating /corner points

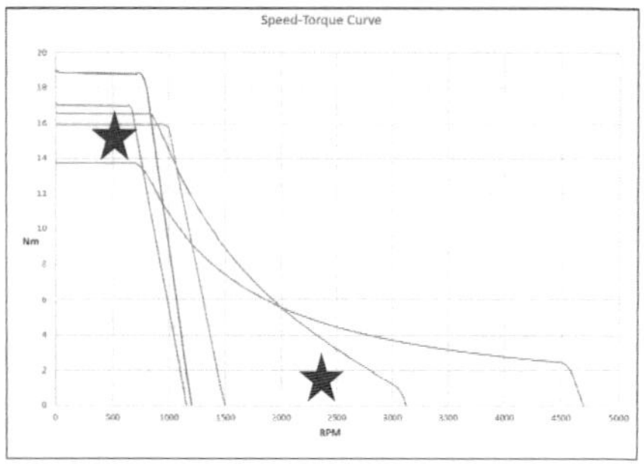

Understand critical requirements

Tradeoffs: What is more important?

Know and understand the system architecture and budgets for current and power. Drive capability

In the end ask a PM motor pro to help with your selection – the more you understand about your requirements, the better fit motor you will get for your system.

Family Tree | Frameless Motors | PM Motor Comparison | **Motor Technology Selection** | Application Examples

Application Examples

Family Tree | Frameless Motors | PM Motor Comparison | Motor Technology Selection | **Application Examples**

Example #1
Surgical Robotic Joint / End Effector

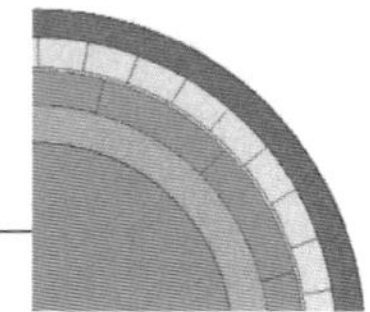

Critical Requirements
1. Performance – Zero speed holding torque.
2. Dynamics – smoothness/ low torque ripple, low cogging, short settling time, holding torque stability.
3. Physical –Large rotor through bore

PM Motor Selection

Direct drive Slotless Motor – smooth, lowest torque ripple, stable holding torque, light weight

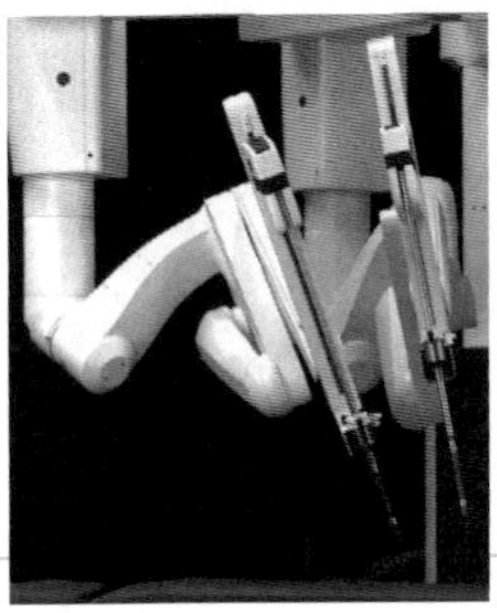

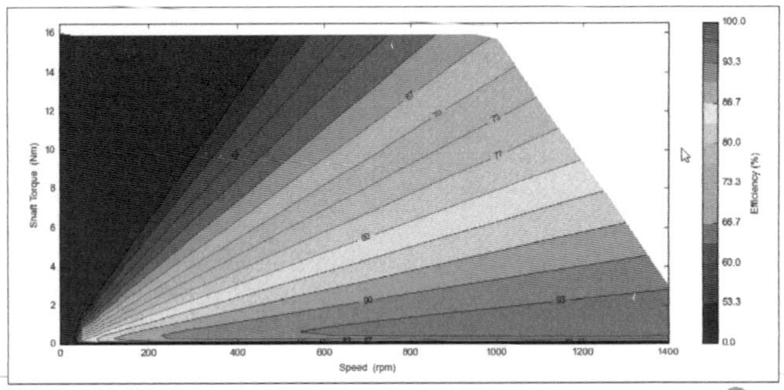

Example #2
Traction Motor with Gearbox / Material Handling Vehicle

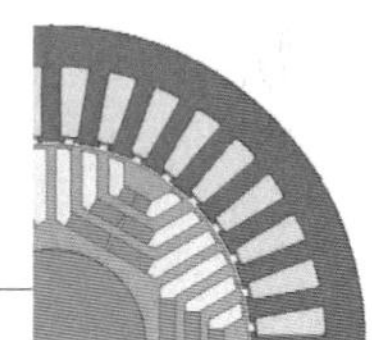

Critical Requirements
1. Performance – high max speed/ base speed ratio, efficiency
2. Dynamics – Acceleration torque
3. Environmental – Shock and Vibe

PM Motor Selection

SRPMA Motor – High speed, efficiency is good for battery life, acceptable peak torques, Good for Shock and Vibe

Electric Pallet Jack

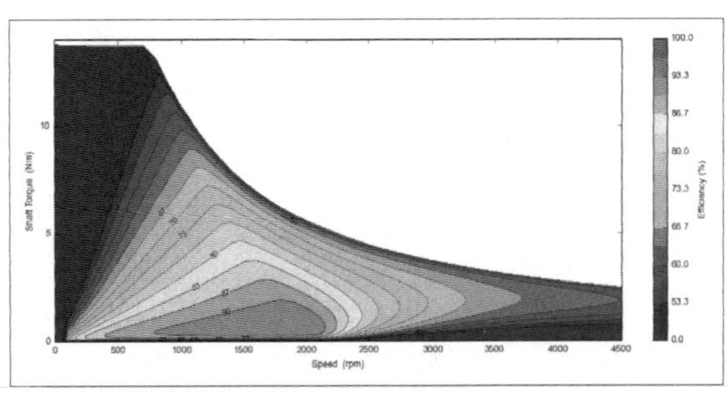

Example #3
Robotic Joint with Harmonic Gearing

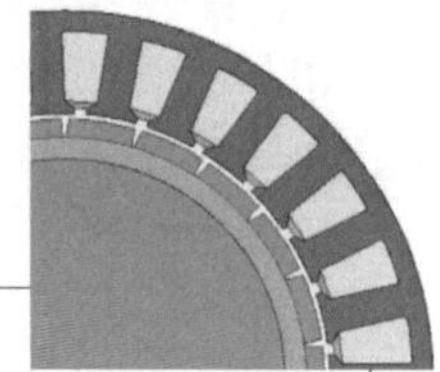

Critical Requirements

1. Max torque in smallest package-torque dense
2. Dynamics – smoothness is important, Acceleration torque
3. Physical – axial length

↔

PM Motor Selection

SMPM – torque dense & low cogging.

Novanta

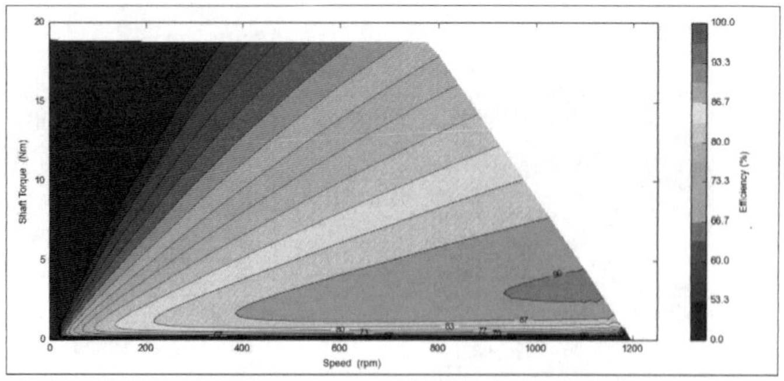

PM Motor Topologies and Frameless Motors

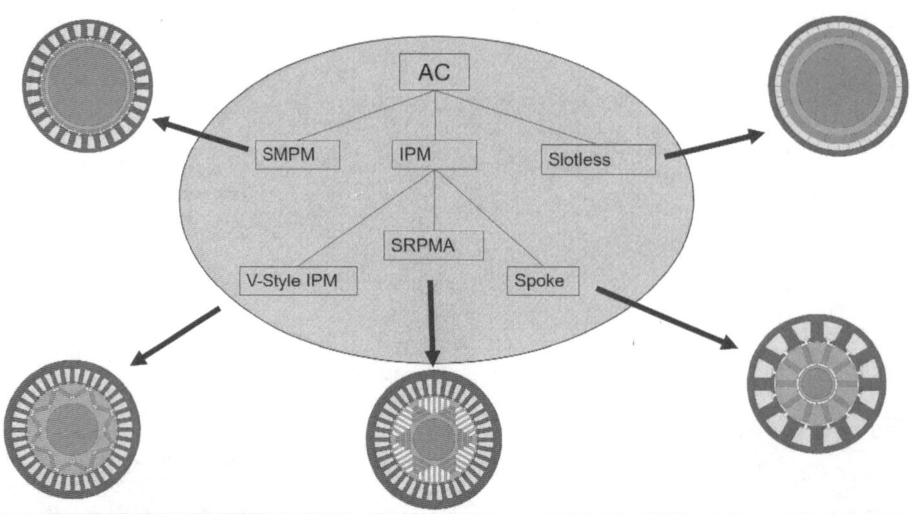

Family Tree | Frameless Motors | PM Motor Comparison | Motor Technology Selection | Application Examples

Thank You For Your Attention!

The Rule of the Inflection Point That Can Improve the Performance of Magnetic Devices

Min Zou

Lab Magnetics, A Quadrant Company

February 9th, 2022

Background

Coulomb's law

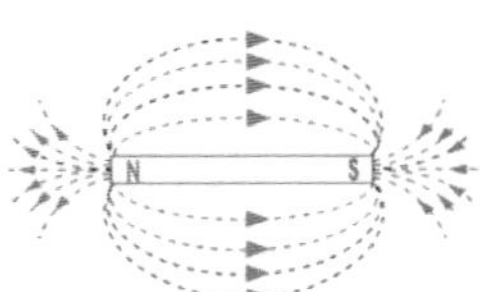

A Magnet has north and south poles.

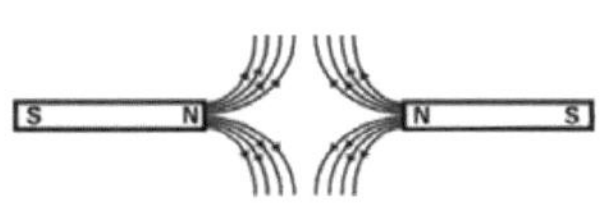

Like poles repel each other

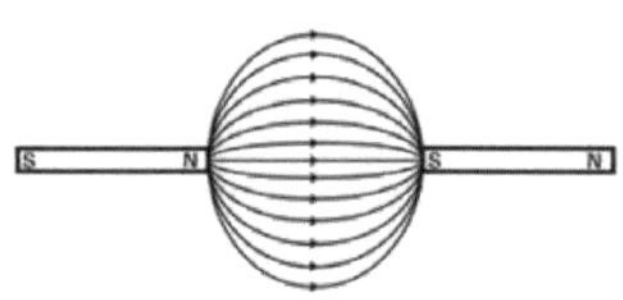

Unlike poles attract each other

Source: National Energy Education Development Project (public domain)

Like Poles Attraction

- *George Mizzell* (2007 and 2019):
  Two NdFeB magnets' like poles attract each other at the center for a pair with different dimensions
- *Y. Zhang and Y. Leng* (2019):
  For a pair of interacting permanent magnets with large different sizes, attraction appears between like poles and repulsion appears between unlike poles

"Can 2 north poles stick together?" https://youtu.be/SSWr0FaNFMU, 2007
"Repelling Magnets - Can 2 South Poles stick together?" https://youtu.be/foOmZcl-MsA, 2019
"Special behaviors of two interacting permanent magnets with large different sizes", 2019, DOI 10.3233/JAE-190057

Force Between Like Poles

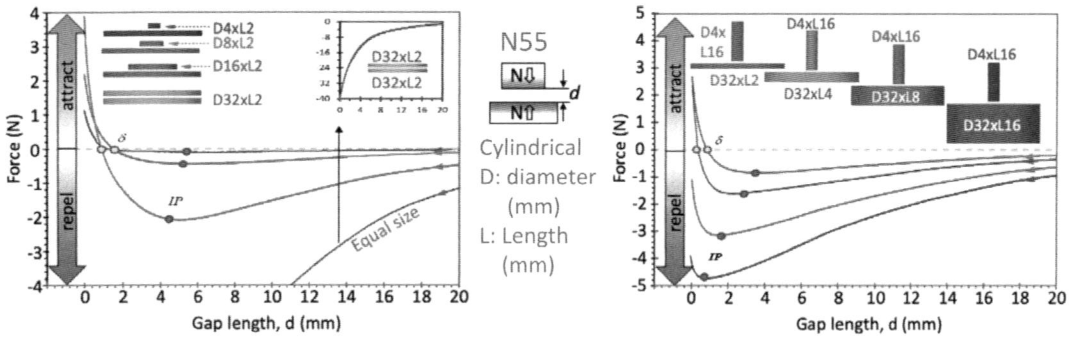

Sci Rep **11,** 12555 (2021)

- Equal sized magnets: Repulsive force only
- Unequal sized magnets:
  - Like-poles attraction when d < δ
  - Inflection point (IP) in every curve

Green Film Observation – Localized Demagnetization

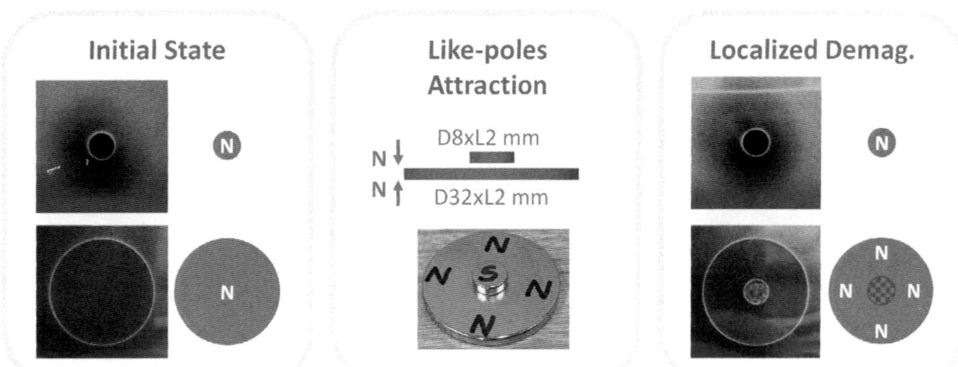

Sci Rep **11,** 12555 (2021)

✓ NO violation of Coulomb's law

✓ One magnet reverses the polarity of the other magnet

Mechanism of Localized Demagnetization

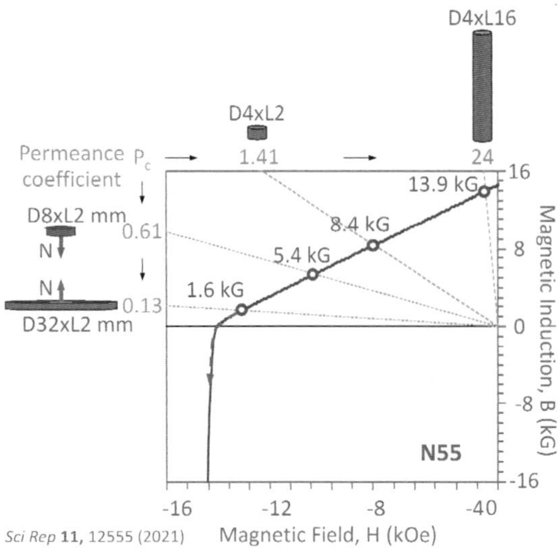

Sci Rep **11,** 12555 (2021)

- Higher L/D → Higher P_c → Higher B_d → lower $|H_d|$
  - Stronger surface magnetic field
  - Stronger resistance to demagnetization
- Lower L/D → Lower P_c → Lower B_d → Higher $|H_d|$
  - Weaker surface magnetic field
  - Weaker resistance to demagnetization

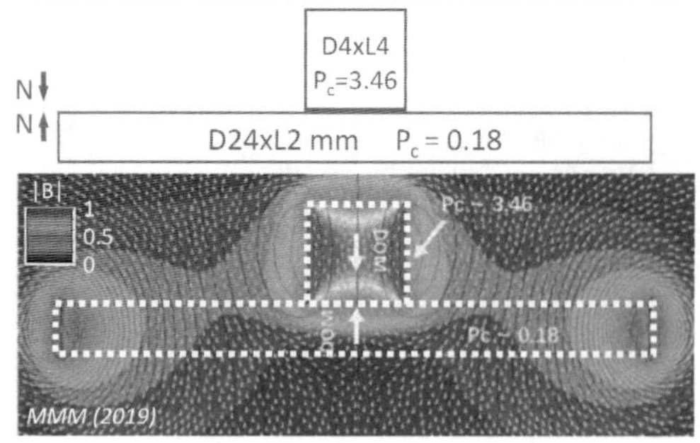

Surface Flux Density - Localized Demagnetization

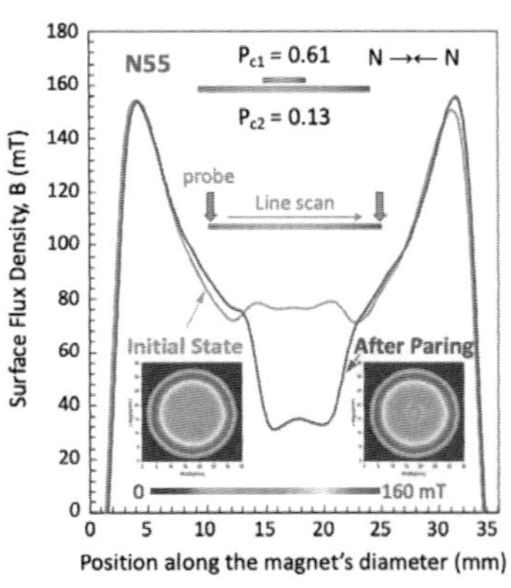

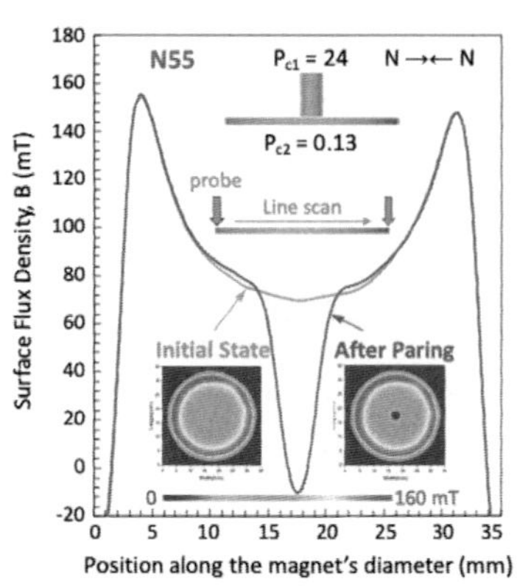

Sci Rep **11,** 12555 (2021)

- Higher L/D → Higher P_c → Higher B_d → lower $|H_d|$
  - Stronger surface magnetic field
  - Stronger resistance to demagnetization
- Lower L/D → Lower P_c → Lower B_d → Higher $|H_d|$
  - Weaker surface magnetic field
  - Weaker resistance to demagnetization
- **Higher P_{c1}/P_{c2} → Higher degree of localized demagnetization**

- Surface flux was measured 1.2mm above the magnets' surface with an XYZ scanner equipped with a Hall probe
- In the force measurements, when the gap is as close as 0.05mm, and the *LD* is much larger.

Effects of P_c ratio and Magnet Types

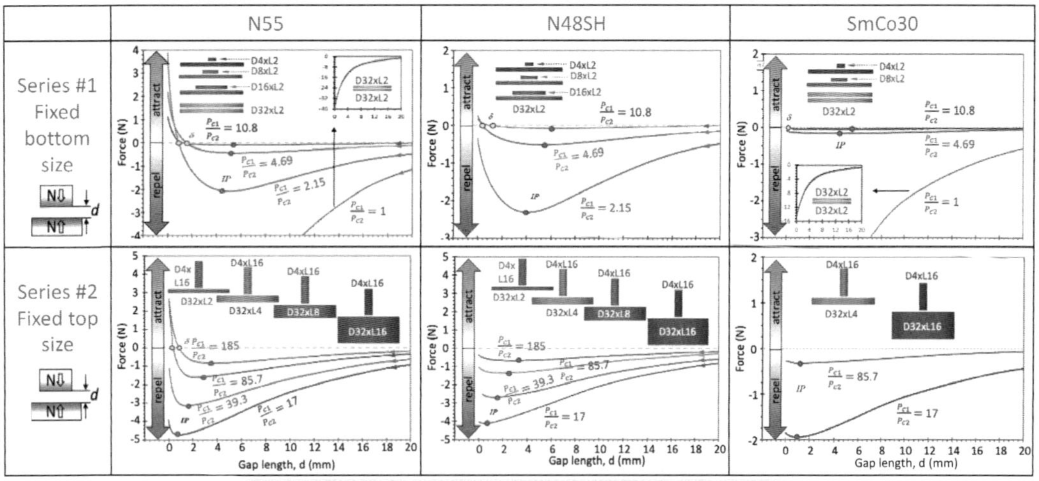

- Different P_c ratio → different inflection point locations
- Different magnet types → appearance of attractive force

Effects of P_c ratio and Magnet Types

$$\Delta F = |(F_{@d<0.5} - F_{@IP})/F_{@IP}|$$

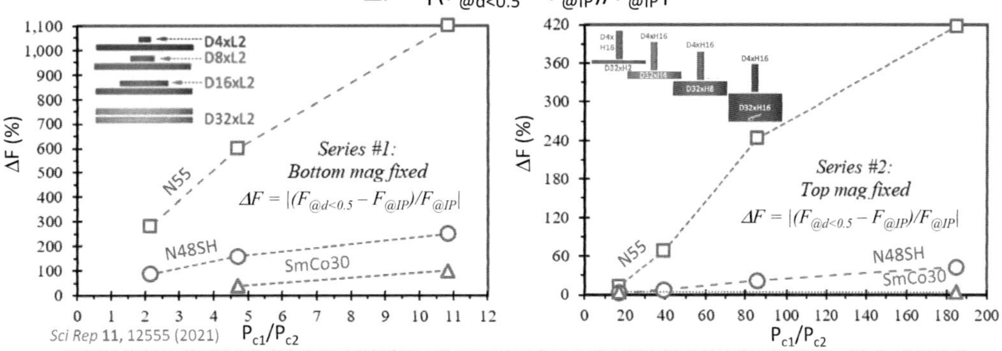

- A larger ΔF indicates a greater degree of localized demagnetization.
- The localized demagnetization is weaker in the N48SH and SmCo30 magnets than that of the N55 magnets.

Effects of Magnet Types - N55, N48SH, and SmCo30

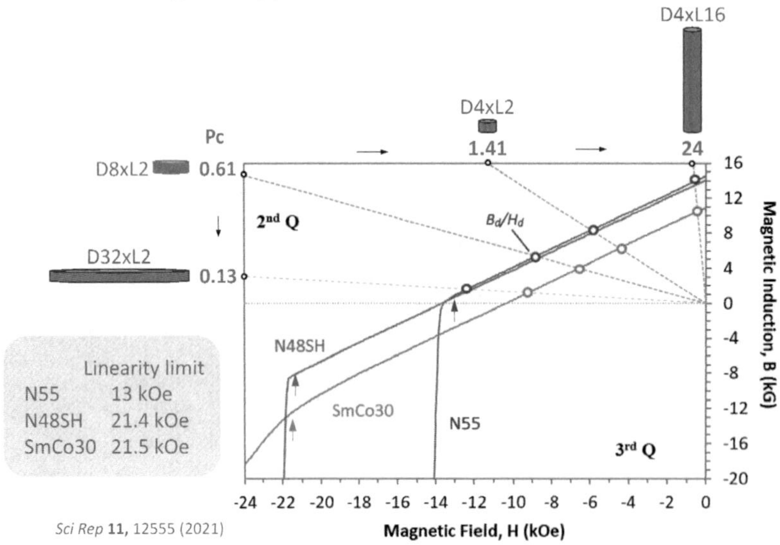

Sci Rep **11**, 12555 (2021)

Force between Permanent Magnet and Electromagnet

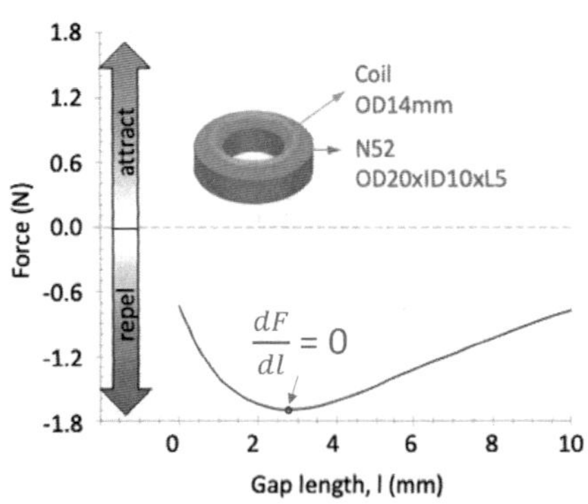

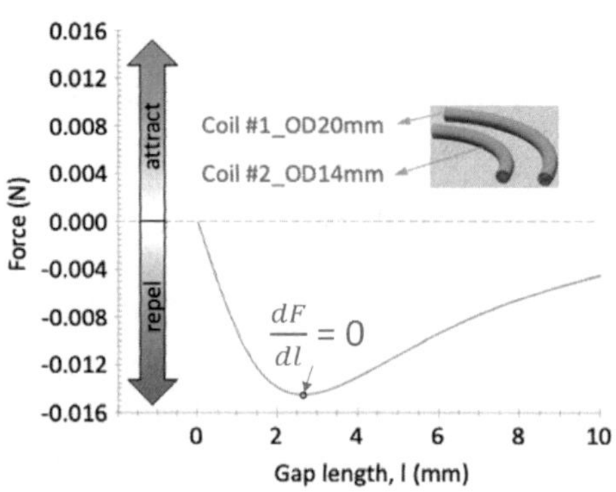

- Non-monotonic behavior
- Appearance of inflection point

Potential Application – Voice Coil Motor

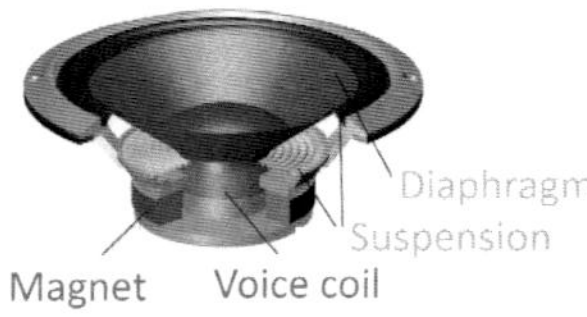

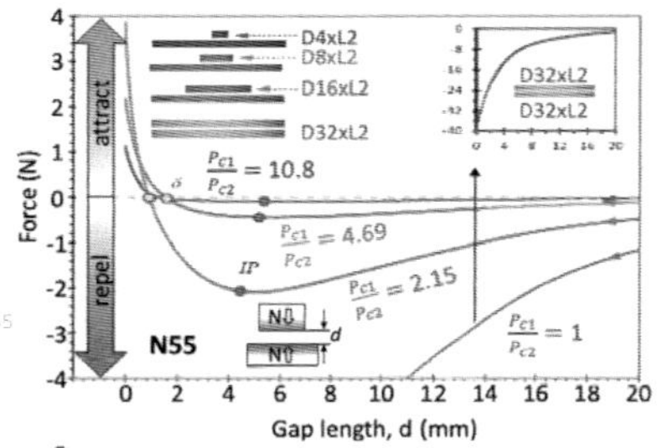

- Magnet dimensions
- Coil dimensions
- Distance between magnet & coil

Big Impact to performance

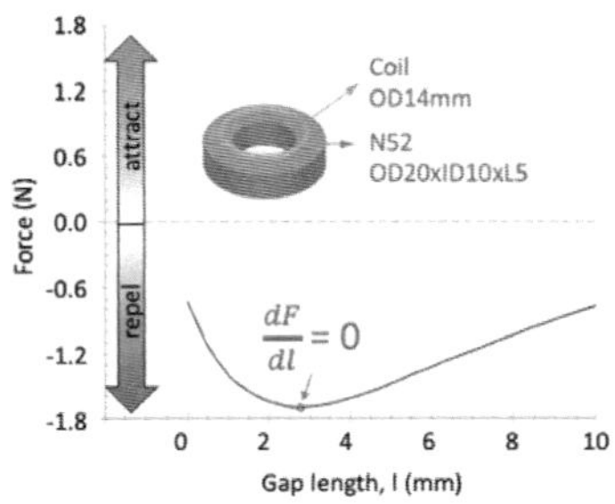

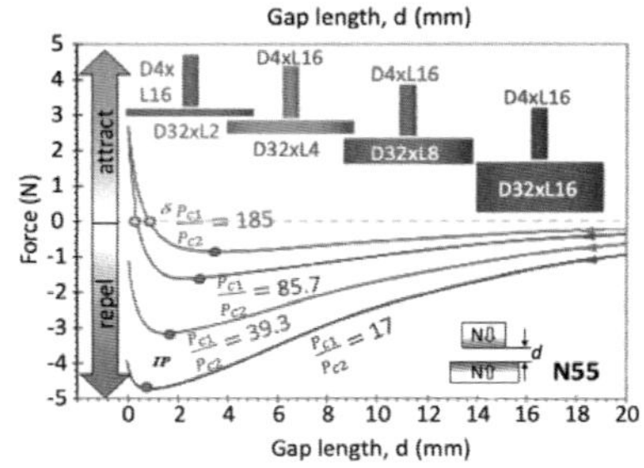

Like Poles Off-Center Repulsion

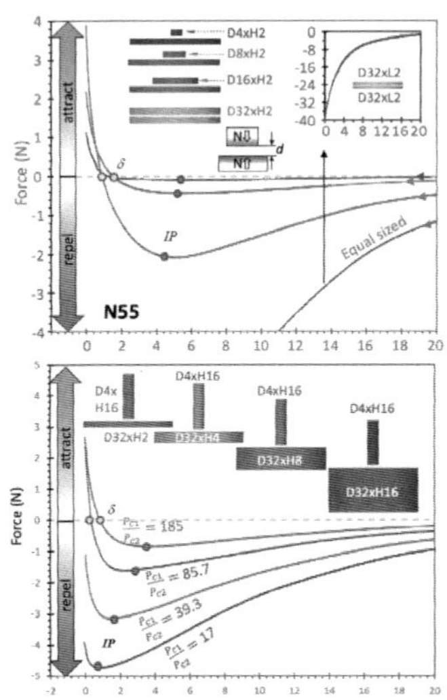

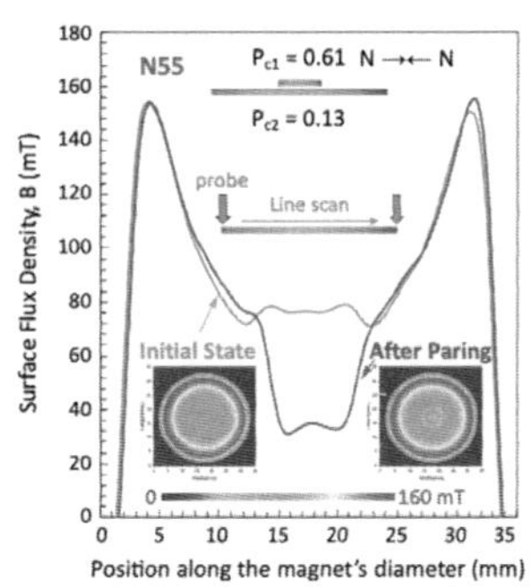

Sci Rep **11**, 12555 (2021)

- Low surface flux density @ center → Vulnerable to demagnetization
- Like-poles:
  - Attract - in-center
  - Repel - off-center

Potential Application – Mechanical Devices

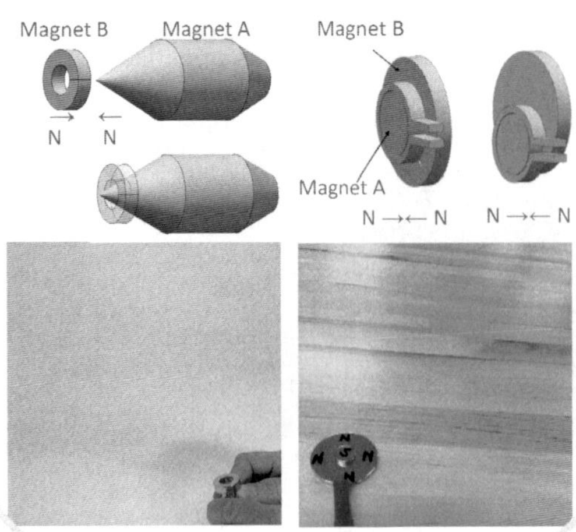

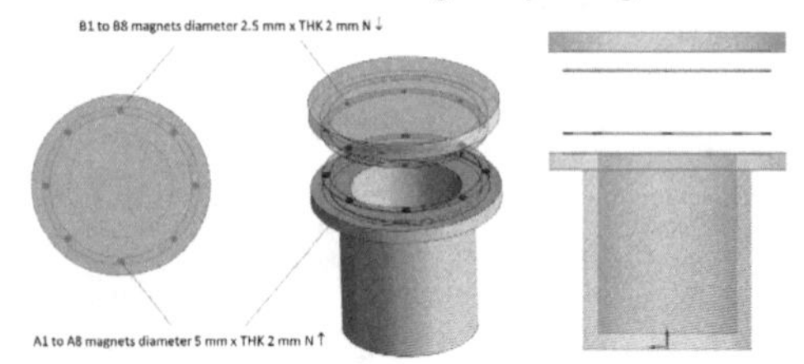

- Two like poles attract each other in the center, and repel off-center
- Repulsive force for propulsion
- Attractive force for sealing, repulsive force for opening of containers

Patent Pending; USPTO Application #63/265,205

Potential Application – Vibrating Device

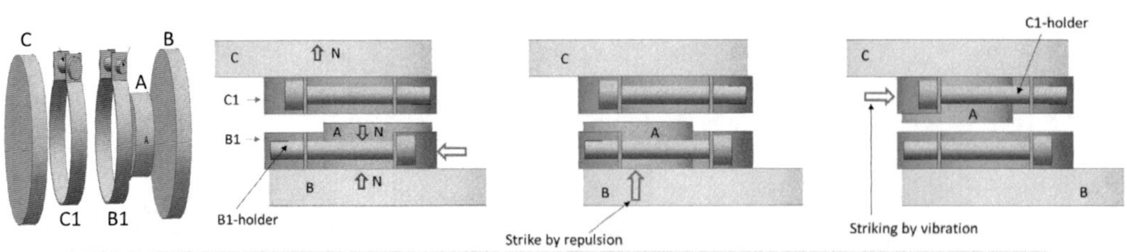

- Conventional electromagnetic vibrator:
  - ac current directional change → electromagnet polarity change → alternative attraction and repulsion between permanent magnet and electromagnet or both electromagnet
  - ac power supply → operation cost, weight and volume limit
- Vibrator device based on localized demagnetization:
  - Magnets' position in and out of central alignment → alternative attraction and repulsion between two permanent magnets with different dimensions
  - No ac power supply needed for alternating attraction and repulsion → reduce energy usage

Patent Pending; USPTO Application #63/265,205

Potential Application – Vibration-based Electric Generator

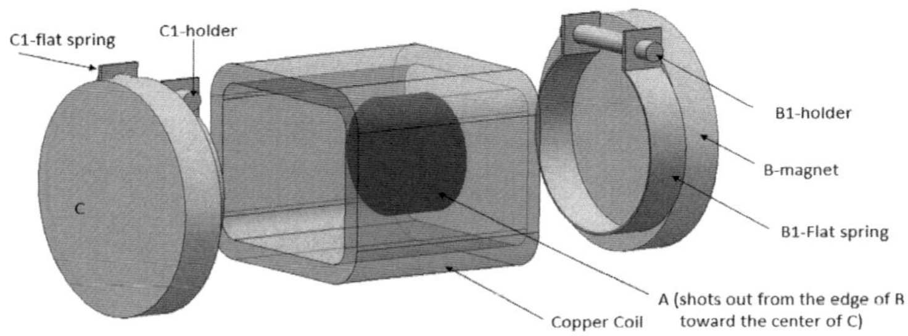

- Change magnet's relative positions in and out of central alignment → alternative attractive and repulsive forces between the magnets
- Movement of magnets → changes of electric fields in its surrounding area → induces electric current

Patent Pending; USPTO Application #63/265,205

Potential Application – In-situ Magnetic Patterner

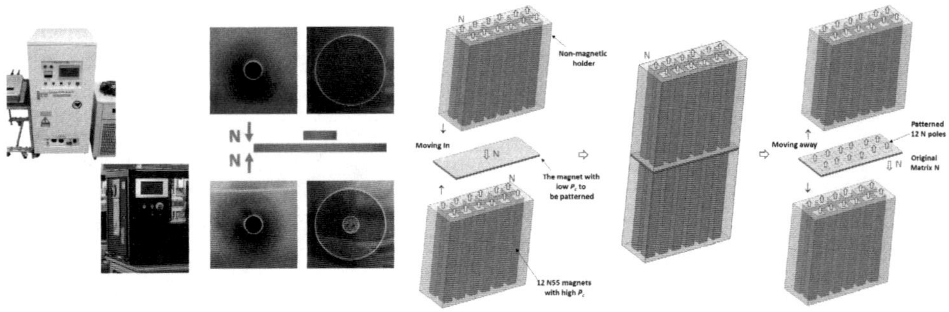

- In-situ magnetizing of multiple magnets at once or magnetizing one magnet into multiple poles after assembly are needed.
- Most in-situ magnetizers require complicated and costly coil winding fixtures with a pulse magnetizer with a large bank of capacitors.
- In-situ Magnetic Patterner using localized demagnetization without an external power source.

Patent Pending; USPTO Application #63/265,205

Summary

Observations

- Like-poles attraction between unequally sized magnets
- Localized demagnetization
- Inflection points in force vs gap length curves

Understandings

- Working points
- Permeance coefficients
- BH curve

Applications

- Mechanical: Propulsion, Vibration, Sealing and opening
- Electrical: electrical generator, voice coil motor
- Magnetic: in-situ multipole patterner

QUADRANT

Provide comprehensive magnetic solutions from early prototype to iterative development

Design & Engineering
- Magnet product design
- Modeling
- Prototyping
- Optimization

Precision Manufacturing
- Tailored services
- Rapid tooling
- Quick turn

Automation Technology
- Assembling
- Magnetizing
- Testing
- Assembling

Magnetizing System
- Conventional
- Automated
- Programmable Mag-Printer

Products & Solutions
- Magnetic materials
- Magnetic assemblies
- Haptic modules
- Motors
- Alloy parts by MIM, CNC & stamping

https://www.quadrant.us

AUTHOR INDEX